¶ *My Dearest Minette*

Henrietta, Duchess of Orleans. Miniature by Samuel Cooper.
By courtesy of the Board and Trustees of the Victoria and Albert Museum, London.

My Dearest Minette

The Letters between Charles II
and his sister
Henrietta, Duchesse d'Orléans

With a Commentary by

Ruth Norrington

Peter Owen
London & Chester Springs

¶ *for my dearest Caroline*

PETER OWEN PUBLISHERS
73 Kenway Road London SW5 0RE
Peter Owen books are distributed in the USA by
Dufour Editions Inc. Chester Springs PA 19425–0007

First published in Great Britain 1996

ISBN 0–7206–0991–7

A catalogue record for this book is available
from the British Library

Printed and made in Great Britain by Biddles
of Guildford and King's Lynn

Contents

Acknowledgements

Among the many people I wish to thank for their assistance during the preparation of this book, I would particularly like to express my gratitude to the following: His Grace the Archbishop of Canterbury and the staff of Lambeth Palace Library for giving me access to Minette's letters; His Grace the Duke of Grafton; The Lord Clifford of Chudleigh; Professor Richard Hutton of the University of Bristol; Dr Elizabeth Ralph, former archivist of the City of Bristol; David Leitch, curatorial officer of The Royal Commission of Historical Manuscripts; Mr John Berkeley of Berkeley Castle; Mr John Shreeve of Blackwell's Research Department, Oxford; the staff of the Bodleian Library, Oxford; Dr Roger Mettam, University of London; Mr John Barratt, formerly of the History Department, Clifton College; Miss Priscilla Wrightson; Mr Michael Hodges; Mr Patrick Taylor; Miss Anne Anson and Mrs Pauline Dolan for their excellent work in preparing the manuscript for the publisher. Above all I would like to thank my husband Sir Patrick Reilly, Fellow of All Souls, Oxford, for his assistance in my researches at the Bodleian Library, his translation of Bossuet's Funeral Oration on Minette, and his continual interest in my work on this book; his encouragement has enabled me to complete it.

R.N.

Chronology

1644 Birth of Princess Henrietta Anne Stuart ('Minette') at Exeter.
1645 Battle of Naseby: Royalist army defeated by Parliamentarians.
1646 Escape to France of Lady Dalkeith and Minette.
1648 The civil wars of the Fronde in France.
1649 Trial and execution of Charles I.
1650 Charles II's uprising in Scotland, followed by the defeat of his forces by Oliver Cromwell at Dunbar and in 1651 at Worcester.
1659 First known letters from Minette to Charles.
Treaty of the Pyrenees ended the war between France and Spain.
1660 The Declaration of Breda (April) leading to the Restoration of Charles II (May).
Death of Henry, Duke of Gloucester (September) and the Princess Royal, Mary of Orange (December).
1661 Cavalier Parliament (to 1679).
Marriage of Minette to Philippe, Duc d'Orléans.
1662 Birth of Marie Louise, Minette's eldest child.
Marriage of Charles II to Catherine of Braganza.
Sale of Dunkirk by England to the French.
Peace treaty between France and Holland.
1664 Birth of Minette's son, Philippe Charles, Duc de Valois.
1665 Second Anglo-Dutch War (until July 1667). England won the naval battle of Lowestoft (June 1665), but lost the 'Four Days' Battle' in the Thames (June 1666), and had

	part of its fleet destroyed by the Dutch at Chatham (June 1667).
	Peace treaty of Breda between England and Holland/France (July 1667): England kept New Amsterdam, renaming it New York.
	Great Plague in England.
1666	Declaration of war between England and France.
	Fire of London.
	Death of Anne of Austria and Philippe Charles, Duc de Valois.
1668	Triple Alliance of Holland, Sweden and England.
	Treaty of Aix-la-Chapelle between France and Spain.
1669	Birth of Minette's last child, Anne Marie.
	Death of Henrietta Maria, Dowager Queen of England.
1670	Secret Treaty of Dover between Charles II and Louis XIV.
	Death of Minette at St Cloud on 30 June.

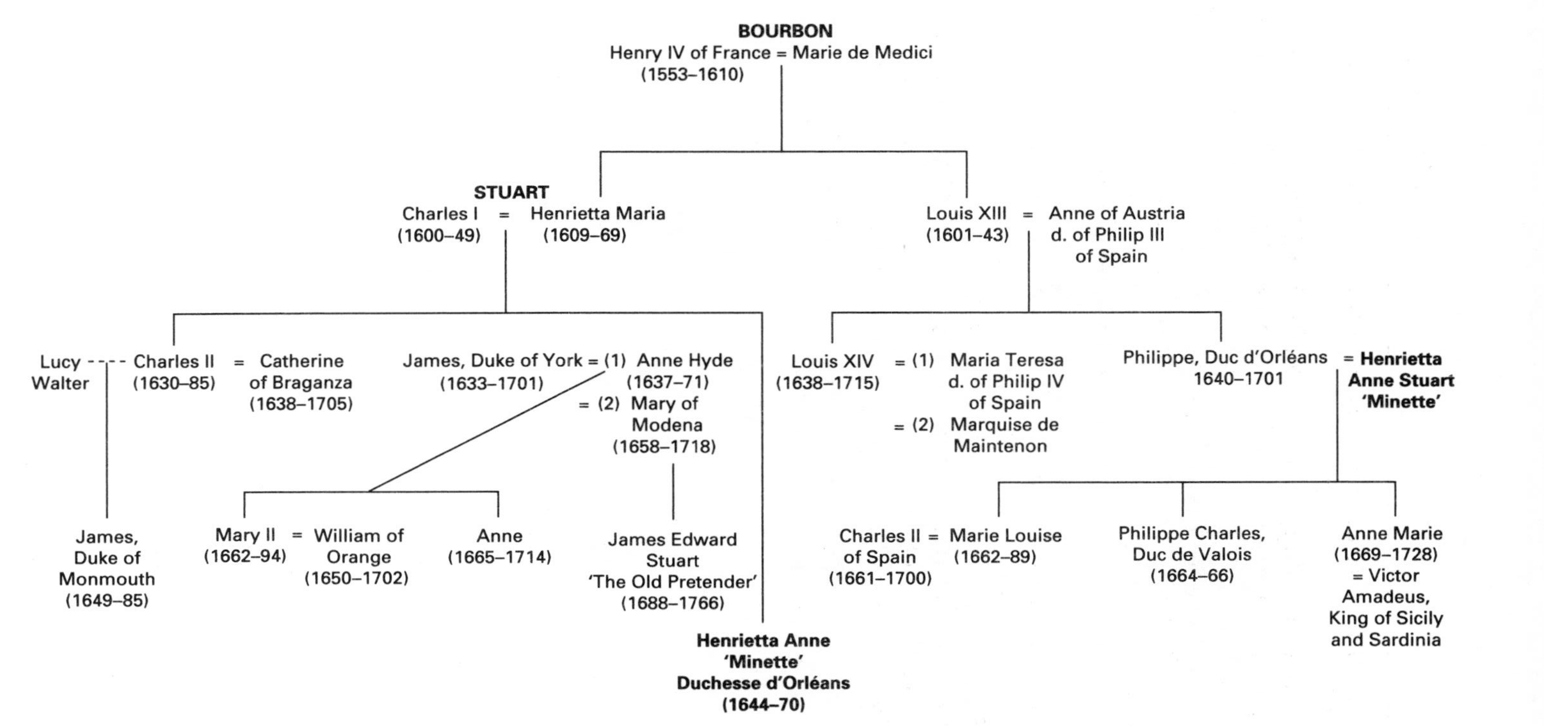

THE HOUSES OF STUART AND BOURBON

Note on the Text

In the correspondence between Charles II and his sister Minette (Henrietta, Duchesse d'Orléans), the vast majority of Charles's letters to Minette were written in English. Although at the beginning of the correspondence Charles tried to persuade Minette to improve her native language by writing to him in English, she always resisted this, and all her letters to him are in French.

Although in the text here I have retained Charles's lively and idiosyncratic English, with its contemporary and often erratic spellings, I have in places where his meaning is obscure 'corrected' the spelling and punctuation in order to make the letters intelligible to the modern reader.

Minette's written French was correspondingly poor in grammar and punctuation, and I have therefore used the translations made by Margaret Duncan and Cyril Hughes Hartmann. On the occasions when Charles wrote to Minette in French, we naturally lose some of the flavour of his language in translation. In the latter stages of the correspondence he uses French only if he expects Minette to pass on the letter to her brother-in-law Louis XIV, or her husband the Duc d'Orléans.

Of Charles's letters, ninety-eight are in the archive of the Ministère des Affaires Étrangères, Quai d'Orsay, Paris; five are in the British Library; and two (copies) are in the Public Record Office, London (State Papers, Foreign, France).

Twenty-three of Minette's letters are in the Lambeth Palace Library, London (Codex Tenison 645); eight are in the Public Record Office (State Papers, Foreign, France); and one is in the Clifford Papers, from Ugbrooke Park, now in the British Library.

Ruth Norrington

Chapter 1

Une Enfant de Bénédiction: Henrietta Stuart

On 21 July 1644, a small christening party entered the nave of Exeter Cathedral and made their way to the new font which had been placed in the centre of the aisle especially for the baptism. Lady Dalkeith, Lady Paulett and Sir John Berkeley were the sponsors for the child, and Dr Laurence Burnell was to perform the ceremony according to the rites of the Church of England, by order of the King.

Thus Henrietta Stuart, the youngest child of King Charles I and Queen Henrietta Maria, made her first brief public appearance when she was five weeks old. She was born in the storms of the Civil War, and none of her family was able to be present at the ceremony.

During her early years her life was threatened by the severe attacks of convulsions that she had suffered from birth. The letters in this first section of the book speak for themselves; of the tumultuous and tragic circumstances which had led to her birth in Exeter, so soon afterwards to be besieged by her father's enemies, and of her dramatic escape from her native land at the age of two, to join her mother in France. Her governess, Lady Dalkeith, is the heroine of this early part of Henrietta's life: the health and safety of the young Princess was entirely due to the loving care and the courage of this devoted and intelligent woman. Anne Elizabeth Dalkeith was the daughter of Sir Edward Villiers, half-brother of the Duke of Buckingham, the favourite of both James

I and Charles I. She was a tall, extremely beautiful woman, a great confidante of the King and Queen, who had asked her to be the governess and guardian of the future royal baby. She was married to Robert Dalkeith, who became 8th Earl of Morton in 1648.

The King and Queen's decision to make Lady Dalkeith the guardian of their youngest child was a wise one, for she was to have a profound and beneficial influence on Henrietta's formative years. The arduous job of caring for the little Princess in the harrowing circumstances of a civil war was taken on at great sacrifice to herself and her own family. She had to leave her husband and four young children – William, Robert, Anne and Margaret – for many years. Her husband died in 1649, only a year after inheriting his father's title, and while his wife was in France with the Princess. Two years later she begged permission to return to her orphaned family, which was granted. Sadly she died of a sudden attack of fever in 1654, when Henrietta was ten years old, so never saw her beloved charge again.

A similar sacrifice was made by Queen Henrietta Maria; accompanied by Lady Dalkeith, she said goodbye to her husband at Abingdon in April 1644. This was the last time she and the King saw each other. She was seven months pregnant, and in very poor health, suffering from some form of acute arthritis which made the journey towards Exeter an extremely painful one. They stopped in Bath, where the Queen had hoped to stay for a time to take the waters. The cost of the candles used by the Queen on this occasion appears to be the only reference in the city archives to the Queen's visit. 'Item: Payed for candles for the Queen's comminge to Towne £0-6-8.'[1]

¶ *Queen Henrietta Maria to King Charles*

Bath, 21 April 1644[2]

My dear Heart,

Fred Cornwallis will have told you of our voyage as far as Abury [Avebury] and the state of my health. Since my coming hence I find myself ill, as well as in the ill rest I have, as in the increase of my rheum. I hope this day's rest will do me good. I go tomorrow to Bristol to send you back the carts many of them have already returned . . . Farewell, my heart. I cannot write more than that I am absolutely yours.

The appalling conditions in Bath, due to an outbreak of the plague, made the Queen hasten on her journey. Leaving the infested city she passed through the loyal town of Axbridge, where the bells were rung in her honour. An entry in the church warden's accounts of 1644 states: 'Paid to Richard Stroud for beere for the ringers at the coming of the Queen to Axbridge . . . £0-12-0.'[3] The party arrived in Exeter on 1 May, and placing herself under the protection of Sir John Berkeley, the Queen took up residence in Bedford House, a property belonging to the Russell family, near the Cathedral.

The King was seriously alarmed by his wife's letter, and his heartfelt note to his own physician is touching in its brevity.

¶ *King Charles I to Sir Theodore Mayerne*[4]

Mayerne, for love of me, go to my wife.

The Queen, although not a favourite with the doctor, added her plea.

¶ *Queen Henrietta Maria to Sir Theodore Mayerne*

Exeter, May 1644[5]

Monsieur de Mayerne,

My indisposition does not permit me to write much to entreat you to come to me, if your health will suffer you; but my malady will I trust, sooner bring you here than many a line. For this cause I say no more but that, retaining in my memory the care you have ever taken of me in my utmost need, it makes me believe that if you can, you will come, and that I am, and shall be ever Your good mistress and friend,

Henrietta Maria R.

Madame Peronne, a highly competent midwife from France, who had been at the birth of some of the Queen's former children, also arrived in Exeter, in time to assist when the Queen gave birth to a daughter on 16 June. The baby was extremely delicate, and Henrietta Maria's own poor health showed no signs of improvement. Two weeks after the birth she decided that the only chance to save her baby from the threat from the advancing Parliamentary troops was to leave her in the keeping of Lady Dalkeith and Sir John Berkeley, and escape herself to France. Parliament had for some time endeavoured to capture the Queen, knowing that in such circumstances the King would try to rescue her. Having made this courageous decision, she wrote to her husband from Exeter just before her departure.

¶ *Queen Henrietta Maria to King Charles*

Exeter, 28 June 1644[6]

> I will show you by this last action that there is nothing that lies so near my heart as your safety. My life is but a small thing compared with that. For in the present state of affairs your condition would be in great peril if you came to my relief, and I know that your affection would make you risk all for my sake. And so I prefer to risk this miserable life of mine, a thing worthless enough in itself, saving in as far as it is precious to you. My dear heart, farewell. The most unhappy creature in the world who can no longer hold a pen.

After a hazardous journey, the Queen reached Falmouth. News reached her that the little Princess was extremely ill with convulsions, so the Queen sent her own physician, Sir John Winton, back to Exeter to attend her daughter. She sailed for France on 14 July.

Twelve days later, unaware of the Queen's flight, and in an attempt to rescue her, the King arrived in Exeter. His little daughter had been baptized five days earlier and had been named Henrietta after her mother; her second name, Anne, was to be given to her after her arrival in France, in honour of the Queen Regent, Anne of Austria. Her eldest brother, the future Charles II, nicknamed her Minette, by which name she will now be called here.

On this first visit to his daughter the King was accompanied by the Prince of Wales. The young Prince Charles was fourteen years old. The stability of his family life had been rudely interrupted by the Civil War, and this was his first meeting with the sister who in future years was to be his closest confidante. His father was able to stay only one night on this first visit to his daughter, but on 17 September he returned and stayed for a week. During this time he arranged for the excise duties of Exeter to be assigned to her household, and appointed Dr Fuller to be her chaplain. In these few precious days he saw Minette for the last time.

Prince Charles returned to Exeter in August 1645, when the Princess was fourteen months old. She had survived the dangerous illnesses of her infancy under the loving care of Lady Dalkeith. Charles was met by a lively little girl whose joy at meeting her brother, the first member of her family that she would have been aware of, was equalled only by his delight in her. The deep affection between brother and sister started in her infancy, and was to have a far-reaching effect on their future lives.

The Prince stayed in Exeter for a month on this occasion. Just after he left, the armies of Fairfax and Waller besieged the city. All his efforts to relieve it were in vain, and life became extremely difficult for Henrietta's household. Lady Dalkeith tried in vain to get away from Exeter to Cornwall before the siege. In spite of her efforts, Queen Henrietta Maria remained seriously worried about her infant daughter, and blamed her governess, most unjustly, for the fact that the Princess and her household were trapped in the city, surrounded by enemy troops. Sir Edward Hyde came hotly to the defence of Lady Dalkeith and wrote to Lord Jermyn, who was with the Queen in France.

¶ *Sir Edward Hyde to Lord Jermyn*[7]

In reply to your postscript concerning the Princess and her governess, I think it will break her heart when she hears of the Queen's displeasure; which pardon me for saying, is with much severity conceived against her. Your motto seems to be that an unfortunate friend is as bad as an unfaithful one. I'll be bold to say, let the success be what it will, that the governess is as faultless in the business as you are, and has been as punctual as solicitous, and as impatient to obey the Queen's directions, as she could be to save her soul. She could not act her part without assistance; and what assistance could she have? She had just got the Queen's letter, when the Prince was last at Exeter, about the end of September; she showed it to me and asked my help. . . . The governess would have procured a pass to bring the Princess to Cornwall, had not letters been taken at Dartwell, by which the designs of transporting her transpired. You may now conclude the governess could as easily have beaten Fairfax, as prevented being shut up in Exeter, from whence I hope she will yet get safely with her charge, to whom I am confident she hath omitted no part of her duty.

As winter wore on, the condition of the garrison and inhabitants became extremely grave. On 3 April Sir John Berkeley, the Governor, was forced to listen to terms of surrender, which included those concerning the little Princess. They were either that she was to remain safely in Exeter, or that the governess with her charge and all the household plate, money and goods were to go to any place they chose within twenty days of the completion of the treaty. Carriages would be provided at a reasonable cost; future maintenance be allowed by Parliament, and a messenger from the governess allowed to go to the King to find out his pleasure concerning the child. The Agreement of Exeter was signed on 13 April 1646.

The contents of the King's reply to Lady Dalkeith were conveyed in a letter written by her to General Fairfax, and which Fairfax forwarded to the Speaker of the House of Commons in London.

¶ *Lady Dalkeith to Sir Thomas Fairfax, General of the Parliamentary Forces*

19 April 1646[8]

Sir,

I have prevailed with Mr Asburnham to acquaint you that I have his Majesty's allowance to remain with the Princess for some time about London, in any of his Majesty's houses. I have judged Richmond the fittest. This bearer will inform you of those particulars concerning the settlement of the Princess in that place, wherein I conceive your assistance and recommendation to the parliament to be necessary, which his Majesty will acknowledge as a service and I as an obligation to.

Sir,

Your Humble servant
A. Dalkeith.

The plight of the little Princess and her household was not lost on one parliamentary soldier who reported her departure from Exeter thus: 'The Princess Henrietta, the last of the royal offspring, but the first that was in any town when it stooped to the obedience of the parliament, came out with her governess upon the entering of our force, and we hear is gone with Sir John Berkeley to Oxford.'[9] The rumoured destination of Oxford was unfounded, and passing through Salisbury, the Princess and her governess finally arrived at the royal palace of Oatlands, near Weybridge in Surrey.

Sir John Berkeley had also had quarters in Bedford House in Exeter. This colourful personality was about thirty-six at the time, and was a devoted admirer of Lady Dalkeith. Having safely delivered her and her royal charge to Oatlands, he remained with them until their escape to France. He was a man of charm and persuasion, and as a result of his popularity with the royal family he became governor to James, Duke of York, in 1652. Sir John asked Lady Dalkeith to marry him after the death of her husband in 1649 and they became engaged. She asked Sir Edward Hyde's opinion on the marriage, and on his advice broke off the engagement. Sir John never forgave Hyde for depriving him of such a lively wife, and retained a deep and lasting animosity towards him. Hyde reciprocated this dislike, as he later tried to destroy Berkeley's influence with the Duke of York, but there he was unsuccessful.

Life at Oatlands was not easy. The revenues that the Princess's household had lived on from the excise duties of Exeter came to an end, and the terms agreed by the Parliamentarians at the surrender of Exeter were not honoured. Lady Dalkeith financed the expenses of the household out of her own funds for three months. After several attempts to obtain the promised maintenance she wrote in desperation to the committee of the County of Surrey at Kingston.

¶ *Lady Dalkeith to the Committee in the County of Surrey*

May 1646[10]

Gentlemen,

Whilst I was on my way hither, I despatched several letters to Sir John Fairfax, and the Speakers of both Houses, to desire a speedy signification of the Parliament's intentions concerning the Princesse's family, which I had brought towards London, with some difficulty and charge to myself, the more willingly because I judged it agreeable to the desires of the Parliament. Their more weighty affairs have hindered them from giving the despatch which is most necessary to our condition. I desire therefore that you would favour me with your best assistance herein, and in the meantime that you would cause some temporary order to be settled out of the receipts of this county for the Princesse's household, according to a list this bearer will give you, which will be a very great service to his majesty and a favour to

Your humble servant. A. Dalkeith

The King had instructed Lady Dalkeith that under no circumstances must she be parted from the Princess. She was profoundly disturbed when it became obvious from the reply she had to her letters that the members of Parliament had no intention of honouring their representatives' promises at the Agreement of Exeter. Instead they passed an order in the House of Commons on 24 May that the Princess should be taken to London and placed with her brother and sister in St James's Palace, that the whole of her retinue should be dismissed, a committee appointed to take care that she wanted for nothing suitable to her birth and quality, and that a proper allowance be made for her support.

Lady Dalkeith was horrified. She was totally committed to her promise to the King and Queen that she would never part from Henrietta until she was safely handed over to her parents. She therefore wrote one last letter to the Speaker of the House of Commons. She made clear in it why it was of such great importance that she should remain with her charge.

At the end of June the Princess and Lady Dalkeith were joined at Oatlands by Prince Rupert, who was preparing to leave England for France, via Dover. In fact, he left the country on 5 July, just under three weeks before the escape of Lady Dalkeith and the Princess. They must have discussed the plans for their departure with him, and obviously decided that it would be too dangerous for them all to travel together.

Lady Dalkeith's last letter to the Speaker went unanswered. Her great fear that she might be forcibly parted from Minette made her take the serious decision to convey her young charge secretly to France to join her mother. Her plans were told to two members of the household who were to accompany them, Thomas Lambert and Elinor Dyke, and the Princess's French valet who was to accompany them in the disguise of Lady Dalkeith's husband. The faithful Sir John Berkeley was also in the plot. Lady Dalkeith disguised herself in a shabby old gown and cloak, with a bundle of rags stuffed into one shoulder to hide her elegant figure. Minette was dressed, much to her disgust, in ragged boy's clothes, and given the name of Pierre. Thus the little party set out, probably on 24 July, to walk the hundred or more miles to Dover.

Lady Dalkeith carried the child on her shoulders the whole way. Her charge made the journey more hazardous by constantly telling the passers-by that she was not Pierre but the Princess of England. Her indignant childish prattle, though not without its humour, caused her poor governess great alarm. They were followed at a safe distance by Sir John Berkeley. So good were their disguises that they were still undetected when Berkeley put them on the packet for France. The household at Oatlands were unaware of the escape, and were very alarmed when they discovered on 25 July that the Princess and her governess were missing. A letter shortly arrived for them from Lady Dalkeith, telling them 'that I have removed her highness to a better air, whither you may, if you will, follow her'. Her faith in the loyalty of the household was rewarded, for the escape was kept secret from Parliament for three days. No attempt was made to follow them, many members thinking that the Princess's flight to France was a good thing, as they would not have to provide her maintenance any more.

The two-year-old Princess would have had no recollection of her mother, whom she had not seen since she was two weeks old. But by the time she and her governess arrived in France, her brother Prince Charles, and her cousin Prince Rupert, whom she had so recently seen at Oatlands, were with the Queen at St Germain. Minette must have been delighted to see both of them again.

Lady Dalkeith, having handed the child over to her ecstatic mother, collapsed with exhaustion, and was gravely ill for some time. She was rightly treated as a heroine by the Court. The two servants who accompanied them, if it is possible to read between the lines of two entries in the Domestic State Papers of Charles I, were not quite so well rewarded for their loyalty.

The first, from Elinor Dyke, is dated 1 September 1663, and is a petition from her for arrears of wages due to her for six years' service – a sum of £25 – board wages at Exeter, and £7 for silver lace for Princess Henrietta. The second is dated 1666: 'Thomas Lambert and Mary, his wife, petition for the customs on 2000 pieces of Holland linen, to enable them to drive a trade in their old age. Were obliged to save their lives by leaving the country six years ago, for their diligence in conveying the Princess, from the barbarous enemies to the Queen Mother in France, are injured by searches in their millinery ware for French commodities.' Because of the great love that King Charles II had for his sister, it is to be hoped that their petitions were answered.

Cyprien de Gamache, who became the Princess's tutor and spiritual adviser, gives a vivid description in his diary of the safe arrival of the two refugees:

> Intelligence of the whole affair was despatched to the Queen, who quickly sent her carriages; and the governess with all her train reached Paris safely, and respectfully placed in the hands of her majesty the precious deposit, which she had so happily preserved amidst so many awful dangers. Oh the transports of joy, Oh the excessive consolation to the heart of the Queen. She embraced, she hugged and kissed again and again the royal infant.
>
> Many thanksgivings did she render to God for his mercy, and regarding the princess as a child of blessing [une enfant de bénédiction], she resolved with the grace of God, to have her instructed in the Catholic and Roman religion, and to use all her efforts to obtain the consent of the King her husband.

The first news that Charles I had heard of the safe arrival of his daughter in France came to them on their arrival in Paris, when the King's delight and deep gratitude was conveyed to Lady Dalkeith.[11] Sir Richard Browne, the English Ambassador, and brother-in-law of John Evelyn, was one of the first diplomats to meet the escapees:

¶ *Sir Richard Browne*

Dispatch on 17 August 1646[12]

> I was yesterday at St Germain, to kiss the sweet little Princess Henrietta's hands; the manner of the Lady Dalkeith's bringing her Highness away from Oatlands is a pretty romance.

Browne was Ambassador in Paris for nineteen years, until the Restoration in 1660; so he watched with great interest the youngest daughter of the King growing from infancy into childhood. Sadly, like Elinor Dyke and the Lamberts, he seldom if ever received any salary for his devotion.

Chapter 2

Oh Me, My Brother! Oh Me, My Mother!

Born in the storms of war, this royal fair,
Produced like lightning in tempestuous air,
Though now she flies her native isle, less kind
Less safe for her than either sea or wind,
Shall when the blossoming of her beauty's shown
See her great brother on the British throne,
When peace shall smile, and no dispute arise,
But which rules most, his sceptre or her eyes.

Edmund Waller

For the first two years after her arrival in France with Lady Dalkeith, Minette enjoyed a comfortable life with her mother in the Louvre, where certain apartments had been allotted to them, and in the Palace of St Germain, which they had as a country residence. Queen Henrietta Maria retained all the state due to a crowned head, and kept a large household of ladies and gentlemen-in-waiting, and drove about in fine carriages attended by guards and footmen. Under ordinary circumstances the pension of 30,000 livres per month which she was allowed by the French crown would have been adequate for her needs. But as Mademoiselle de Montpensier, daughter of Gaston, Duc d'Orléans, and first cousin to Louis XIV, Charles and Minette, comments in her memoirs, Henrietta Maria's style of living was diminished because she had parted with nearly all her money and sold her jewels and plate to assist her husband. Much to Minette's delight, the Prince of Wales and Prince Rupert were also members of the household, and naturally it was a meeting place for all the exiled Cavaliers who had lost everything in the royal cause.

Mademoiselle describes the Prince of Wales at this time as very tall for his age, with a fine figure, dark complexion, and beautiful black hair. The two years that Minette had with her eldest brother in Paris forged a close bond between them that was to flower into the most important relationship in their lives. Prince Charles was studiously neglected by the French, and he became a great drain on his mother's dwindling resources. During this period he suffered a prolonged attack of fever which put him out of action for a long time, and the wild life he led with his friends the Duke of Buckingham and Lord Percy added to his mother's worries. He left Paris in July 1648 to sail from Helvoe, taking 19 English ships and 20,000 men. This abortive attempt to return to England ended instead with Charles's return to Holland. He contracted smallpox, but recovered, and the time spent with his sister Princess Mary of Orange and away from his mother's apron-strings gave him a good opportunity to develop a mind of his own, and to take stock of his position.

The damaging civil wars of the Fronde broke out in 1648, and once more Minette and her mother were to find themselves in a state of siege. They were asked to vacate the Palace of St Germain by the Queen Regent, who was anxious for the safety of the young king. They decided to return to their apartments at the Louvre. This was a time of considerable hardship not only for Queen Henrietta and her daughter but for the whole French court. Mademoiselle de Montpensier describes the plight of the courtiers thus: 'Those who had beds had no hangings and those who had hangings were without clothes.'

This was the second occasion in her short life that Minette had been the prisoner of a siege in time of civil war. She and her mother were visited in the Louvre by Cardinal de Retz in early January 1649. He was appalled to find them without food or fuel, Minette in her mother's bed, trying to keep warm. As his failure to send the Queen her allowance was partly the cause of her plight, guilt made him react promptly, and fuel and food were produced at once. As he remarked, 'Posterity will hardly believe that a Queen of England and granddaughter of Henri Quatre and her daughter wanted firewood in this month of January in their house.'

Rumours of the trial of Charles I reached the household in early February, but for several weeks his wife remained in ignorance of the appalling truth. Desperate for information, she sent a member of her court to St Germain, and it was the sad task of Lord Jermyn to break the tragic news to her of the execution of her husband. She was so speechless with shock and despair that her courtiers gravely feared for her reason. Eventually the loving little daughter, with her childish prattle, broke down the Queen's frozen condition, and the tears at last flowed. Minette had not seen her father since she was a few weeks old, and obviously had no recollection of him, but the grief of her mother for his loss was very real to his highly sensitive little girl. She was not quite six years old when her father was executed. If it had not been for Minette, Queen Henrietta would have retired for life to the Convent of the Carmelites in the Fauberg St Jacques. As it was, she went there for several weeks, leaving Minette in the safe hands of Lady Dalkeith (now Countess of Morton) and Father Cyprien.

There is a letter in the Clarendon papers dated 12 April 1649 from Charles II to the Earl of Morton acknowledging the services of his wife to the Princess Henrietta, desiring that she may continue in that charge and that the Earl will provide her with sufficient maintenance for herself and her children: a clear indication of Charles's impecunity at the time.[1] Further evidence of this is provided in the Clarendon papers for September 1649. It would appear that Sir John Berkeley had put in a claim to the Crown for the £500 he had lent to the Countess of Morton some years earlier for the care of the Princess Henrietta. Apparently Sir John was not paid the sum owed to him until that year.

Charles II, who had been recognized as King by the States General, returned to Paris in the summer of 1649, to comfort his mother. They were invited to join the French Court at St Germain, and in spite of the hazardous conditions on the streets of Paris, Henrietta and her mother, with Charles riding beside the coach, with his hand on the door to protect them from the mob, arrived there safely. Charles stayed with his mother and sister until September, when he left for Jersey. In May 1650, he landed in Scotland, in another abortive attempt to regain the throne.

Minette's childhood was surrounded with sorrow. Soon after Charles left France, the tragic news reached the exiled court of the death of Minette's elder sister Elizabeth at Carisbroke Castle, at the age of fifteen. Two months later her brother-in-law, the Prince of Orange, died of smallpox, adding another burden to a household already overwhelmed with grief.

Queen Henrietta was determined to bring up her beloved youngest daughter in the Roman Catholic religion, and from the moment of her arrival in France, Minette's instruction in the faith began. She was placed under the spiritual care of her mother's Capuchin chaplain Father Cyprien de Gamache. He wrote, 'As soon as the sparks of reason began to glimmer in the mind of that precious child, the Queen honoured me with the command to instruct her.' From a very early age Minette developed a deep love for the Catholic Church, and her religion became a dominating force in her life. She would also have been aware of the profound political significance religion had in the lives of her family, and her brother Charles's disapproval of her mother's efforts to bring her up in the Catholic faith; moreover, her mother's disastrous attempt to convert her brother, the Duke of Gloucester, was not lost on the little girl.

Her adored governess was her first target for a conversion from Protestantism to Roman Catholicism. Lady Morton always came with her to her instructions from Father Cyprien, and she commented to Minette that, 'Father Cyprien is working so hard at the catechism as much on my account as your royal Highness . . .' It is interesting to read Father Cyprien's early insights into Minette's character:

> I recollect that one day, the Queen her mother, seeing her with pleasure so warm in the cause of religion, said to her, 'My dear, as you have so much zeal, why do you not convert your governante?' 'Madam', answered the Princess, 'I do as much as I can in that way'. 'And what is that', rejoined the Queen. 'Madam', answered the Princess, in her infantine innocence, 'I embrace my governante, I kiss her, I say to her "Lady Morton, be converted, be a catholic, you must be a catholic to be saved. Father Cyprien tells me so very often; you have heard him as well as I; be a good lady, and I will love you dearly".'

The childish pleading was a forerunner of that later crusade which had such an important effect on her life and that of her eldest brother when she sought so earnestly to convert him and his country to Catholicism. Lady Morton very nearly succumbed to Minette's persuasiveness, but in 1651, two years after the death of her husband in Scotland, she felt that she had to return to her children, whom she had neglected for so long. Her promise that on her return to France she would embrace the faith was not to materialize, as she died of a sudden violent fever in 1654.

Late in 1652 the young Duke of Gloucester was released from Carisbroke Castle by Cromwell, and set sail for Holland. At the request of his mother he joined her in Paris, and for a short time her three sons, Charles, James and Henry, as well as Minette, were resident in the Palace of St Germain. Charles left Paris for Germany in 1654, and wanted to take Gloucester with him. But the Queen begged him to let the young boy stay with her for his education. This proved to be a bad decision.

Queen Henrietta Maria immediately set out to convert the boy to Catholicism with the aid of her new confessor, the Abbé Montagu. He was the second son of Sir Henry Montagu, First Earl of Manchester, a fanatical convert, and master of court intrigue. He not only had the ear of Henrietta Maria, but also of the Queen Regent, and last but by no means least, Minette. He persuaded the Queen Regent to break up Henrietta Maria's household at the Louvre, where an Anglican chaplain had been installed, and move her to the Palais Royal, where any form of Anglican worship was forbidden. Henrietta Maria lost her independence by this move, and the Anglican members of her household and her two sons, the Duke of York and the Duke of Gloucester, had to attend services at the house of Sir Richard Browne, who still maintained his ambassadorial privileges. At this time, the Abbé Montagu was also assisting Queen Henrietta Maria to establish her convent at Chaillot in a villa that had been built for Catherine de Medici. It was here that the Queen and Minette began to spend months on end, and here that the campaign to make the Duke of Gloucester a Catholic was conducted. Plans were made to send young Gloucester to a Jesuit college, but he refused to go. Charles II was deeply angry with his mother over what he looked on as a flagrant disregard for his father's wishes, and a dangerous move for the safety of the crown. He wrote a strong letter to his young brother:

¶ *Charles II to the Duke of Gloucester*

Cologne, 10 November 1654[2]

Dear Brother,

I have received yours without a date, in which you tell me that Mr Montagu, the Abbot of Pontoise, has endeavoured to pervert you from your religion. I do not doubt but you remember very well, the commands I left with you at my going away concerning that point. I am confident that you will observe them; yet your letters that come from Paris say, that it is the Queen's purpose to do all she can to change your religion, in which, if you hearken to her, or to anybody else in that matter, you must never think to see England or me again; and whatsoever mischief shall fall on me or my affairs from this time, I must lay all upon you as being the cause of it. Therefore consider well what it is to be, not only the cause of ruining a brother who loves you so well, but also your king and country. Do not let them persuade you either by force or fair promises; the first they never dare nor will use, and for the second, as soon as they have perverted you, they will have their end, and then they will care no more for you.

I am also informed there is a purpose to put you to the Jesuits' college which I command you, on the same grounds never to consent unto; and whensoever anybody goes to dispute with you in religion, do not answer them at all; for though you have reason on your side yet they, being prepared, will have the advantage of anybody that is not upon the same familiarity with argument as they are. If you do not consider what I say unto you, remember the last words of your dead father, which were, to be constant in your religion, and never to be shaken in it; which if you do not observe this shall be the last time you will hear from,

Dear Brother, your most affectionate brother

Charles II.

The Duke of York, the Princess of Orange and the Queen of Bohemia all added their strong advice to him to resist his mother's attempts to convert him.

Gloucester's refusal to comply with her wishes caused a terrible rift in the royal family and Henrietta Maria told him she never wished to see him again. He was dismissed from her household, and in spite of his pleadings she angrily abandoned him on the steps of the Palais Royal, refusing to give him her blessing.

While the Queen proceeded to vespers at Chaillot, her son returned to the Palais Royal to find his apartments stripped of his possessions, his servants dismissed and his horses turned out of the royal stables. Members of the court came to his assistance. Lord Hatton gave him lodgings, and Lord Jermyn showed his great generosity in selling his George, the last jewel he possessed, to give him funds for his journey to his brother Charles. The Duke came back to the Palais Royal that night, before the Queen's return from vespers, to say goodbye to his little sister. She was grief-stricken at the thought of parting from this younger brother who had become such a good companion. Her heart-breaking cry, 'Oh me, my brother! Oh me, my mother! What shall I do? I am undone for ever', gives an intense insight into this little girl's perceptive and loving character. Neither she nor her mother were to see him again.

According to Lord Hatton the issue of the Duke of Gloucester's religion rocked the exiled court. The great contrast between his early captivity under Cromwell and the adulation he received on his arrival in France had made him a rather insufferable young man.[3] Queen Henrietta Maria was at this time nearly unhinged with sadness and tribulation. This tragic family rift was for her a disaster, filling her with remorse that her last words to her young son, who was to die so soon afterwards, were ones of anger and hate.

Having now driven her three sons from her, Henrietta Maria remained in the Palais Royal with her much loved youngest daughter, and although the girl was only eleven years old the Queen started schemes for marrying her to her young cousin, Louis XIV. Minette was growing into a very intelligent and charming girl. A great deal of trouble was taken with her education, and she outshone all the other princesses. She was very fond of music, reading and poetry. She sang well, played the guitar and harpsichord, and was a beautiful dancer. Madame de Lafayette observed that as she was educated as a private person, she was full of sweetness and humanity. The lessons of adversity had not been wasted on her. 'You could see by her very perfections that she had been trained in the school of misfortune.' Her excellent governess, Lady Morton, must take much of the credit for this blossoming. Minette was the pet of the royal household in exile, and adored by her three brothers. But it was to Charles, who was the only member of her family that she remembered from her earliest days, that her deepest love was given. His love for her, which was perhaps the finest and profoundest element in his life, flowered in these pre-Restoration days in France, and remained steadfast until her tragic death. She was greatly loved at the Convent at Chaillot, where she spent so many of her childhood years. She used to wait on the Abbess and Filles de Marie, and everyone found her a very intelligent and engaging child.

The Queen Mother, however, was worried that Minette led too secluded a life, and at the early age of nine she was allowed to attend the ball given by Cardinal Mazarin for his niece Anna Martinozzi, on her marriage to the Prince of Conti. Minette appeared in the grand ballet. The subject was the nuptials of Peleus and Thetis. The royal prologue was dominated by the resplendent figure of Louis XIV as Apollo. His appearance was followed by the small figure of Minette in the character of Erato, the muse of the lovers, crowned with roses and myrtles. Her introductory speech was a huge success, and this first appearance gave her a love of the theatricals, masques and ballets which became so much a part of her life at the French Court.

Her appearance in 1655 at a private dance at the Louvre was not so successful. The Queen Mother thought the King should open the dance with his young cousin, but Louis did not like dancing with little girls and said so, and only very reluctantly did he comply with his mother's wishes. Minette's name appears frequently in court gazettes from this time onwards. She went to the crowning of the King at Reims with her two elder brothers, but during these very formative years, she spent most of her time either at the Palais Royal, Chaillot, or at Colombes, a pretty house that Queen Henrietta had bought as a country residence.

In 1656 her sister, the Princess of Orange, came to stay with them in Paris. The entertainments that were laid on at the French Court for this occasion gave Minette much pleasure. At a ball given for her by the Duke of Anjou, her future husband, and the Queen Mother, she was led out by King Louis, giving rise to more hopes that Minette might become his future wife. In 1657 Minette accompanied her mother to Bourbon-aux-Bains during September and October. The Queen's health was so improved by the treatment that they returned the following year with her brother and sister-in-law, the Duke and Duchess of Orléans, uncle and aunt of Louis XIV and parents of Mademoiselle de Montpensier, known as *une grande Mademoiselle* because of her great height.

We are fortunate to have several descriptions of Minette from people who knew her well. They vary from the over-courtly words of Father Cyprien de Gamache to the more honest opinions of Sir John Reresby and Madame de Motteville. They all in their way give us a vivid account of what kind of person Minette was at the time she wrote the first known letter to her brother Charles II. Father Cyprien de Gamache wrote of her:

> She is a princess of extraordinary merit, not only for the graces and beauty of the mind with which nature, prodigal of her gifts, has most liberally enriched her, but much more for the holiness of religion, and the sentiments of piety that have been shed abroad in her heart.

Madame de la Serre becomes more fulsome about her person:

> It is difficult to portray a countenance without defect; perfect beauties dazzle the eye of the beholder and cause the pencil to fall from the hand that would describe them. Her figure is rich, her bearing grave, her hair most beautiful, her brow a mirror, representing the majesty of her race, and her eyes matchless; in short the sun sees nothing to equal her. The beauty of her soul can only be compared to that of her countenance. Her disposition is so good that from the moment of first learning to follow virtue, she needed no other guide. She speaks so agreeably that the pleasure of hearing her is no less than that of seeing her; in singing, Echo alone can equal her, and in other accomplishments she is unrivalled. She has the mind, the voice, the beauty of an angel; let it not be thought strange that heaven enriches her with its rare treasures; who can express her goodness, grace, sweetness and wisdom? She possesses a thousand other qualities, least of all is that of Princess.

Madame de Brégis gives us more personal details of her appearance:

> To begin with, her height, I must tell you that this young princess is still growing, and that she will soon attain a perfect stature. Her air is as noble as her birth, her hair is of a bright chestnut hue, and her complexion rivals that of the gayest flowers. The snowy whiteness of her skin betrays the lilies from which she sprang. Her eyes are blue and brilliant, her lips ruddy, her throat beautiful, her arms and hands well made. Her charms show that she was born on a throne, and is destined to return there. Her wit is lively and agreeable. She is admired in her serious moments, and beloved in her most ordinary ones; she is gentle and obliging, and her kindness of heart will not allow her to laugh at others as cleverly as she could if she chose. She spends most of her time in learning all that can make a princess perfect, and she devotes her spare moments to the most varied accomplishments. She dances with incomparable grace, she sings like an angel, and the spinet is never so well played as by her fair hands. All this makes the young Cleopatra the most admirable princess in the world, and if fortune will untie the fold that wraps her eyes, to gaze upon her, she will not refuse to give her the greatest of earthly glories, for she deserves them well. I wish them for her more passionately than I can say.

In 1659 the twenty-five-year-old courtier Sir John Reresby, who had recently been converted to Catholicism, arrived at the court in exile in Paris to pay his respects to Queen Henrietta and her daughter. It is apparent that he was a firm favourite with the young princess and in his memoirs he writes of her thus:

> As I spoke the language of the country and danced pretty well, the young princess, then about fifteen years of age, behaved towards me with all the civil freedom that might be; she made me dance with her, played on the harpsichord to me in her highnesses chamber, suffered me to wait on her as she walked in the garden, and sometimes to toss her in a swing between two trees, and, in fine suffered me to be present at all her innocent diversions.[4]

Chapter 3

My Dearest Minette

The first known letter from Minette to Charles II is not dated, but must have been written some time after 28 October 1659, the date of the signing of the Treaty of the Pyrenees, which brought to an end the long conflict between France and Spain. Charles was at the time on the Spanish border, attempting to get the support of Spain for his cause. The bearer of the letter was Murrough O'Brien, 6th Baron and 1st Earl Inchquin, a convert to Catholicism, who was later to become the steward of Queen Henrietta's household. Charles, who had been unwelcome in France for so long, has decided to take the opportunity of King Louis' and Cardinal Mazarin's absence to go to Paris to see his mother and sister, and to make up the deep quarrel he had had with her over her attempt to convert the young Duke of Gloucester. Like most of Minette's letters, this one is in the Lambert Palace Library, and shows her characteristic rounded, large childish hand. It still has her personal seal attached to it and the faded brown ribbon ties, and like all her letters to Charles it is in French. It was written from the Queen's country house at Colombes.

Although some of the letters between Minette and Charles were carried by private courier, as this one was, much of their correspondence went by the weekly post between Paris and London, particularly Minette's letters, which went by the 'ordinaire', leaving Paris on Sundays. The Ambassadors complained of the great unreliability of the service. Letters were opened, particularly in

France, and the packet ship was often delayed, and sometimes actually foundered. Charles later warned his sister, after two of her letters went astray in the post, not to trust the service with anything confidential.

¶ *Minette to Charles*

Colombes, November 1659[1]

I would not let My Lord Inchquin leave, without assuring Your Majesty of my respect, and thanking you for the honour you do me, in writing to me so often. I fear that this may give you too much trouble, and I should be sorry if your Majesty should take so much for a little sister, who does not deserve it, but who can at least acknowledge and rejoice in the honour you do her. I hope the peace will give you all the happiness you desire, and then I shall be happy, because of the love and respect I bear Your Majesty. It is a cause of great joy to me, since it gives me the hope of seeing you, which is most passionately desired by your very humble servant.

This visit to Colombes was the first time Charles had seen Minette for five years. She had changed out of all recognition, and he first greeted the wrong young girl by mistake. Minette has become a captivating creature with her beautiful auburn hair, bright blue eyes and colourful complexion. In all the sorrows of her short life, she had always been surrounded by love, which she gave and received with her whole heart. Everyone who met her warmed to this loving personality, and Charles was completely captivated by her. It was from the time of this visit that the correspondence began between the two which was to continue until her death. The following letter from Charles was probably written on his way back to Cologne after this visit:

¶ *Charles to Minette*

20 December[2]

For my deare, deare sister, Henriette
The kindness I have for you will not permit me to lose this occasion to conjure you to continue your kindness to a brother

that loves you more than he can express, which truth I hope you are so well persuaded of, as I may express these returns which I shall strive to deserve. Dear sister be kind to me, and be confident that I am entirely yours. C.

Although all Minette's letters to Charles are in French, nearly all Charles's letters to her are in English. He had been trying to persuade her to write to him in English, but she had refused and had begged him to write to her in French. Her English at this time was poor, and although it improved, she was never as fluent in her native tongue as he would have liked. On this occasion it appears that Charles gave way to her, and his next letter to her is in French. The girl Janton, whom Charles mentions in this letter and in the following one, must have been a great friend of Minette, and probably a former member of her mother's household. She has never been identified as a mistress of Charles, but at this time she certainly seems to be an intimate member of his household, with what was described as a delightful voice. His reference to the scapular that Minette promised to send him is fascinating. These objects of Catholic piety were worn over the shoulders, hidden from view, as a sign of devotion to a particular religious order. It would imply that Charles was not as firmly against the Roman Church as some historians have implied. Madame de Bordes was Minette's *femme de chambre* and attended her throughout her life. After his sister's death, Charles sent for her to come to England to be dresser to his wife.

The date of this letter is probably 1660, although he was also in Brussels in 1659. But the mention of Janton in both this letter and the following one, which is definitely dated 1660, suggests that this one also belongs to that year.

¶ *Charles to Minette*

Brussels, 7 February 1660[3]

For my dearest dearest sister

I begin this letter in French by assuring you, that I am very glad to be scolded by you. I withdraw what I said with great joy, since you scold me so charmingly, but I will never give up the friendship that I have for you, and you give me so many marks of yours that we shall never have another Quarrel but as to which of us shall love the other most. But in this I will never yield to you. I send you this letter by the hands of Janton, who is the best girl in the world. We talk of you every day, and wish we were with you a thousand times a day. Her voice has almost entirely returned and she sings very well. She has taught me La Chanson de ma queue 'I prithee, sweet harte, come tell me and do not lie', and a number of others. When you send me the scapular I promise to wear it always, for love of you. Tell Madame Boude that I will soon send her my portrait. Just now the painter is away, but he returns in a few days. Tell me, I beg of you, how you spend your time, for if you stayed in Chaillot in this miserable weather you must have been not a little bored.

For the future please do not treat me with so much ceremony, or address me with so many Your Majesties, for between you and me there should be nothing but affection. C.R.

Between this letter from Charles and the following one, great events occurred. Four days after it was written General Monk arrived in London at the head of his army, and at his request the members of the Long Parliament (The Rump) who had been driven out in 1648 returned, and Parliament was dissolved a month later. Monk started negotiating with Charles for his return. The King had moved to Breda to be with his sister Mary, and his next letter to Minette was written from there. Although he was deeply involved in negotiations for the Restoration, he still had time to write to his sister in reply to a letter of hers of 23 April, which is, alas, missing. It would appear that she was worried and a little jealous of Charles's proximity to a rival for her place in his heart. Perhaps the enigmatic Janton was the cause of this. He certainly mentions her again in this letter, which like the previous one was written in French. Her other rival may have been Barbara Palmer, the future Lady Castlemaine, who had arrived at Breda with her husband, and had already captivated Charles's heart.

¶ *Charles to Minette*

Breda, 29 April 1660[4]

I wrote to you last week and meant to send my letter in Janton's packet, but she had already closed hers, so I had to give my letter to Mason. I have received yours of the 23rd, which is so full of marks of affection that I know not how to find words in which to express my joy. In return, I must assure you that as I love you as much as possible, and that neither absence, nor any other cause will alter the affection I have promised to bear you, in the smallest degree. Never fear that others who are present shall get the advantage over you, for, believe me, no one can share the love I cherish for you.

I have sent to Gentseau to order some summer clothes, and have told him to take the ribbons to you, for you to choose the trimmings and feathers. Thank you for the song that you have sent me, I do not know if it is pretty, as Janton has not yet learned it. If you only knew how often we talk of you, and wish you were here, you would understand how much I long to see you, and do me the justice to believe that I am entirely yours. C.R.

On 1 May the new Parliament, called the Convention, heard the Declaration of Breda read out to them, and voted unanimously for the restoration of the Monarchy. Charles showed masterly diplomacy in his dealings with General Monk and the Parliamentary Commission who met him at The Hague. On 23 May, accompanied by his two brothers, he embarked on the Royal Navy's flagship, the *Naseby*, whose name was quickly changed to *Royal Charles*, and sailed for Dover. His following short letter to Minette was written in haste from Canterbury, on his way to London. This letter, in French, was in the collection of M. Donnadieu, and is now in the British Museum. The bearer was Edward Progers, the King's *valet de chambre*.

¶ *Charles to Minette*

Canterbury, 26 May 1660[5]

I was so tormented with business at The Hague, that I could not write to you before my departure, but I left orders with my sister [the Princess of Orange] to send you a small present from me, which I hope you will soon receive. I arrived yesterday at Dover where I found Monk with a great number of nobility, who almost overwhelmed me with kindness and joy for my return. My head is so dreadfully stunned with the acclamation of the people, and the vast amount of business, that I know not whether I am writing sense or nonsense. Therefore pardon me if I say no more than that I am entirely yours . . . For my dear sister.

Charles's present to Minette of a splendid side-saddle trimmed with green velvet trappings, embroidery and gold lace was received with great joy, not only for its intrinsic beauty but as a visible sign of the sudden and wonderful change in her brother's fortunes: a present from a King who had certainly come into his own. The gift is mentioned in the Warrants of 10 August 1660, in the Lord Chamberlain's office at St James's. Minette's delight with the gift is expressed in her next letter, written two weeks later, still from Colombes. This is the only letter of hers which has the year date.

¶ *Minette to Charles*

Colombes, 15 June 1660[6]

I have received the letter you wrote me by Mr Progers which gave me no little joy, for to know that you were arrived in England and at the same time that you have remembered me gave me the greatest joy imaginable, and in truth I would I were able to express that I think and you would see that it is true that nobody is more your servant than I.

To the King.

The royal courtiers thronged round Queen Henrietta and Minette, all anxious that the royal ladies would put in a good word for them to Charles, and the next few letters we have from Minette show that they did not plead in vain. The bearer of these letters, M. Fevrier, was a popular astrologer at the French Court, casting horoscopes and performing conjuring tricks to entertain the ladies. Minette obviously had no hesitation in sending him to her brother for his amusement. The young Louis XIV had been down to the south of France to meet his Spanish bride. On their return they stopped at Fontainebleau and Vincennes. The Queen Mother took Henrietta Maria and Minette to meet her. On 12 August the King's younger brother Philippe, known as 'Monsieur', gave a ball at St Cloud for them. He opened the dancing with Minette. Rumours were already abounding of a possible marriage between these two cousins.

¶ *Minette to Charles*

Colombes, 17 August 1660[7]

I must write to you by M. Fevrier, who is going to England, in the assurance that he will deceive more than half the kingdom. He even hopes to begin with you! We are soon going to Paris to see the entry of the Queen, which takes place on the 26th of this month. I would offer to tell you all about it, if my Lord St Albans were not staying here over that time. He will acquit himself of the task far better than I can, although I am more than anyone your most humble servant.

Although Louis XIV had looked on his young cousin as a little girl, his brother Philippe, who had now succeeded his uncle as Duc d'Orléans, was clearly captivated by her, and as 1660 progressed it became obvious that he was very much in love with Minette. Queen Henrietta Maria wrote to her daughter, Mary of Orange, on 20 August, telling her that she thought that the betrothal of Minette to Monsieur was almost settled, only waiting for the official consent of Charles. On 24 August, Anne of Austria formally called on the Queen to ask for the hand of her daughter in marriage to Anne's son. The Queen immediately wrote that day to Charles asking for his consent. In her letter she states that, 'Your sister is by no means averse to the idea, and as for Monsieur, he is very much in love and extremely impatient for your answer.' On the surface this looked like a brilliant match for the sixteen-year-old Minette. Madame de Lafayette, who was very close to the Princess, writes in her *History of Madame Henriette of England*, 'What the English Princess possessed in the highest degree was the gift of pleasing, together with what we call grace and her charms were distributed throughout her person, revealed alike in her actions and her wit, and never has princess been able to make herself so equally beloved of men and adored by women.'

Her future husband, a glittering figure at his brother's court, is described by Madame de Lafayette in not such glowing terms. 'Monsieur, the King's only brother, was no less attached than he to his mother, the Queen. He was by inclination as much disposed to the pursuits of women as the King was adverse to them. He was well made and handsome, but with a stature and type of beauty more fitting to a princess than to a prince and he had taken more pains to have his beauty admired by all the world than to enjoy it for the conquest of women despite the fact that he was continuously amongst them. His vanity, it seemed, made him incapable of affection save of himself.' In spite of his growing homosexual tendencies, the Duc d'Orléans was certainly in love with his future wife before they were married.

As Madame of France, Minette would have her heart's desire to live out her life at the French Court, unlike so many less fortunate princesses who had to leave their native country for good when they married, never to return.

The following letter from Charles, dated 27 August, has no year date, but may well have been written about this time, when due to her preoccupation with her betrothal and with the wedding of Louis XIV, Minette had lapsed in her letters to her brother. His devotion to her shines out in this short, loving note:

¶ *Charles to Minette*

27 August[8]

I should thinke myself much to blame if I let this bearer see you without a letter from me. I know not whether the long time we have been asunder doth not slacken the kindness you had for me, I am sure neither that or anything else can alter me in the least degree towards you. Deare sister, be kinde to me for assure yourself there is no person living will strive to deserve it more than him that is and ever will be most truly yours.

For my deare Sister,
C.

After Charles's consent to his sister's marriage was given, the betrothal was officially celebrated by a state banquet arranged for the young couple by Cardinal Mazarin, who led Minette into the banqueting hall. She was dressed in a dazzling white dress, but it was already noted by many people, not least the King, that she was unnaturally thin. Louis teased his brother about it, saying he was marrying the 'bones of the Holy Innocents'.

Queen Henrietta was determined to take Minette to England before her marriage, and arrangements for the visit to take place at the end of October and early November were being finalized when the Duke of Gloucester became ill with smallpox, which was prevalent in London at the time. He appeared to be making a good recovery when he suddenly collapsed and died on 13 September. This was a cruel blow to the King, who had dearly loved his youngest brother, a boy of great promise. It was also a bitter blow to his mother, who remembered with deep remorse her treatment of Gloucester the last time she saw him, when she had virtually thrown him out of her house. The loss to Minette of her young brother, who had been such a loving companion for her during his time in France, was intense, as it was for Princess Mary of Orange, who was on her way to England when she heard the news. A great sadness marred the excitement of the family reunion.

The early death of the Duke of Gloucester, considered the most able of the three royal brothers, had far-reaching effects on the future of the House of Stuart and made it even more imperative that the King should marry and have children as soon as possible. Such was Minette's grief for her brother that it was some time before she could bring herself to write to Charles. Her poignant letter speaks for itself:

¶ *Minette to Charles*

Colombes, 10 October 1660[9]

Since I last wrote to you so cruel a misfortune has occurred that until this hour I could not make up my mind to speak of it to you, not finding fit terms in which to do so. The sorrow which it has caused you is so just that one can but take one's part in it, and I have the honour to share it equally with you. Besides, I think it best to be silent, which I shall be when I have told you that the thing I desire most on earth is to have the happiness of seeing you, which I hope will be soon; and then I shall be able to show you how much I am your very humble servant, which all kinds of people may tell you, but assuredly there are few who are so as truly as I.

To the King.

Charles II had several other marriage proposals for Minette. They were from Emperor Leopold II, the King of Portugal, the Duke of Savoy, and even Prince Rupert. But he was quite satisfied with the idea of a marriage between Minette and her first cousin, the Duc d'Orléans, and the Comte de Soissons, as Ambassador of France, arrived in England at the end of October to prepare the formal proposal and marriage contract.

Queen Henrietta and Minette left Paris on 29 October, for the journey to England, stopping the night of All Saints Day, 1 November, at Beauvais, where they attended Mass in the cathedral. Monsieur had been loath to part with his beloved Princess, and begged the Queen to bring her back as soon as possible. The Duke of York met them in Calais with a large fleet, and escorted them onto his flagship. They set sail for Dover, but very calm seas delayed them, and they did not arrive until two days later. Charles and Minette were delighted to be in each other's company again, and a great banquet was held in Dover Castle, where the four remaining children of Charles I sat down to dine together for the first time on English soil since the early days of the Civil War.

The following day they travelled to Canterbury, then on to Rochester. The Queen had objected to the arranged formal entry into London by water. Maybe it brought back too many memories of her arrival that way as Charles I's young bride. Instead they came by road, crossing Lambeth Bridge to Whitehall on 12 November. The following day Minette was too tired to appear in public, and she stayed in her private apartments, dressed in a negligée and a mob cap, and a brightly coloured Indian robe, playing ombre with the Duke of York and the Princess Royal, Mary of Orange. She received the Comte de Soissons in these informal surroundings, much to his delight.

From her first arrival, Minette captured the hearts of the English with her winning ways. The House of Commons sent a deputation to present her with a gift of £10,000. She was never to receive the money. As she wryly put it to Ralph Montagu years later, 'The King made bold with it.' Samuel Pepys and his wife were presented to her by Mr Fox soon after her arrival. Apparently he did not like her hair style, 'frizzed up to the ears', as he put it, and considered his own wife much handsomer.

In November the Comte de Soissons made the formal demand to the King for her hand. The main clauses in the agreement were that the two spouses promised to unite their faith to each other in the presence of the Roman Church, and that the King would give his sister a dowry of £40,000 and a present of £20,000, part in jewellery and part in kind. The French King and his brother agreed to give the Princess 40,000 livres a year for life, and the Château of Montargis, magnificently furnished, for her own residence. When Monsieur had become Duc d'Orléans the King had given him the Duchy's property, along with St Cloud, Valois and Villers-Cotterets. The Duke and his wife were to hold their property in common, and if she died childless her heirs could only claim her dowry, not the gifts from Charles. Montargis, which is east of Orléans, does not seem to have been visited by Minette.

Although very different in character and religion, Minette and Mary of Orange enjoyed each other's company enormously. Mary was not so enamoured with her native country as her young sister and kept to her apartments most of the time. She was violently opposed to the Duke of York's marriage to Anne Hyde, one of her former Maids of Honour.

Just as preparations were afoot for the celebration of a royal family Christmas, and Minette was enjoying the balls and fêtes given in her honour, disaster struck the house of Stuart for the second time that year. On 20 December, Princess Mary was taken very ill in her apartment. The dreaded smallpox was diagnosed, and the Queen, fearing that Minette would contract the disease as well, removed her at once to St James's Palace. She herself wished to remain behind with her eldest daughter, but Charles would not hear of it, partly for the sake of her health, and partly for fear that she might attempt to convert Mary to Catholicism.

Obviously Minette was deeply upset by being parted from her brother and sister, and maybe a little jealous, after all Charles's attention to her, that his time now was totally spent with Mary. On the evening of her arrival at St James's Palace, she received a short loving note from Charles to comfort her.

¶ *Charles to Minette*

20 December 1660[10]

The kindness I have for you will not permit me to lose this occasion to conjure to you to continue your kindness to a brother that loves you more than he can express, which truth I hope you are so well persuaded of, as I may expect those returns which I shall strive to deserve. Deare sister, be kind to me, and be confident that I am entirely yours. C.R. For my deare sister, the Princess Henriette.

Unable to attend her daughter herself, the Queen sent her own French doctor to her. A staunch advocate of blood-letting, it would appear that this well-meaning man did, in fact, cause the death of the Princess. She appeared to be recovering well from the illness when he advocated a fierce course of bleeding for her; the already weakened patient immediately collapsed, dying on Christmas Eve, aged twenty-nine. At the end of this eventful and tragic year for the royal family, Minette's grief was particularly harrowing; for during these last weeks of her stay in England she had become devoted to her sister.

Chapter 4

Madame of France

What was to have been a Christmas full of joy for the united royal family found them in deep mourning for the Duke of Gloucester and the Princess Royal. Queen Henrietta Maria, fearful for the health of Minette and with repeated agitated messages from the Duc d'Orléans for their speedy return, decided to shorten the visit and return to France.

On 9 January 1661 they embarked at Portsmouth on the man-of-war *The London*. They were accompanied by the Duke of Buckingham, who had fallen deeply in love with Minette during her short stay in England, and had persuaded the King to let him accompany the Queen and Princess to France. The ship ran into bad weather almost as soon as it set sail, and had to return to Portsmouth in a severely damaged state. Minette had already been taken very ill. At first it was thought to be seasickness, but her alarming symptoms continued on dry land, and the smallpox was feared. In fact it was measles, and she owed her recovery from the illness to her refusal to be repeatedly bled by the French physicians. She had been convinced that bleeding had been the cause of the early deaths of her brother and sister. One of the royal household attending the Princess during this frightening illness wrote on 24 January:

> The expectation we here are now in is the health of my dear Princess, which till this morning, I apprehended, she having

> had since blood letting and purging, almost constant fever; but God be praised they are both now so well appeased, that if our French physicians give nature a time to recover its strength before embarkment, I hope all will have been for the best, notwithstanding the still remaining drought in her highness's mouth.[1]

They arrived at Le Havre on 31 January. Buckingham, who made no effort to conceal his passion for Minette, was causing considerable embarrassment to the Queen with his excessive show of concern for her health. To get him out of the way she despatched him to Paris to give Monsieur advance news of their arrival; soon afterwards, at the instigation of Monsieur, he was sent home.

Avoiding Rouen, where there was rumoured to be an outbreak of smallpox, they went to the château of Henrietta Maria's cousin, the Duc de Longueville, who entertained them very royally. From there they moved on to stay with her Almoner and confidant, the Abbé Montagu, at his splendid Abbey of St Martin. They were dazzled by his magnificent collection of jewellery, paintings and porcelain. The King and Queen made a private trip out to the Abbey to greet them, accompanied by Monsieur who was ecstatic with joy to see Minette again in good health.

The French royal family returned to St Germain, but Monsieur came back the following day to escort Queen Henrietta and Minette to Paris. The King and Queen welcomed them officially at St Denis, and conducted them from there to the Palais Royal. The official welcome over, the Queen and her daughter retired to the Convent at Chaillot to await the Papal dispensation for the marriage, which was required as the betrothed couple were first cousins. There was considerable delay over its arrival from Rome, because the first application had failed to mention exactly what the couple's relationship to each other was. The document eventually arrived on 9 March.[2]

There is no known correspondence between Charles and Minette from the time of the King's letter to her of 20 December 1660, during Mary of Orange's last illness, until a year later – 14 December 1661. This is unfortunate, as 1661 was a very significant year for Minette. Her marriage to the Duc d'Orléans, her disillusionment with him, her probable affair with Louis XIV, and the birth of her first child all occurred during this time. Whether the absence of correspondence results from her preoccupation with her new role as Madame of France and the intrigues that followed her marriage, or from the fact that the letters were so politically sensitive that they were destroyed, will never be known.

Monsieur's impatience to be married as soon as possible increased. The delay was caused by it being the season of Lent, the fact that the Princess was still in mourning for her brother and sister, and that the letter had not arrived from England empowering Lord Jermyn as ambassador extraordinary to sign the marriage articles on behalf of Charles II. All these causes for delay were at last brushed aside, and the marriage contract was signed at the Louvre on 30 March. The following morning Minette went to confession at the Church of St Eustache, and Monsieur to the chapel at St Germain l'Auxerrois. That evening the betrothal was solemnized in the great drawing-room of Queen Henrietta Maria in the Palais Royal, in the presence of the King and Queen, the Queen Mothers of France and England, Mademoiselle of France, the Prince and Princess of Condé, the Duc d'Enghien, the Duc de Vendôme, Lord Jermyn, the Earl of St Albans and a few select members of the court. The marriage took place the following day, 1 April, in the presence of the same people, in the private chapel of Queen Henrietta Maria in the Palais Royal. Although the Abbé Montagu had hoped to perform the ceremony, it was the Bishop of Valence, Grand Almoner to Monsieur, who officiated. It was followed by a private and informal supper given by Queen Henrietta Maria. Although we have no correspondence between Minette and Charles about the time of the wedding, there is a letter written the day after by Louis XIV to his cousin, Charles II.

My brother,
Having always considered the marriage of my brother with your sister the Princess of England, as a new tie which would draw still closer the bonds of our friendship, I feel more joy than I can express, that it was yesterday happily accomplished; and as I doubt not that this news will inspire you with the same sentiment as myself, I was unwilling to delay a moment in sharing my joy with you, nor would I lose the opportunity of this mutual congratulation, to confirm to you by these lines that I am, my brother very sincerely your good brother Louis.[3]

Madame de Motteville gave a vivid description of Minette at the time of her marriage:

> The Princess of England was above middle height; she was very graceful, and her figure which was not faultless, did not appear as imperfect as it really was. Her beauty was not of the most perfect kind, but her charming manners made her very attractive. She had an extremely delicate and very white skin, with a bright, natural colour, a complexion so to speak, of roses and jasmine. Her eyes were small but very soft and sparkling, her nose not bad, her lips were rosy, and her teeth as white and regular as you could wish, but her face was too long, and her great thinness seemed to threaten her beauty with early decay. She dressed her hair and whole person in a most becoming manner, and she was so lovable in herself, that she could not fail to please. She had not been able to become queen, and to make up for this disappointment, she wished to reign in the hearts of worthy people, and to find glory in the world by her charms, and by the beauty of her mind. Already much sense and discernment might be traced in her mind, and in spite of her youth which had hitherto hidden her from the public, it was easy to judge, that when she appeared upon the great theatre of the court of France, she would play upon it one of the principal parts.[4]

The training which Monsieur had received throughout his childhood, supervised by the Queen Mother and Cardinal Mazarin, deliberately encouraged him to indulge in every frivolity and feminine pursuit. The more effeminate he was, the less threat he would be to his elder brother. Such a background inevitably made it almost impossible for him to make a success of his marriage, in spite of his belief before his marriage to Minette that he was violently in love with her. No one was more conscious of this than Minette's cousin, Prince Rupert, who tried in vain to make Charles withhold his sanction for the marriage. Whether she herself had given deep thought to the personal side of marriage was doubtful. She found Monsieur an amusing companion, he was apparently very much in love with her, and her brother approved of the match. It was an excellent alliance for England and France. This obviously satisfied her. Mademoiselle de Montpensier was less impressed with the Duc:

> The more I knew of him, the more I was of the opinion, that he was a character to think more about his own beauty and attire than to raise himself by great action, and render himself considerable; so that I loved him very well as my cousin, but I could never have loved him as my husband.[5]

A few days after the marriage, Monsieur decided that it was time to take his wife to his apartments at the Tuileries. Father Cyprien describes the tearful parting between Minette and her mother.

> When Monsieur came to fetch this princess to take her to his apartment in the Tuileries, there was general mourning in the Palais Royal; sighs, tears and sobs of the Queen and of Madame, made some weep, melted the hearts of others and pained all. It took some time to moderate the grief of those royal personages and Madame desired that the service which I had rendered to the Queen her mother might not prevent me from seeing her, and continuing the same offices which I had performed for her before her marriage.[6]

The young couple were greeted by the royal family at the Tuileries with lavish presents and entertainments, and Minette's sorrow at parting with her mother was soon forgotten in the whirl of activities and admiration, and her new role as Madame of France. However, the Duc's love for her died within a fortnight of marriage, and was replaced with a growing jealousy of her which was to cloud, and eventually ruin her life.

On 14 March, at the Holy Thursday ceremony of the washing of the feet of the poor, Minette took the place of the sickly Queen; she did so all through that summer, and on many future occasions. The Court left Fontainebleau shortly after Easter, but Minette and her husband stayed behind for a short time to receive the congratulations of foreign courts on their marriage. Francheville writes of her at this time:

> The Princess of England, the King's sister-in-law, brought to court the charm of sweet and animated conversation, sustained

> by the reading of good works, and by a sure and delicate taste. She perfected herself in the knowledge of the language, which, at the time of her marriage, she still wrote badly. She inspired a fresh emulation of spirit, and introduced at court a politeness and grace of which the rest of Europe had hardly any idea. Madame had all the wit of her brother Charles II, embellished by the charm of her sex, by the gift and the desire of pleasing.[7]

Her afternoons were spent with a clique of sprightly and intelligent young ladies, and they were joined in the evenings by Monsieur and his friends. Among her closest friends at this time was the widowed Duchess of Châtillon, Bablon as she was nicknamed, a great favourite of Charles II. There was also the Duchesse de Crequi, and Mademoiselle de Mortemart, better known in later years as Madame de Montespan, and Madame de Monaco, sister of Monsieur's favourite, the Comte de Guiche. Another, who was to remain near her for the rest of her life, was Madeleine de la Vergue, the young Marquise de Lafayette, one of the most intellectual ladies of the Court, who was to write so vividly of Minette.

The young married couple paid a brief visit to Queen Henrietta Maria at Colombes before visiting the exquisite St Cloud, which had been enlarged and embellished by the King for their marriage. In these beautiful surroundings, Minette was to spend many happy hours, wandering with her friends in the formal gardens which had been laid out by Le Nôtre, and bathing in the river. All her life she was a keen swimmer, and she encouraged her ladies to join her. Their first stay there was a short one.

Louis XIV was already, in the short time since her return from England and marriage to his brother, fascinated by his sister-in-law. As she saw her husband's affection for her die, so Minette was flattered and delighted with the increasing admiration and attention she was getting from the King. As their romance flowered during the summer at Fontainebleau, so the dark shadow of Monsieur's jealousy, firstly of the Duke of Buckingham, who had been despatched home, but chiefly of her relationship with his brother, grew. It was not Minette's love for the King that bothered him but the King's love for her, which made him feel deeply neglected. Louis XIV wrote to her at St Cloud, begging her to come to Fontainebleau.

¶ *Louis XIV to Madame*

Fontainebleau[8]

If I wish myself at St Cloud it is not because of its grottos or the freshness of its foliage. Here we have gardens fair enough to console us, but the company which is there now, is so good, that I find myself furiously tempted to go there, if I did not expect to see you tomorrow, I do not know what I should do and could not help making a journey to see you. Remember me to all of your ladies, and do not forget the affection that I have promised you, which is, I can assure you, all you could possibly desire, if indeed you wish me to love you very much. Give my best love to my brother. To my sister. Fontainebleau. Friday.

The stay at Fontainebleau was magical. In the palace where Mary Queen of Scots had spent much of her early life, her great-granddaughter revelled in the elegance of the place and the lavish entertainments laid on by the King largely for her benefit. She was an excellent horsewoman, and she and the King spent many blissful hours riding alone in the forests around the palace, where their mutual affection for each other grew to dangerous proportions and aroused comment from the Queen, the Queen Mother, Monsieur, and other members of the Court. The Queen's ill health and lack of spirits placed on Minette the burden of leading the entertainments with the King, adding fuel to the gossip. Louis' admiration of her charm, intelligence, wit, as well as her learning held him in thrall all that summer, and if his adulation turned her head a little, it was not surprising.

The contrast between Louis and his brother became more and more painfully obvious to her. She became reckless about her strong feelings for the King, and there is little doubt that she became his mistress. The absence of letters at this time between her and Charles II is a great loss, though there are contemporary letters and accounts which show that the situation between them had become so serious that Queen Henrietta Maria and the Queen Mother were alarmed. Madame de Motteville was a close confidante of Queen Henrietta Maria and the Queen Mother, and it is apparent from her memoirs that the two Queens had spoken to her of their concern, and asked her to speak to Minette about it.

> This young princess should have confided in me, as well on the account of the honour which the Queen of England did me in treating me kindly and believing me attached to her interests, as of the assiduous services I rendered her in my intercourse with the Queen her mother-in-law. I spoke to her about it; and as she was gentle and complaisant, I thought that she was willing to follow my advice . . . for had she only deprived herself of the walks which mitigated against propriety, and might injure her health, and seemed to the King to give them up voluntarily, the King would have commended her for it, since what is reasonable always inspires esteem in those who are guided by reason . . . but her natural sentiments were opposed to prudence; Madame heard with the ear the councils I gave her, but the impulses of her heart rejected them. The Queen of England . . . was uneasy about what was passing at Fontainebleau, and about the Queen Mother's dissatisfaction with Madame.[9]

Queen Henrietta Maria wrote to Madame de Motteville at this time of her worries about her daughter, ending her letter with the words, 'You have with you my other little self who loves you well, I can assure you. I beg of you to remain her friend. I know you will understand what I mean.'

The obstinate, coquettish side of Minette's character, which was to cause her much trouble, was already showing itself. It seems impossible that Charles did not know what was going on at the French Court between Louis and his sister, and as correspondence between them at this time must have taken place, its absence in the archives makes it fairly obvious that both parties thought that it should be destroyed.

On 11 June Monsieur gave a brilliant ball succeeded by an even more splendid affair given by the Duke of Beaufort in the park. Dancing took place in a salon of foliage and the trees were lighted with innumerable lamps. The Queen Mother, perhaps to try and break up the liaison, took the young couple on a visit to Madame de Chevreuse at Dampierre, and shortly after Queen Henrietta arrived on a visit, obviously to see what her daughter was up to. She stayed for a week, and the couple accompanied her on her return as far as Vaux de Vicomte, the magnificent residence of M. Fouquet, who was so shortly to fall from grace.

To divert attention from his affair with Minette, Louis started paying attention to her Maid of Honour, Louise de La Vallière. What started as a ruse to draw attention away from Minette soon developed into an affair, and before very long the King found himself genuinely in love with the shy young lady. Naturally Minette was piqued with this turn of events and turned her attention to the handsome, gallant Comte de Guiche. At this time she became pregnant and her health rapidly deteriorated. The endless round of balls and ballets had taken its toll of her fragile constitution, and she was ordered to bed by her doctors. In this next letter from Charles to Minette, he shows deep concern for her health. Lord Crofts of Saxham was a Gentleman of the Bedchamber and guardian of Charles's illegitimate son by Lucy Walter, who was known as James Crofts until he was created Duke of Monmouth in 1663. Reading between the lines in this letter, the 'full account' which was given to Charles by Lord Crofts may have been of the termination of Minette's affair with Louis, and his reference later in the letter to her good relationship with the King, in spite of the tumultuous summer, would seem to confirm this. In this letter Charles uses his pet name for his sister for the first time in the correspondence.

¶ *Charles to Minette*

Whitehall, 16 December 1661[10]

I have been in very much paine for your indisposition, not so much that I thought it dangerous, but for fear that you should miscarry. I hope now that you are out of that fear too, and for God's sake, my dearest sister have a care of yourselfe, and beleeve that I am more concerned in your health than I am in my owne, which I hope you do me that justice to be confident of, since you know how much I love you. Crofts hath given me a full accounte of all you charged him with, with all which I am very well pleased, and in particular with the desire you have to see me at Dunkerke the next summer, which you may easily believe is a very welcome proposition to me; between this and then we will adjust that voyage I am sure I shall be very impatient till I have the happiness to see my chere Minette againe. I am very glad to find that the King of France does still continue his confidence and kindness to you, which I am so sensible of, that if I had no other reason to grounde my kindness to him but that, he may be assured of my friendship as long as I live, and pray upon all occasions, assure him of this. I do not write to you in French, because my head is now dosed with businesse, and 'tis troublesome to write anything but English, and I do intende to write to you very often in English, that you may not quite forget it.

For my dearest sister.
C.R.

Minette stayed resting in her apartments under doctor's orders until well into March. This did not stop her entertaining all her friends from morning to night, and even having ballets performed there, one devised by herself, and one in which the King, Queen and Monsieur took part.

The next letter from Minette to Charles is not only the first we have that has her new seal attached as the Duchesse d'Orléans, but also the first since her marriage. Mrs Stuart, the bearer of it, was the widow of Walter Stuart, third son of the first Lord Blantyre. The letter introduces her and her enchanting daughter Frances to the English Court, where Frances was destined to become the lady-in-waiting of Charles's bride, Catherine of Braganza, and one of Charles's greatest loves, although, much to his dismay, she would never become his mistress. She had been brought up entirely in France, was extremely beautiful in rather a childish way, wonderfully dressed, and from her arrival, completely won Charles's heart.

¶ *Minette to Charles*

4 January 1662[11]

I would not lose this opportunity of writing to you by Mrs Stuart, who is taking over her daughter to become one of the Queen your wife's future maids. If this were not the reason for her departure, I should be very unwilling to let her go, for she is the prettiest girl in the world, and one of the best fitted of any I know to adorn your Court. Yesterday I received your letter in reply to those I sent you by Crofts. I cannot tell you what joy I feel at the mere thought of seeing your majesty once more. There is nothing in the world I wish for more. Believe me, when I say that I remain your very humble servant.

The Comte de Guiche appeared again in Minette's life encouraged by one of her less desirable Maids of Honour, Montalais. She was a born intriguer and carried passionate love letters from de Guiche to Minette, and secreted him into her apartments disguised as a fortune-teller. Flattered by his attentions, and bored by the long weeks of inactivity, she very unwisely encouraged him, arousing yet again Monsieur's deep jealousy, and a great deal more court gossip. At the same time, Louis' passion for her maid de La Vallière also reached alarming proportions, and Minette felt that she should ask her to leave the Tuileries. She went to the Convent of St Cloud, but the distraught King soon fetched her back and begged Minette to reinstate her, as a reward promising not to carry out the threatened banishment of de Guiche.

On 27 March, at three in the morning, Minette gave birth to her first child, a daughter. A contemporary account states that she was so bitterly disappointed that it was not a son that she told her attendants to throw the baby out of the window. The Marquis de Vardes, who was himself deeply jealous of de Guiche, persuaded the latter's father, the Maréchal de Gramont, to ask the King for a military appointment for his son, to get him away from Minette and out of the country. After taking a secret farewell of her, de Guiche left France to take up his command of the troops in Lorraine, and Minette duly dismissed Montalais. On 21 May Minette's daughter was christened in the Chapel of the Palais Royal by the Abbé Montagu. She was named Marie Louise. The disastrous beginning to Minette's marriage, and her probable affair with her brother-in-law so soon afterwards, have given rise to speculations that Marie Louise was, in fact, the child of Louis XIV, which may have been one of the reasons why Minette was so angry that she was not a boy. Queen Anne of Austria's deep devotion to this little girl, who came to live with her, and who inherited the main bulk of her fortune, adds interest to this argument. Charles II was married to his Portuguese bride, Catherine of Braganza, on the same day as his niece's christening, and Minette received a letter from him written two days later, telling her the news.

¶ *Charles to Minette*

Portsmouth, 23 May 1662[12]

My Lord of St Albans will give you so full a description of my wife as I shall not goe about to doe it, only I must tell you that I think myselfe very happy. I was married the day before yesterday, but the fortune that follows our family is fallen upon me, car Monsieur le Cardinal m'a fermé la porte au nez, and though I am not so furious as Monsieur was but I am content to let those pass over before I go to bed to my wife, yet I hope I shall entertain her at least better the first night than he did you. I do intend on Monday next to go towards Hampton Court, where I shall stay till the Queen comes. My dearest sister continue your kindness to me, and believe me to be entirely yours.

There is clear evidence here that Minette had written to Charles immediately after her marriage, a letter that is missing, telling him of her being unable to consummate her marriage on the wedding night because of her period, and Monsieur's inadequacy as a lover when it eventually was consummated.

Charles II, Minette and Louis XIV all married during the year 1661–2, and in each case the marriage was less than successful. It is not surprising that Louis XIV was bored with his Queen, Maria Teresa, who was dull, ignorant and bigoted, and whose main pleasure in life was eating enormous meals. Charles on his marriage to Catherine of Braganza made it obvious from the beginning that he was fairly pleased with her, but had no intention of leaving off his affair with Barbara Castlemaine, and he even insisted that she was made Lady of the Bedchamber to his bride. The Queen was deeply hurt and angry, and by Minette's next letter we can see that she was also shocked by her brother's behaviour. As to her own marriage, this was in ruins from the earliest days, and she quickly grew to despise and fear the effeminate and spiteful Duc d'Orléans.

This next letter of Minette's mentions the intrigues of the French

Court as well as her knowledge and disapproval of what was going on at the English Court. Charles's postponement of his visit to Dunkirk clearly upset her. Her veiled reference to Monsieur's delight at the news was another indication of his deep jealousy of her relationship with Charles.

¶ *Minette to Charles*

Paris, 22 July 1662[13]

The courier I had sent you, came back two days ago, and brought the worst news I can possibly receive, in telling me that my hopes of seeing you [at Dunkirk] were after all, to be disappointed. Every one here does not share my feelings, and the highest are as much pleased as I am grieved. I should indeed be inconsolable, if you had not led me to hope, and still believe that you keep a little love for your poor Minette, who certainly has more for you than she can express. You tell me that some one has spoken ill of a certain person, to the Queen your wife. Alas is it possible that such things are really said? I who know your innocence can only wonder! But to speak seriously, I beg you to tell me how the Queen has taken this. Here people say that she is in the deepest distress and to speak frankly I think she has only too good reason for her grief. As to this kind of thing, there is trouble enough here, not as with you through the Queen but through mistresses. I have told Crofts all particulars. If you are curious to know them, he can tell you. Adieu, I am more your servant than anyone in the world.

At the end of July, Queen Henrietta Maria returned to England. Minette's sadness at the parting was soon forgotten in the hectic court life. She was quickly becoming involved in a mesh of romantic intrigue, not only in her own life but her ladies', and the King's. Considering her youth, extreme attractiveness, and affectionate personality, and the total failure of her recent marriage, this is not surprising.

Charles begins his next letter with profound apologies for not writing more often. He mentions his mother's safe and happy arrival, and indicates that a spirited correspondence went on between Henrietta Maria and Minette, which is now lost. In a letter to her mother Minette has told her of the quarrel between herself and King Louis, obviously a continuation of the discord which had arisen over her wish to dismiss Louise de La Vallière. This time another Maid of Honour of her household, and friend of de La Vallière, was involved. Minette was capable of great jealousy, and she angrily threatened to dismiss Mademoiselle d'Artigny when she heard that d'Artigny had not only had a secret visit from the Comte de Guiche before his departure, but was also pregnant, presumably by him. De La Vallière pleaded with the King for her friend but without any success, and it was finally the Marquis de Vardes, who was beginning to have much influence on Minette, who persuaded her to keep her.

¶ *Charles to Minette*

Whitehall, 8 September 1662[14]

I am soe ashamed for the fault I have committed against you that I have nothing to say for myself, but ingenuously confesse it, which I hope in some degree will obtain my pardon, assuring for the time to come I will repair my past failings, and I hope you do not impute it in the least degree to wante of kindness, for I assure you there is nothing I love so well as my dearest Minette, and if ever I failed you in the least, say I am unworthy of having such a sister as you. The Queen has tould you I hope, that she is not displeased with her being heere. I am sure I have done all that lies in my power to lett her see the duty and kindnesse I have for her. The truth is, never any children had so good a mother as we have, and you and I shall never have any disputes but only who loves her best, and in that I will never yield to you. She has shewed me your letters concerning your quarrel with the King, and you were much in the right. He has too much ingenuity not to do what he did. If I had been in his place I should have done the same. The Chevalier de Gramont begins his journey tomorrow or next day; by him I will write more at large to you. I am doing all I can to gett him a rich wife here. You may think this is a jeste, but he is in good earnest and I believe he will tell you that he is not displeased with his usage heere, and with the way of living; and so farewell, my dearest Minette, for this time. – I am entirely yours, C.

The autumn of 1662 was an important turning point in Minette's life. Her disillusionment with her marriage and deep dislike of, and disgust at, her husband and his behaviour drove her into a round of intrigues which eventually aroused grave court gossip. Her brief, idyllic and maybe consummated affair with King Louis was followed by another with the Comte de Guiche, who was deeply in love with her, and who was accordingly forced to leave France. The Marquis de Vardes' name was also connected with hers. De Vardes, First Gentleman of the Bedchamber to Louis XIV, was the most dangerous and treacherous of her admirers. He had been the lover of the Comtesse de Soissons, and of Madame d'Armagnac, whose husband was another of Minette's unwanted admirers. As soon as de Guiche had left the country, de Vardes was determined to make Minette his mistress. He blackened his absent friend de Guiche, and aroused Monsieur's jealously by drawing attention not only to his own follies, but also to those of another admirer, Marsillac. Meanwhile, he insinuated himself into the confidence of a very gullible Minette, who was so taken by him that she even started showing him Charles's letters. There was a certain naïvety about Minette, as in her attitude to de Vardes, which caused her a great deal of trouble in her short life. She genuinely had no idea that de Vardes was not still the lover of the Comtesse de Soissons, and she was dangerously encouraging in her attentions to the man. A chance remark of hers about her fondness for de Guiche made de Vardes realize that he had no hope of getting her as his mistress and made him her implacable enemy. From that time onwards he was determined to poison the King's mind against her. He told Louis that she was carrying on a treasonable correspondence with her brother, and inspired Minette with distrust of the King. This dangerous and damaging situation went on until just before the birth of her son, in July 1664.

The flirtatious side of her character was uppermost during this time. After the birth of her child, the more serious side to Minette's nature started to develop, and her dislike of the disapproval of others which her flirtations had caused, made her pause to take stock of herself. The most overwhelming emotion was her deep love for her brother, and this was to become the ruling passion of her life. Charles's love for her was also of a remarkable quality, exceeding in intensity and durability his affection for any of his mistresses.

The closeness between brother and sister encouraged Charles to use Minette as a private, powerful intermediary between himself and the King of France. His desire to make France his ally against the Dutch, a nation Charles had never liked, prompted him to write the next, rather formal letter to her in French, with the hope that the French King would read it. A more private note written on the same day mentions his hopes of paying off some of his debts to her – the £10,000 given to her on her visit to England after the Restoration, and the £40,000 still owed for her dowry. He had recently negotiated the sale of Dunkirk to the French, and hoped to use part of this money for the purpose. That these debts were never fully wiped out is obvious from Monsieur's attempts to recover them for her daughter in 1670, after Minette's death.

¶ *Charles to Minette*

Whitehall, 26 October 1662[15]

I shall not need to say much to you by this bearer, Mr Montague, he is so well instructed as he will inform of all that passes here. I will only tell you that nothing but pure necessity and impossibility hath kept me hitherto from paying what I owe you, but I will now put it into so certayne way, as you shall begin to see the effects of it very speedily, and I assure you it hath more troubled me the not being able to pay it than the want of that sum can be to you. The man that makes the lunettes d'aproche [magnifying glass] has been very sicke, which is the cause I have not sent you one all this while, but now he promises me one very speedily. I will say no more to you at this time, because I will not prevent the bearer in what he shall say, only I will trust nobody but myself in telling you how truely I am yours. C.

In Minette's next letter, of 20 November, she refers to Bablon, a very attractive, black-eyed, young widow, and a great friend of Charles, Elizabeth-Angelique de Montmorency-Bouteville, Duchesse de Châtillon. Bablon wished to improve her poor financial position by getting licence from Charles to export alum from England. This chalky substance was used as make-up by the ladies of the court. The letter was carried to Charles by the Comte de Vivonne, with the compliments of King Louis. Unlike most of Minette's letters, this one is among the French Foreign Papers in the Public Record Office. It would appear that she had written to Charles about Bablon before, and judging from Charles's reply, two of her letters to him about this time are missing.

¶ *Minette to Charles*

Paris, 20 November 1662[16]

I am almost glad of giving you an opportunity of doing Bablon a service. She has begged me to recommend her affair to you, and I assure you, I do it most willingly, for I am very fond of her, and know that she is much attached to both of us, which is a good reason that you should do your best for her, even if you have forgotten old days. Bablon and I, we both of us thank you beforehand since we have no doubt that you will do what we ask. If you want more news Vivonne [brother of Mademoiselle de Mortemart, later Madame de Montespan] will give it you. He is a great friend of mine and I have told him to tell you all you wish to know. I am sure that he will do this, if you say that it is my wish. I have not written to you since I received your letter by M. de Montagu. I will only say that I am very well satisfied with what you have done, and if I have not told you so before, it is because I am afraid of wearying you as much with my thanks as I had done with my prayers before. This is all I will say, excepting that I am your very humble servant. To the King of Great Britain, my brother.

Charles always had a soft spot in his heart for his former loves and the fascinating Bablon was no exception. Although he was not very hopeful of getting the licence she wanted, as is obvious from his next letter, he did in fact succeed, and with a typical touch of humour, had it made out in her nickname to 'The Duchesse de Chastillon or Bablon'. This letter was taken to Minette by Monsieur Vivonne.

¶ *Charles to Minette*

Whitehall, 4 December 1662[17]

You may easily believe that any request which comes from Bablon will be very quickly despatched by me. I am striving all I can to take away the difficulties which obstruct this desire of hers, which in truth are very great, all those things being farmed, and 'tis not hard to imagine that people on this side the water love their profit as they do every where else; I have sent to enquire farther into it, and within five or six days will give you an account, for I am very unwilling not to grante Bablon's desires, especially when they come recommended by you. In the meane time I refer you to this bearer, Monsieur Vivonne, who will tell you how truly I am yours, C.R.

During Queen Henrietta Maria's stay in England, Minette wrote constantly to her mother; in consequence, her correspondence with Charles suffered. This is particularly sad, for as previously mentioned, none of these letters to her mother has survived.

The Queen of France gave birth to a daughter, Madame Anne Elizabeth de France, on 18 November 1662, but like so many of Louis XIV's children, her life was a short one. She died on 30 December, in the middle of the Christmas festivities – yet another victim of the French doctors' practice of literally bleeding their patients to death. The Court gaiety hardly paused for her funeral. Two outstanding entertainments dominated their lives. On Twelfth Night Molière's *L'Ecole des Femmes*, which was dedicated to Minette, was performed. This was followed on 8 January by the magnificent *Ballet des Arts*. The music was by Lully, and the words by Benserade and Baptiste, and Minette was responsible for the production and costumes. She and the King took prominent parts, and four of her most beautiful ladies-in-waiting also performed with her, Mlle de La Vallière, Mlle de Tonnay-Charente, who was then engaged to the Marquis de Montespan, Mlle de Sevigné, and Mlle de Saint-Simon. It was such an enormous success that it was repeated five times during that winter either at the Palais Royal or at the Louvre.

Minette wrote a short note to Charles towards the end of January, which was carried by Ralph Montagu to the King. Montagu had been in France since October, and was entranced with the French Court, and even more by Minette herself. The man Bruno referred to in this note is probably a nickname given to young Montagu by Minette and Charles. This letter was endorsed by Abbé Montagu in error.

¶ *Minette to Charles*

Paris, January 1663[18]

I will not importune you with a long letter, since Mr Montague is very well informed on everything here and has even had a very pleasant visit thanks to the good treatment he received from those in authority. This is all the more encouraging as there are some people who say the contrary. And so he has left completely satisfied; but as I do not doubt that he will give you an account I will not say any more on this subject and will tell you that Bruno will leave soon to come to you and that I beg you to forgive him if he has not done so sooner, but it was I who detained him and it is on me that you must lay the blame. As I do not think that your rage will be very great I take the affair upon myself and finish by assuring you that I am your very humble servant.

To the King.

Charles would dearly have loved to emulate the French Court, and put on ballets and masquerades, but as he was the only man at the English Court who knew how to dance, he had to give up the idea. His suggestion that Lord St Albans should take to the floor must have caused Minette a great deal of merriment. He was not the most elegant of men. In fact Andrew Marvell had referred to him in his poem 'Last Instruction to a Painter' as having 'drayman's shoulders and a butcher's mien'. In spite of his dislike of his wife Monsieur's jealousy of her was becoming a serious problem, and was causing Charles and his sister grave concern. The picture Charles paints in this next letter of Lord Aubigny and his wife's two chaplains dancing country dances in her bedroom must have amused Minette when she read about it, and is an indication that Catherine of Braganza was beginning to enjoy herself.

¶ *Charles to Minette*

Whitehall, 9 February 1663[19]

Mr Montagu is arrived heere, and I wonder Monsieur would let him stay with you so long, for he is undoubtly in love with you, but I ought not to complain, he having given me a very fine sword and belt, which I do not beleeve was out of pure liberality but because I am your brother; he tells me that you pass your time very well there. We had a designe to have a masquerade heere, and had made no ill design in the generall for it, but we were not able to goe through with it, not having one man here who could make a tolerable entry. I have been perswading the Queene to follow the Queen Mother of France and goe in masquerade before the carnival be done, I believe it were worth seeing my Lord St Albans in such an occasion. My wife hath given a good introduction to such a business, for the other day she made my Lord Aubigny [the Abbé Lodovico Stuart d'Aubigny] and two other of her chaplins dance country dances in her bedchamber. I am just now called for to goe to the Play, so as I can say no more at present but that I am entirely yours,

C.R.

Outbreaks of colds and flu, particularly in the winter when the weather turns warmer, seem to be as common to the England of the mid-seventeenth century as they are today. It is obvious by this short note from Charles that he and his mother have both succumbed to a germ. Queen Henrietta, true to form, resorts to the favourite French remedy of bleeding as a cure for her acute headache, in spite of the fatal effect it had in the past on two of her children.

¶ *Charles to Minette*

Whitehall, 5 March 1663[20]

I writ to you yesterday by de Chapelles, who will tell you what a cruell cold I have gott, which is now so general a disease heere, after the breaking of the frost, that nobody escapes it, and though my cold be yett so ill, as it might very well excuse me writing, I thought it necessary to let you know that the

Queene, my mother, findes an absolute ease of the headache which she has had all night, by being lett blood this afternoon, and she finds so great benefitte by it, as I hope her cold will in two or three days be gone, especially if the weather continues so faire and warme as it is today. Excuse me that I say no more at this time, for really this little holding downe my head makes it ake, my dearest sister I am entirely yours. C.R.

In the spring of 1663 Minette had a miscarriage, probably due to the very hectic Court life she had during and after Christmas, which had a damaging effect on her health. Charles's illegitimate son James Crofts was now fourteen years old. In February he was created Duke of Monmouth, and in March, a Knight of the Garter. He took precedence at Court over all the other Dukes who were not of the blood royal. Charles, always anxious to get his illegitimate children off his hands by marrying them to great wealth, decided that Anne Scott, the Countess of Buccleuch, one of the richest heiresses in England, would make the young Duke of Monmouth a suitable wife. She was barely twelve years old. Anne and James were married on 20 April, and were created the Duke and Duchess of Buccleuch.

Anne of Austria, the Queen Mother, had been extremely ill, and in the next letter Charles enquires after her health. It appears that he had sent James Hamilton, a Groom of the Bedchamber, to France on a visit to Minette. He was the eldest son of Sir George Hamilton, and brother-in-law of the Comte de Gramont. Elizabeth Hamilton, his sister, was one of the greatest beauties at the English court. Why James Hamilton went to France on this occasion we do not know, though possibly it was to enquire after the Queen Mother and Minette's health.

¶ *Charles to Minette*

Whitehall, 20 April 1663[21]

You must not by this post, expect a long letter from me, this being Jameses [the Duke of Monmouth] marriage day, and I am goeing to sup with them, where we intend to dance and see them abed together, but the ceremony shall stop there, for they are both too young to be all night together. The letters from

France are not yett come, which keeps me in a paine, to know how the Queen Mother does, I hope James Hamilton will be on his way home before this comes to your handes. I send you heere the title of a little booke of devotion, in Spanish, which my wife desires to have, by the directions you will see where 'tis to be had, and pray send two of them by the first conveniency. My dearest sister, I am intirely yours,

For my dearest sister C.

Hamilton reported back to Charles a week later, but in this next letter little more can be gathered about his mission to Minette, except that the discussions were very personal to her, perhaps on her marriage problems. Charles was very worried about the French Ambassador, Comminges, who did little to promote a good relationship between France and England, and Minette's task in bringing the two countries closer together by using her influence on King Louis was becoming a very important factor in the diplomacy between the two countries. The deep affection Charles felt for his sister shines out in this very warm and loving letter.

¶ *Charles to Minette*

Whitehall, 27 April 1663[22]

Hamilton came last night to towne, and was so weary with his journey, as he was not able to render me a full account of all that you commanded him, yet he hath sayed so much to me, in generall, of the continuance of your kindness to me and the obligations I owe you, that I cannot tell how to expresse my acknowledgements for it. I hope you beleeve I love you as much as 'tis possible, I am sure I would venture all I have in the world to serve you, and have nothing so neere my harte, as how I may find occasions to expresse that tender passion I have for my dearest Minette. As soone as I have had a full account from Hamilton, of all you have trusted him with, you shall heare farther from me, in the meane time be assured that all things which comes from you, shall never go further than my own harte, and so for this time, my dearest sister, adieu.

C.R.

Louis XIV's appointment of the Comte de Comminges as Ambassador was an unwise choice. Comminges loathed the climate, disliked the people, was a hypochondriac, and was often under the influence of opium for his ailments and insomnia. Charles II, who was usually a very shrewd judge of character, made an equally bad mistake in appointing Denzil, Lord Holles to be his ambassador in Paris. He was a man of sixty-four when he took up the appointment. A staunch Protestant, and former Parliamentarian, he disliked France and the French almost as much as Comminges disliked England. Both were excessive sticklers for protocol, and for the three years of his appointment he caused a lot of ill feeling at the French Court, and was continually running to Minette with his troubles.

¶ *Charles to Minette*

Whitehall, 11 May 1663[23]

I hope you have, before this, fully satisfied the King my brother of the sincerity of my desire to make a strict alliance with him, but I must deal freely with you, in telling you that I do not think his ambassador heere, Monsieur de Cominges is very forward in the businesse. I cannot tell the reasons which make him so, but he findes upon all occasions, so many difficultyes, as I cannot chuse but conclude, that we shall not be able to advance much in the matter with him, therefore I am hastening away my Lord Holles with all possible speede, to let the King my brother see that there shall nothing rest, on my parte, to the finishing that entier friendship I so much desire; my wife sends for me just now to dance so I must end, and can only add that I am entirely yours. C.R.

Owing to the Queen Mother's illness, which forced her to stay in Paris until August, the Court remained at the Louvre, the King, Queen, Minette and her husband making excursions out to Versailles and St Cloud. Charles gave Minette a magnificent present of a barge, painted blue, with blue velvet cushions and hangings, embroidered with gold. Some elaborate water parties took place on this enchanting craft, which became a great favourite with the Queen and the Queen Mother, who borrowed it from time to time for trips up the Seine. On one occasion Minette and Monsieur were taking the barge from Paris to St Cloud for the day, when they met, on their arrival, a party of English travellers. The story is delightfully described by a great friend, the Comtesse de Brégis. Minette, very pleased to meet some of her brother's subjects, asked them into the palace, showed them her exquisite boudoir with its lacquered walls, Indian cabinets, and allegorical frescoes, and the alterpiece by Mignard in the Chapel. This was followed by a walk round the dazzling water gardens, an alfresco meal, and finally a slow journey back by starlight in the blue barge. Even Monsieur seems to have enjoyed the surprise visitors.

On a trip to Versailles King Louis caught the measles, apparently from his wife, and became dangerously ill, his life at one point being despaired of. Minette, who had had measles on her visit to England, and so was immune, visited him. On hearing of this Charles immediately put pen to paper. The following letter of Charles's was sent to Minette by the bearer that brought Charles the news of Louis' illness. Charles obviously wanted to use this fast traveller to take the knowledge of his concern to France as soon as possible.

¶ *Charles to Minette*

Whitehall, 27 May 1663[24]

Though I send my Lord Mandeville, on purpose to see how the King of France does, yett this bearer having made such diligence hither, I believe will be first with you, therefore I add these few lines, only to thanke you for giveing me so timely notice of this ill accident, and to desire you upon any change, that you will advertise me of it, which is all I have to say for this time but that I am intirely yours, C.R.

Lord Holles's journey to France was delayed by a bad attack of gout, which did not improve his temper, and he finally set out in June to take up his appointment. This letter was carried by him to Minette and re-emphasizes Charles's determination to use Minette as the unofficial ambassador between him and Louis.

¶ *Charles to Minette*

Whitehall, 24 June 1663[25]

I shall not say much to you, by this bearer, my Lord Hollis, in writting, because I have ordered him to entertain you at large, upon all I have trusted him with, by which you will see the kindnesse and confidence I have for you, for I am sure I will never have a secret in my harte, that I will not willingly trust you with, and there is nothing I will endevour more, than to give you all sortes of testimonies, how truly and passionately I am yours, C.R.

In spite of his poor personal opinion of Monsieur, Charles felt that for Minette's sake and political reasons, he should always keep on outwardly good terms with him. They corresponded fairly frequently, and presents were exchanged from time to time. English horses were much in demand in France, and although Charles did not think the four he was sending good enough for a present from him, he was very willing that they should come as a present from Minette.

Chapter 5

A Web of Intrigue

The intrigues surrounding Minette and her ladies were making life very unpleasant for her and they were aggravated by de Vardes, whose unsuccessful wooing of Minette had turned him against her. He was a very unpleasant and dangerous man, and the scandals referred to in this next letter were centred around the enchanting Bablon, Madame de Châtillon. Her popularity with Minette and Charles had always aroused envy in her associates, and on this occasion the trouble arose over Monsieur's wish that Minette should include the wife of his friend, the Comte d'Armagnac, in her intimate circle. The situation was further complicated by the Comte d'Armagnac falling in love with Minette. Madame de Montespan and Madame d'Armagnac saw a chance in this web of intrigue to discredit Bablon, and they gained the support of Monsieur and the Queen Mother. Monsieur forbade Bablon to see Minette. Minette, guessing that the two ladies were at the bottom of the trouble, countered by forbidding them to come into her presence. She appealed to Louis who took her part against Monsieur, causing him to dislike his wife even more.

Charles very naturally takes Minette's part in the sordid affair, and in scarcely veiled terms blames the Queen Mother for encouraging her son to behave so badly. Charles himself was having more trouble with the French Ambassador, the Comte de Comminges, who was always on the look-out for a slight to his dignity. The latest instance was over his reception at the Lord

Mayor's banquet in London. He arrived very late, and found all the guests already assembled at table. No one rose to greet him officially, and he stormed out without partaking of the meal. He immediately wrote to King Louis, who of course told Minette of the episode. He thought that Comminges was making a fuss over nothing, and told Minette not to bother Charles with the matter. But she had already done so, and told Lord Holles to write at once to Charles and tell him not to worry about it. Charles had already taken steps to defuse the situation, and the Lord Mayor formally visited the Ambassador to apologize to him.

Charles was by this time deeply in love with the beautiful Frances Stuart, who had joined Catherine of Braganza's household earlier in the year. Her childish prattle and love of simple games, coupled with her remarkable good looks and wonderful dress sense, completely captivated Charles. Of all his paramours she was nearest to his heart, although she refused to become his mistress. When the Queen fell dangerously ill, and was not expected to live, all the rumours said that Charles would marry Frances if she died. In fact Catherine survived, thanks to Charles's devoted attention to her and his insistence that she should not be attended by her Portuguese doctors, with their macabre and dangerous remedies. It is an endearing side to Charles's character that although he was so deeply in love with Frances Stuart, when his wife became so ill his devotion to her was outstanding, even if it robbed him of the chance not only to marry a woman he loved, but also, probably, to have some legitimate children.

¶ *Charles to Minette*

Whitehall, 2 November 1663[1]

I could not write more to you by Mon^r Cateux, haveing then the collique, which troubled me very much, but I thanke God 'tis now perfectly over, and pray make my excuse to the King of France and Monsieur, that I write to them in an other hande, for, seriously, I was not able to make use of my owne, Mr Montagu did shew me your letter concerning the businesse you had about Madame de Chatillon, and without being partiall to you, the blame was very much on the other side. I was very glad that the King tooke your parte, which in justice he could not do lesse, I do more wonder that other people who had more yeares did not do the like, and then Monsieur would not have continued so much in the wrong. You will have heard of the unlucky accident that befell the French Ambassadour at my Ld Maior's feast, I was very much troubled at it, my Ld Maior has been since with him, to give him all imaginable satisfaction, and I hope he is now fully persuaded that it was a meere misfortune, without any farther intent, though I must tell you, that the Ambassadore is a man very hardly to be pleased, and loves to raise difficultyes even in the easiest matters.

My wife is now out of all danger, though very weake, and it was a very strange feaver, for she talked idly fouer or five dayes after the feaver had left her, but now that is likewise past, and desires me to make her compliments to you and Monsieur, which she will do her selfe, as soone as she getts strength, and so my dearest sister, I will trouble you no more at this time, but beg of you to love him who is intierly yours.

C.R.

Charles refers in his next letter to his former devotion to Bablon, and his delight that her affair has had a happy outcome. Apparently Monsieur missed the other two ladies, Madame de Montespan and Madame d'Armagnac, so much that he agreed to have Bablon back if the other two could also be reinstated.

¶ *Charles to Minette*

Whitehall, 11 November 1663[2]

I have nothing to say to you by this bearer, Lusan, but to tell you that I have dispatched all, on my parte, in order to the mariage, and I hope the young couple will be as happy as I wish them. This bearer tells me, that all thinges are now adjusted, concerning the dispute about Madame de Chatillon, for whome, you know, I had more than an ordinary inclination, and pray remember my service to her, and tell her that upon all occasions I shall alwais declare my selfe on her side. I have no more to add, but that I am intierely yours. C.R.

The pious pictures which Charles asks Minette for in this next letter were duly dispatched, and much admired by Pepys when he visited the Queen in her bedchamber. Although Charles does not go so far as to poke fun at his wife's excessive piety, he does rather ruefully compare it with his own frivolity and love of the theatre.

¶ *Charles to Minette*

Whitehall, 10 December 1663[3]

My wife is now so well, as in a few dayes, she will thanke you herselfe for the consernement you had for her, in her sicknesse. Yesterday, we had a little ball in the privy chamber, where she looked on, and, though we had many of our good faces absent, yett, I assure you, the assembly would not have been disliked for beauty, even at Paris it selfe, for we have a great many yong wemen come up, since you were heere, who are very handsome. Pray send me some images, to put in prayer bookes. They are for my wife, who can gett none heere. I assure you it will be a greate present to her, and she will looke upon them often, for she is not only content to say the greate office in the breviere, every day, but likewise that of our Lady too, and this is besides goeing to chapell, where she makes use of none of these. I am just now going to see a new play, so I shall say no more, but that I am intierly yours. C.R.

In February 1664 the Queen Mother gave a bal-masqué at the Louvre during Carnival week. Minette was four months pregnant, but still took part. She tripped on one of the ribbons hanging down the front of her dress from its heavily jewelled bodice, and was saved from having a really bad fall, according to Lord Holles in his dispatch to Sir Henry Bennet, by a certain M. Clerambault, who caught her just as she was going to hit a silver grate. She suffered no serious harm, but had to stay in bed with her feet up for nine days. When she was recovered the whole Court left the Louvre, which was having some rebuilding done, for St Germain. Minette and Monsieur persuaded the Queen Mother, who was still very unwell, to make the journey down river to St Cloud in the delightful new barge that Charles had given his sister. It was more comfortable than any the French Court had available.

Charles in this letter shows how deeply he had been concerned to hear of her fall, but relieved to have heard from her that she was unharmed. His dislike of sermons, probably going back to his dreary days in Scotland, and his humorous advice to Minette to follow the family example and sleep through them, is characteristically enchanting.

¶ *Charles to Minette*

Whitehall, 29 February 1664[4]

I was in great paine to heare of the fall you had, least it might have done you prejudice, in the condition you are in, but I was as glad to finde by your letter, that it had done you no harm. We have the same disease of Sermons that you complaine of there, but I hope you have the same convenience that the rest of the family has, of sleeping out most of the time, which is a great ease to those who are bounde to heare them, I have little to trouble you with this post, only to tell you that I am now very busy every day in prepareing businesse for the Parlament that meetes a fortenight hence. Mr Montagu has had the sciatique, but is now pretty well. I thanke you for the care you have taken of the snuffe, at the same time pray send me some wax to seale letters, that has gold in it, the same you seald your letters with before you were in mourning, for there is none to be gott in this towne, I am entierely Yours. C.R.

There was a gap of two weeks between this letter and the following one, during which time Charles was busy preparing his speech for Parliament, which he was to open on 21 March. He intended to recommend the repeal of the Triennial Act of 1641, which stated that a new parliament should be called every three years for at least fifty days' duration. The rebels he had suppressed in Yorkshire late the previous year had stated that under the present Act, the Cavalier Parliament had been dissolved. Fear of further rebellion and a clever speech from Charles persuaded Parliament to repeal the Act and pass a new one stating that there should be a parliament at least every three years, but of no specified duration, and with no mechanism ensuring that it actually met.

The four-month argument on the formal entry of Lord Holles as Ambassador was finally solved, when he had an audience with Louis at St Germain, with the Princess of the Blood being conveniently absent. The masterly compromise was worked out by Charles and Minette to the satisfaction of all concerned, especially Holles, who had found Minette's assistance and advice invaluable. The delicate operation mentioned by Charles in answer to a letter of Minette's, on Julie-Marie de Sainte Maure de Montausier, daughter of the Duc de Montausier, was treated by him in his typical bawdy style. The operation was evidently a success as the lady had five children by her husband, the Duc de Crussol.

¶ *Charles to Minette*

Whitehall, 17 March 1664[5]

I did not write to you the last post because I had so much businesse in order to the parlament as I had no time. This day I receaved a letter from my Ld Hollis in which he gives me an accounte of his audience, which I am very well satisfied with and his whole treatement there, and pray lett the king my brother know how well I am pleased with it, and that upon all occasions I will strive if it be possible to out doe him in kindnesse and frindship. He tells me likewise how much I am beholding to you in all this businesse, which I assure you I am very sensible of, and though it can add nothing to that entier kindnesse I had for you before, yett it gives me greate ioye and satisfaction to see the continuance of your kindnesse upon all occasions, which I will strive to diserve by all the endeavors of my life, as the thing in the world I valew most. The Queene shewed me your letter about the operation done upon Melle Montosier, and by her smile I beleeve she had no more guesse at the meaning then you had at the writing of the letter. I am confident that this will be the only operation of that kinde, that will be don in our age, for as I have heard, most husbands had rather make use of a needle and thread, then of a knife. It may be you will understand this no more then what you writt in your owne letter, but I do not doute you will very easily gett it to be explayned without goeing to the Sorbone therefore I neede add no more but that I am entierly Yours C.

The current session of parliament was proceeding smoothly for Charles, but was marred by Lord Bristol's attempts to impeach Clarendon. Bristol was a brilliant but difficult man, full of contradictions and therefore extremely hard to deal with. Having written violently against the Roman Catholic Church, he became a convert, which precluded him from ever holding very high office. He had been anxious for an Italian marriage for the King, and never forgave Clarendon for his part in bringing about the Portuguese marriage to Catherine of Braganza.

Pepys gives us a good account of the episode that Charles refers to in his next letter. The King was very angry with Bristol's animosity towards Clarendon, and on 13 March Pepys reported that the affair had been hushed up. Three days later, he carries on the story:

> March 17th . . . The King is offended at my Lord Bristol, whom he hath found to have been all this while, pretending a desire of leave to go to France, and to have all the difference between him and the Chancellor made up, endeavouring to make factions in both houses to the Chancellor. So the King did this to prevent the houses from meeting; and in the meantime, sent a guard and a herald last night to have him taken at Wimbleton, where he was in the morning, but could not find him; at which the King was and still is mightily concerned, and runs up and down to and from the Chancellor's like a boy; and it seems would make Bristol's articles against the Chancellor to be treasonable reflections against his Majesty. So that the King is very high, as they say; and God knows what will follow upon it.

Meanwhile Lord Holles was working hard upon a treaty with France, having surmounted the petty troubles of his formal entry.

¶ *Charles to Minette*

Whitehall, 24 March 1664[6]

The Parlament has sat ever since Monday last, and if they continue as they have begun, which I hope they will, I shall have great reason to be very well pleased with them. The Lords' house has refused all sortes of addresses from My L^{d} of Bristol, upon the account of his disobeying my proclamation, and not rendreing himselfe, as he is therein commanded, and this day his wife brought a petition to the house doore, but could not gett one of the Peeres to deliver it; the other adresse, which he sent the first day of the meeting, was sent sealed to me, without ever being opened, and the truth is, 'tis rather a libell than a petition; what his next eforte will be, I cannot tell, but I beleeve he will add to those crimes and follyes he has already committed. As it is, he has put it out of any of his frindes power, to mediate for him. The house of Commons are now upon breakeing that wilde act of the Trieniall bill, which was made at the beginning of our troubles, and have this day voted it, so that now it wants nothing but puting it into forme. The truth is, both houses are in so good humour, as I do not doute but to end this sesion very well. By the letters I have receaved from My Ld Hollis, he has, by this time, demanded commissioners to treate with him, and I hope that treaty will go on, to all our satisfactions; I am sure there shall be nothing wanting, on my parte, to bring it to a good conclusion. My Ld Hollis writes such lettters of you, as I am affraide he is in love with you, and they say his wife begins already to be jealous of you. You must excuse me, as long as the parlament sitts, if I miss now and then a post, for I have so much businesse, as I am very often quite tired, and so, my dearest sister, I am intierly yours. C.R.

The letter of 28 March is a delightful mixture of state affairs, personal chat about mutual friends, and a discussion of fashions in the size of sealing wax amongst the Court ladies. Charles still has the Lord Bristol affair much on his mind, and speaks very strongly about his annoyance that he did not arrest him before he escaped out of England.

Charles seems very pleased with the business of the Parliament: the old Triennial Act has been repealed, and plans for the new Act are going well. Minette has told him in a previous letter of Bablon's marriage to the German Prince, Christian Louis, Duke of Mecklenberg. Charles, since his stay in Germany before the Restoration, never liked Germans or Germany, so he does not enthuse on the match. Apparently Bablon herself was determined not to let marriage get in the way of her life in France, and after a short visit to Germany she was back again at the French Court, with Minette. Guy Patin wrote that her husband sent three things back to Louis XIV in France – his collar of the Saint Esprit, his wife, and his religion.[7] (The Duke had had a brief conversion to Roman Catholicism while he was in France, but reverted to Lutheranism on his return home.) This letter is attributed to the year 1663 in the volume at the Quai d'Orsay, and that date has hitherto been accepted. But it undoubtedly belongs to 1664. The repeal of the Triennial Act was voted on in the House of Commons on 28 March 1664. Moreover, the Duchesse de Châtillon's marriage took place in February 1664.

¶ *Charles to Minette*

Whitehall, 28 March 1664[8]

You may be sure, that I would not have missed so many posts, but that I have been overlayd with businesse. I give you many thanks for the concerne you shew in my Ld Bristol's businesse; you see I have had reasonable good successe in that matter, I have only failed in not takeing him, but you know how hard 'tis to finde out one who is cunning enough, in so great a towne as this. I was very neere it once or twice, I am just now informed that he is gon out of England, how true 'tis I cannot tell, but that shall not make me the lesse watchfull against his mischiveous purposes, nor make me lesse diligent in seeking after him. The bill passed in the house of commons for the repeale of the Trieniall bill, and all thinges goes on in both houses as I can wish, I am to much Madame de Chatillon's servant, to tell her that I am glad that she is married into Germany; if she knew the country, that's to say the way of liveing there, and the people, so well as I do, she would suffer very much in France, before she would change countries, but this is now past, and I shall desire you to assure her that, upon any occasion that lies within my power, I shall ever be ready to serve Bablon. I thanke you for the wax to seale letters, you sent me by de Chapelles. I desire to know whether it be the fashion in France for the wemen to make use of such a large sise of wax, as the red peece you sent me; our wemen heere find the sise a little extravagant, yett I beleeve when they shall know that 'tis the fashion there, they will be willing enough to submitt to it, and so I am yours. C.R.

Having been reproved by Minette for his treatment of his wife over Barbara Castlemaine, Charles, from time to time in this correspondence, and as in the following letter, takes the opportunity to point out to his sister how kind he is to his wife, and how much time he spends with her. He also alludes to a diplomatic incident in April 1664 over ambassadorial protocol, this time at The Hague, between the young Prince of Orange, Charles's nephew, and the French Ambassador, the Comte d'Estrades. Charles had little love for d'Estrades from the time when he was French Ambassador in London in 1661, and that he was now threatening the peace of Europe over the precedence of his coach seemed particularly stupid and dangerous. Apparently the Prince of Orange's coach had given precedence to d'Estrades on a former occasion, but only due to an error on the part of an ignorant coachman.

¶ *Charles to Minette*

Whitehall, 19 May 1664[9]

I have ben all this afternoon playing the good husband, haveing been abroade with my wife, and 'tis now past twelve a clocke, and I am very sleepy. I thought I should have had a word from you, about this accident which fell out betweene our nephew and Mon^r d'Estrades at the Hage; the secretary I cannot well tell what to say upon the matter, but methinkes hath written both to my Lord Hollis and Mr Montague about it. It is a strange thing, that at the same time that the Princes of the blood in France, will not yeelde the place to my ambassadore there, that the french ambassadore at the Hage should goe out of his way, to make a dispute with my nephew. I would be glad to know your opinion upon this businesse, for it concernes you, in all respects, as much as me. I hope you will pardon me for haveing mist writing to you so many posts, but the truth is, I had very much businesse at the end of the parlament, which hindreed me, and I hope you will thinke my paines not ill imployed, when I shall tell you that never any parlament went away better pleased then this did, and I am sure that I have all the reason in the world to be well satisfied with them, and when they meete againe, which will be in November, I make no dout but that they will do all for me that I can wish, and so good night for I am fast a sleepe. C.R.

The bearer of the next letter was probably the Comte de Gramont. He was a notorious gambler, and Comminges had written to Louis XIV between 19 and 29 May that he had lost a huge amount of money, and was loath to leave England until he had won some of it back. He was also worried about his wife, the beautiful Elizabeth Hamilton, who was having marked attentions from a handsome cousin of hers, a son of the Duke of Ormonde.

Lord Teviot was formerly Governor of Dunkirk, and Charles had created him Earl in 1663. In April of that year he had gone to Tangiers as Colonel of the Tangier Regiment, and was then made Governor. He was killed during a sortie against the Moors, with most of his officers and two hundred of his men. Charles was appalled by the tragedy; at the time this letter was written he had not had confirmation of Teviot's death.

Sir George Downing had been a staunch Cromwellian during the Civil War, and been appointed Ambassador at The Hague in 1657. At the Restoration he made his peace with Charles, blaming his former loyalty to Cromwell on his American upbringing and education. He was retained by Charles as Ambassador at The Hague, made a baronet in 1663, and instructed to obtain redress from the Dutch for the severe damage that was being done to English merchantmen. Clarendon considered him to be a tactless diplomat, and there is no doubt that his heavy handling of a very difficult situation contributed to the outbreak of war against the Dutch in the following year. France had no intention of going back on her treaty with Holland, thus Charles, for the first time in a letter, speaks to Minette of the growing hostility against the Dutch in England, which was bound to affect his hopes of a treaty with France.

¶ *Charles to Minette*

Whitehall, 2 June 1664[10]

This bearer has been so long resolving to leave this place, that I did not beleeve he would goe, till I see now his bootes are on, and he has taken his leave of me, and he gives me but a moment to write this letter, for 'tis not a quarter of an houer since he was looseing his mony at tenis, and he should have been gone, two howers agoe. I am affraide he comes very light to you, for though his wife has her loade, I feare his purse is as empty, haveing lost very neare five thousand pounds within these three monthes. You will heare of the misfortune I have had at Tanger. We are not very certaine that the governer is dead, but I am very much affraide that those barbarous people have given him no quarter; whosoever, he is taken, and what is become of him God knowes. S[r] George Downing is come out of Holland, and I shall now be very busy upon that matter, the States keepe a great braging and noise, but I beleeve, when it comes to it, they will looke twise before they leape. I never saw so great an appetite to a warre as is, in both this towne and country, espetially in the parlament-men, who, I am confident, would pawn there estates to mainetaine a warre, but all this shall not governe me, for I will looke meerly what is just and best for the honour and good of England, and will be very steady in what I resolve, and if I be forsed to a warre, I shall be ready with as good ships and men, as ever was seene, and leave the successe to God. I am just now going to dine at Somerset House with the Queene, and 'tis twelve o'clocke, so as I can say no more, but that I am yours. C.R.

Poor Minette, contemplating an imminent English war against the Dutch, shows in her next letter her despair at the incompetence and foolishness of Lord Holles, who instead of doing his best to further good relations with France, spent all his time and energies in petty fighting for his own privileges. Lionne, the Secretary of State, was one of his targets, and M. le Chancelier the other. Both started by calling him Excellency but when he did not reciprocate the courtesy, they quite naturally, stopped. Holles even addressed le Chancelier by the familiar 'vous', an affront to the dignity of any Frenchman in his position.

¶ *Minette to Charles*

Fontainebleau, 22 June 1664[11]

I have already written to you several times, on the little affairs, which concern my Lord Hollis. I really think you must send him imperative orders to conclude them, if things are not to remain, as I am told they now are. For from him, I do not hear the least thing, since I told him that I did not think him right to vex himself so much over points of no importance. It is the justest thing in the world that he shall have certain privileges, but since these are not according to the custom of the country and the King offers to deprive Comminges of them, to my mind there is nothing more to say. Milord Hollis is offended because Lionne [the Secretary of State] has not addressed him as your Excellency. As a matter of fact, he had always done this, but since the other never styled him so in return, he grew tired and gave it up. The same thing has happened with M. le Chancelier. They agreed to adopt this style, and M. le Chancelier having addressed Milord Hollis as Your Excellency, he replied by a simple Vous, which enraged the other to the last degree. Nothing, however, advances, and I am in despair to think all should be at a standstill for such trifles. I am called to go to the comedy, and can only assure you that I am your very humble servant.

Charles's reply is missing, and the next note we have from him, although brief, thinly disguises the fact that it is Minette, rather than Holles, who will be used as Ambassador for England at the French Court. Charles's apothecary, M. le Fevre, carried this note to Minette on one of his many trips to Paris to buy drugs. His pass for the trip was issued on 15 June.[12]

¶ *Charles to Minette*

Whitehall, 19 June 1664[13]

I writt to you yesterday by the post, whereby you will have a full answer to yours, I shall therefore say little to you now, only that I am so confident both of your kindnesse to me and of your discretion, as I shall ever put the greatest of my secretts into your hands. The cheefe businesse of this letter is to accompany this bearer, Mon^r Le Fevre, my apoticary, who I send to Paris about some businesse which concernes his trade. I will only add that I am Yours. C.R.

A letter from Minette, now lost, told Charles of her intention to invest money in the East India Company for the benefit of her two-year-old daughter, Marie Louise. The company was under the patronage of Louis XIV, and had aroused a lot of interest in France. Charles, in his reply, indicates that he does not think much of the plan. He was increasing his sabre-rattling at the Dutch, and his interests in West Africa, by sending twelve ships to Guinea. Minette also told Charles that her little daughter was getting very like himself, which caused him a great deal of amusement. She was becoming an enchanting but very wayward child, very difficult to manage. Louis XIV adored her, and was one of the few people around her who could control her. Perhaps he knew that she was, in fact, his child. At a very young age Marie Louise married Charles II of Spain. She was deeply unhappy, and her tragically early death, probably from poison, was reminiscent of her mother's sad end.

Charles refers again to his attempts to deal with the fractious Lord Holles. With his usual charm, he manages to combine in this interesting letter his deep love of Minette and concern for her affairs, his dry, shrewd humour, and his passion for the English navy.

¶ *Charles to Minette*

20 June 1664[14]

This bearer, Mr Walters, being one of my servants, and having asked me leave to go into France to see the country, I would not let him kiss your hands, without a letter. I see you are as hot upon setting up an East India Company, at Paris, as we are here upon our Guinea trade. We are now sending away eight ships thither, to the value of £50,000, and I have given them a convoy of a man-of-war, lest the Dutch in those parts might do them some harm, in revenge for our taking the fort of Cape Verde, which will be of great use to our trade. I hope my niece will have a better portion than what your share will come to, in the East India trade. I believe you might have employed your money to better uses, than to send it off so long a journey. I hope it is but in a compliment to me, when you say my niece is so like me, for I never thought my face was even so much as intended for a beauty. I wish, with all my heart, I could see her, for at this distance I love her; you may guess, therefore, if I were upon the place, what I should do! I am very sorry that Lord Hollis continues these kind of humours; I have renewed, by every post, my directions upon it, and have commanded him to proceed in his business, and not to insist upon trifles. I am newly returned from seeing some of my ships, which lie in the hope, ready to go to sea, and the wind has made my head ache so much, as I can write no longer, therefore I can say no more but that I am yours. C.R.

The Dutch Ambassador, Van Gogh, tried to give Charles the impression that the last thing his country wanted was open war with England. But his suggestions for avoiding a conflict were so out of the question for Charles, whose ships were ready to sail for West Africa, that he decided to send Sir George Downing back to Holland at once to make his position quite clear.

The scandal of the Duc de Navailles, obviously mentioned by Minette in her last letter, was another example of the dangerous mischief-making of Mazarin's niece, the Comtesse de Soissons. An early mistress of Louis XIV, and at the time of this letter the discarded mistress of de Vardes, deeply jealous of de La Vallière, she had gone to the Queen to tell her of de La Vallière's affair with Louis, and then went to Louis to say that it was the Duchesse de Navailles who had told the Queen of the affair. The Duchess was a woman of very high principles, so much so that to protect the Queen's ladies who were in her charge, she had bricked up the door into the Maids of Honour's apartments, thus stopping the King visiting a current mistress, Mademoiselle de la Motte Houdancourt. Louis was already angry with her over this, and was looking for a chance to get rid of her and her husband. The opportunity finally came during a stay at Fontainebleau, when the Duke, who was in command of the Light Horse, asked the King for accommodation for his troops. The King told him to pay for them himself, and during the argument that followed, he and his wife were dismissed from Court. The pair were very highly thought of for their integrity and honourable behaviour, and the whole affair was frowned upon by the Court, particularly the Queen and the Queen Mother. Madame de Fiennes, a less harmful mischief-maker than de Soissons, and a great favourite of Queen Henrietta Maria, was going to England to try to obtain a position as Captain in the Guards for her young, good-looking, but not very clever husband.

¶ *Charles to Minette*

Whitehall, 27 June 1664[15]

The last letter I writt to you, I had so great a paine in my head, as I could not make an end of my letter. I did intend to have tould you then, of the Holland Ambassadore's being arrived heere; he had two private audiences before his publique one. If his masters be but as aprehensive of a warre with us, as he in his discourse seemes to be, I may expect to have very good conditions from them, and I have reason to beleeve by the letter they writt to me, there feares are no lesse at home. For, after takeing great paines to assure me of the great affection they have for me, they desire by all meanes that I will not lett my ships, which I am prepareing goe out to sea, least, by the indiscretion of some of the captaines, the quarrell might be begun. And they promise me, that they will not send out more men of warre, but such as are of absolute necessity to looke to the East India fleete and fishermen, and they desire me, that I would likewise give it under my hande, that those ships which I sett out may not fight with theres. You may guesse, by such a simple proposition, whether these people are not affraide! I have made no other answer to all this, but that I do intend, very speedily, to dispatch Sr George Downing into Holland, and by him, they shall have a returne of all this. I am very sorry for Mon^r^ de Navaile's misfortune, I see Madame de Fiennes will rather venture the stormes at sea, then those suden gustes with you at land! I do not doute but that your wether there, is as hott as ours heere, no body can stirre any where, but by watter, it is so very hott and dusty. I am just now cald away, by very good company, to sup upon the watter, so I can say no more but I am entirely Yours. C.R.

Minette's second child was due at the end of June, but was in fact born after one hour's labour on 16 July. To the great delight of Monsieur and herself, and the whole Court, the child was a son; he was named Philippe Charles and created Duc de Valois. The same day Monsieur immediately wrote to Charles to tell him the good news.

¶ *Duc d'Orléans to Charles II*

Fontainebleau, 16 July[16]

I should fail in the duty which I owe Your Majesty, if I did not hasten to inform you, that your sister was this morning safely delivered of a very fine boy. The child seems to be in excellent health, and will, I hope, grow up worthy of your Majesty's friendship, which I ask you to bestow on him. I wish you the same joy with all my heart. I send Boyer, my first maître d'hôtel, with this.

Louis, equally delighted, also wrote at once to Charles.

¶ *Louis XIV to Charles II*[17]

We have this morning received the accomplishment of our wishes, in the birth of a son, whom it has pleased God to give my brother; and what renders this blessing the more complete is the favourable state of health of both mother and child. With all my heart I congratulate Your Majesty, and to understand my joy, you need only be pleased to consider the greatness of your own, for my tenderness towards my brother and sister is not less than even that of your Majesty.

Charles, at the time of receiving this good news, was suffering from one of his many bad chills, this time caught by removing his wig and waistcoat while reviewing the Fleet at Chatham, on a very warm day. Nevertheless he sat down at once to write his congratulations to Minette, before immediately reverting to the subject so near to his heart, the Dutch treatment of the navy, followed by his distrust and dislike of the East India Company. The misdating of this letter may be due to the effects of Charles's chill.

¶ *Charles to Minette*

14 July 1664[18]

My feaver had so newly left me, and my head was so giddy, as I could not write to you on monday last, to tell you the extreame joye I have at your being safely brought to bedd of a sone. I assure nothing could be more welcome to me, knowing the satisfaction it must be to you, and all your concernes shall ever be next my harte. I thanke God I am now perfectly quitt of my feavour, though my strength is not fully come to me againe, for I was twise lett blood, and in eight dayes eate nothing but watter-grewell, and had a greate sweat, that lasted me almost two dayes and two nights. You may easily beleeve, that all this will make me a little weake! I am now sending Sr George Downing into Holland, to make my demandes there, they have never yett given me any satisfaction for all the injuryes there subjects have done myne, only given good words and nothing else, which now will not be sufficient, for I will have full satisfaction, one way or other. We have six East India ships arrived heere this weeke, which bring us newes of a great losse the hollanders have receaved there, three of there ships, which trade to Japon, being cast away, whereof two richly laden, and besides this, they had sent 24 saile upon some designe in China, who are all blocked up in a river in that country, so as they cannot escape. This will coole the courage of the East India company at Amsterdam, who are yett very impertinent. I am just now come from seeing a new ill play, and it is almost midnight, which is a faire howre for a sicke man to thinke of goeing to bed, and so, good-night. C.R.

Just before Minette's confinement the Comtesse de Soissons, who thought herself gravely ill at the time, begged Minette to come and see her. She proceeded to unburden herself of de Vardes' treachery to Minette, really concealing her own part in it. Minette, with her usual kindness, comforted the Comtesse, but was deeply shocked and angry to hear how de Vardes had deliberately been sabotaging her relationship with Louis and Monsieur.

De Guiche, who had recently returned from Poland, also got to hear of de Vardes' despicable behaviour, and threatened to fight him. De Vardes panicked and although it was so soon after the birth of her son, begged Minette to see him. She was desperately anxious to get to the bottom of the whole affair, so gave him an audience. He immediately set a trap for her again, by producing a letter for her from de Guiche. Minette, by now well on her guard, refused to accept it. Louis had forbidden her to correspond with him. She became extremely angry, and de Vardes fell at her feet in contrition, but she dismissed him. Hardly had he left her than the King appeared, and Minette was able to pour out the whole miserable story to him. He confirmed that the de Guiche letter had been a trap, and was delighted that she had not fallen into it. He spoke very kindly to her, and promised to punish de Vardes severely.

It is a tragedy that Minette's long letter to her mother, which Charles mentions in this next correspondence, has vanished. In it she apparently had described the whole business in great detail. Perhaps the letter was destroyed for diplomatic reasons. Charles was very angry over the affair, and refers to it here. He had decided to send James Hamilton to Minette with his formal congratulations; these followed this more intimate letter, which was taken to Minette by Boyer, Monsieur's Maître d'Hôtel, who apparently resembled a woman of their acquaintance.

¶ *Charles to Minette*

Whitehall, 22 July 1664[19]

The Queene shewed me yesterday your long letter, in which I perceive you have been very ill-used, but I am very glade to finde that the K. is so kinde and just to you. I did not thinke it possible that some persons could have had so ill a part in that matter, as I see they have had by your letter. I shall have by this a better opinion of my devotion for the time to come, for I am of those bigotts, who thinke that malice is a much greater sinn then a poore frailety of nature. I shall send James Hamilton to you and Monsieur, in two or three dayes, to performe my compliments, I must give Boyer that time before him, because I beleeve my messenger is the better rider-post, and so might be at Paris before him. My wife thinkes that Boyer is very like a faire Lady of your acquaintance, he will tell you who it is. I will say no more to you at present, because I shall write more at large to you by J. Hamilton, only againe I must give you joye for your sonne. C.R.

James Hamilton did not arrive until the middle of August. Meanwhile, Lord Holles had reported on the health of Minette and her little son. She had put on weight and was looking very well and so was the baby. After a short stay at Vincennes, Minette and her husband went for a month to Villers-Cotterêts, where she had a course of asses' milk to build up her strength. Soon after the birth of her son, her daughter Marie Louise went to the household of the Queen Mother who offered to take care of her early education.

Charles makes it clear in his next, long letter to Minette that he has been hurt by a previous letter from her, where she laid the blame on the English for the failure to arrange an alliance between France and England. Rightly or wrongly, he feels that he is not to blame for the grave shortcomings of the English and French Ambassadors, but promises that Lord Holles's behaviour will improve. Holmes's capture of Cape Verde had reduced the political situation between England and Holland to one dangerously near war. In the Treaty of 1662 between France and Holland, France was bound to come to the assistance of Holland in time of war, thus putting her friendship with England in grave jeopardy. The highly confidential nature of this letter shows clearly that Charles is now completely dependent on Minette to continue the very delicate negotiations between the two countries. His reference to her being an Exeter woman is a gentle reminder to her that she is herself English.

¶ *Charles to Minette*

23 August 1664[20]

I tould you in my two last that I would write to you more at large upon the subject of your two letters by the Comte de Gramont and James Hamilton. The truth is, I am sorry to see you beleeve that the faute is on our side, that the aliance with France is not farther advanced; 'tis true there has been very unlucky accidents which have fallen out, that have retarded it, as the dispute with the princes of the blood at my Ambassadore's entry, and, since that, others of the like nature, but if the ambassadores on both sides have had the misfortune to render themselves unacceptable where they negociate, why must it be thought their masters' faute? I assure you, if I had made that the rule, I must have long since concluded that France had very little inclination to advance in the treaty, but you shall see now that my L[d] Hollis will goe on very roundly in the matter, so as there shall be no neglect on our part, and when the generall treaty is concluded, it will be then the proper time to enter upon the particular one, of that kindnesse and frindship which I have always desired there should be betweene the King, my brother, and my selfe. But, now that I am upon this matter, I must deale freely with you, and tell you that nothing can hinder this good aliance and frindship which I speake of, but the King, my brother's, giving the Hollanders some countenance in the dispute there is betweene us. I assure you, they would not be so insolent as they are, if they had not some such hopes. My L[d] Hollis will give you true state of that businesse wherein you will finde how much the Hollanders are in the wrong. I meane the two companyes of the east and west India, against whome my complaints are, and the States hitherto have given them more countenance and assistance than they ought to have done. I must confesse I would be very glad to know what I may expect from France, in case the Hollanders should refuse me all sorte of reason and justice, for upon that, I must take my mesures accordingly. I am very glad that the King, my brother, is so kinde to you, there can be no body so fitt to make a good correspondent and frindship betweene us as your selfe, I take the occasion of this safe messenger to tell you this, because I would not have this businesse passe through other hands than yours, and I would be very willing to have your opinion and counsell how I shall proceede in this matter, I do not doute but you will have that care of me, that I ought to expect from your kindnesse, and as you are an Exeter woman; and if you are not fully informed of all things as you complayne of in your letters, it is your own faute, for I have been a very exact correspondent, and have constantly answered all your letters, and I have directed my L[d] Hollis to give a full account of our dispute with

Holland, if you will have the patiance to heare it. I shall sum up all, in telling you that I desire very much to have a strict frindship with France, but I expect to finde my account in it, as 'tis as reasonable that they should finde theres, and so I shall make an end of this long letter, by assuring you that I am intierly yours. C.R.

Although Minette's reply to this is missing, she was evidently pleased with it, and Charles was encouraged to continue in a similar vein. Although Downing continued to tell Charles that the Dutch did not want war, the feeling at home was certainly for a fight. James, Duke of York, a governor of the Royal Africa Company, was eager to get into battle with them, the general population were overwhelmingly in favour, and only elder statesmen like Clarendon and Southampton urged caution. Charles's prime worry was finance. The Dutch had set off for Guinea in an attempt to recapture the Gold Coast territory that Sir Robert Holmes had taken, and Charles decided to send Prince Rupert after them, considering that the Dutch attack in Guinea was an overt action of war. In August Holmes had spread his action against the Dutch across the Atlantic, and ousted the Dutch from the New Netherlands and their settlement of New Amsterdam, renaming it New York. On his return, because of the strong representations of the Dutch against him, he was put in the Tower, pending investigations. He was released in the following March and received a general pardon. Some considered that he was responsible for the Dutch War, others that he was a wise, brave and clever man.

¶ *Charles to Minette*

Whitehall, 19 September 1664[21]

I am very glad to finde you are satisfied with my Long letter. I do assure you I will ever behave my selfe so in all that concernes a good inteligence with france, as you shall be satisfied with me, but when I have sayd this I expect the same forwardnesse on there side, and that I may finde the effects of those good words you mention. If the King my brother desire to have a strict frindship with me there is no body so proper to make it as yourselfe, and I am sure I will put all my interest into your hands, and then you shall be the judge who desires most the good alliance. I receaved just now my letters out of Holland by which I finde they make all the hast they can to gett out there fleete for Guiny, and I am useing all diligence to put P: Robert in a condition to follow them in case they goe, and as they have alwayes hetherto made the first step in there preparations for warre, so I am resolved they shall now send first, that all the world may see I do not desire to begin with them, and that if there comes any mischife by it, they have drawne it upon there own heads. The truth is they have no great need to provoke this nation, for except my selfe I beleeve there is scarce an Englishman that does not desire pationatly a warre with them. I do expect with impatiancy to heare some thing from you upon the subject of my long letter that I may know what I may depend upon. I am confident the coniuture will be such before it be long, wherein I may be useful to France, and I tell you freely I had much rather make my frindships where you are, and with those I know, then with others, but it will be impossible for this nation to be idle when they see there neighbours busy, and I canot deny to you it agrees with my humour likewise. I write thus freely to you that you may know the truth, for I assure you I consider your interest in it, and so my dearest sister good night for tis late. C.

Pray make my compliments to Monsieur and though I do not trouble him often with letters, yet there is nobody more truly his, then I am. C.

With the full authority of her brother behind her, Minette approached Louis directly on the long-standing affair of a firm treaty between England and France. Louis, glad to be getting near to an amicable agreement, mentioned a treaty which he signed on his accession to the throne in 1644 at Lord Goring's request, ratifying a treaty of 1610, as a good basis for negotiation. Minette wrote to Charles with the good news that such a treaty existed. Charles admits in this next letter that he had never heard of it, blames the difficult times in 1644, and asks for a copy.

¶ *Charles to Minette*

Whitehall, 3 October 1664[22]

I have receaved yours of the 7 from Vincenes but just this moment as the post is goeing away, and therfore can say nothing to you now, the paper in your letter referring to a treaty which I never saw, it being made when I was P: of Wales, and at a great distance from the King my father. I shall imediatly looke out for that treaty, but for feare I shall not be able to finde a copy of it heere, it being made in a disorderly time, pray gett a copy of it and send it imediatly hether, that so there may be no time lost. In the meane time I shall only add that I am very glad to see the King my brother so ready to made a good frindship with me, and pray assure him that nothing can be more welcome to me, then a strict frindship betweene us. I have no more time left me only to assure you that I am intierly Yours. C.

Charles obviously found the treaty of 1610 among his papers and read it before the copy he had asked for arrived from Minette. It is apparent from the next letter that he thinks it has little relevance to the present situation. To put it into order to meet the present requirements of the two countries would be more trouble than drafting a new one. The postscript refers to the fact that Louis had lent Charles his famous garden designer, Le Nôtre, who was helping him with one of the gardens of a royal residence. He must have inspired him with his love of fountains and waterfalls.

¶ *Charles to Minette*

17 October 1664[23]

I have receaved yours of the 21st, with a copy of the treaty of 1610, the same I mention to have read heere, with the proces-verbal of the ceremonyes passed at my Ld Gorings swering this, and all other treatyes then subsisting between France and us, which, as I have sayde, cannot come home to the present case now before us. This makes me still remaine in the conclusion, that we must lay for a foundation the project my Ld Hollis hath now given in, and add to it other private articles of mutuall defence and succour, as may be easily agreed upon betweene us, and this will not be a worke of much time, if our mindes be according to our professions, and so I am yours. C.R.

Pray lett le Nostre goe on with the modell, and only tell him this adition, that I can bring water to the top of the hill, so that he may add much to the beauty of the desente by a cascade of watter. C.R.

The strong political tone of their recent correspondence is interrupted by this next letter from Minette, which is taken up entirely with personal affairs. It concerns the discovery of some jewellery belonging to the English royal family in the possession of some jewellers in Paris. Not only did the collection consist of the pieces Minette mentions in her next letter, but also a magnificent sapphire, a crystal ship set with rubies and diamonds, and some very rare tapestries. Some of the rubies may have been those that Queen Henrietta Maria pawned in France to help pay for the Civil War.

Minette heard of this jewellery several months before writing this letter, but hoping to restore the treasure to Charles as a surprise she had kept her negotiations about it fairly secret. However, Lord Holles had also heard of the collection, and started procedures to get it restored to his master himself. He wrote about it to the Abbé Montagu, who showed his letter to Minette. Terrified of offending the peppery Ambassador, Minette immediately wrote to him explaining why she had not mentioned the jewels before. The fact that they both had been working independently for the recovery, plus the treachery of one of Minette's ladies, were two reasons why the jewellery was never recovered. Charles, the person most concerned, seemed little affected by the loss, maybe because his mind was too occupied with more important matters at this time. Another reason for the failure of this attempt to recover such valuable objects was that they had passed through so many hands before reaching the French jeweller in question, making a claim for return of stolen property almost impossible. If Queen Henrietta Maria had been in Paris, she could have identified them herself, as she knew the Royal Collection so well. For once Lord Holles did not take offence.

Queen Henrietta Maria, a connoisseur of fine architecture, was making substantial alterations to Somerset House, her splendid mansion overlooking the Thames. Minette shares a good joke with Charles when she tells him of Louis and his wonderful idea at Versailles of giving land there to wealthy courtiers, and getting them to pay for the building of their own accommodation.

¶ *Minette to Charles*

Versailles, 24 October 1664[24]

I have always delayed to inform you of a discovery that I made six months ago, of certain jewels which are said to have been stolen from the King, our father, and I should not mention it now, only that the Ambassador has lately been informed of it, and will no doubt have written to you. Since this is the case, I can no longer give you the surprise which I had planned, so I will tell you that the suspected parties, who have been arrested by my orders, confess to having once had the jewels in their possession, but as they have now passed into different hands, there will, I fear, be some difficulty in recovering them. But, cost what it may, I am determined they shall not escape me, and I hope before long to restore them to you. There is a very handsome hat-band of diamonds, also a garter, a great many rings, and a portrait of Prince Henry, set in very large diamonds. The Queen will be able to tell you whether she remembers them, for the King had nothing which she did not know of. I have nothing to say in reply to your last letter. I have so often spoken to you on the same subject, that it would be troubling you to begin again. To give you some news, in return for what you tell me about the Queen's building, I must tell you that the King is making a grand building here, which will adorn the place very much, and which joins the fore court in the shape of a triangle. The best of it is, that it will cost him nothing, for he gives the ground to several persons of quality, who will build at their own expense, and will be very glad to have houses on this site. This is all that I have to say to you.

The next letter from Charles begins with personal news. He again asks Minette to be kind to the Gramonts, who are returning to

France. Charles had a great admiration and affection for Gramont's wife, the former Elizabeth Hamilton, beautiful niece of the Duke of Ormonde. He mourns the fact that she has lost her lovely figure in childbirth, and as an expert in these matters, fears it will never return. Charles's almost casual reference to the taking of New Amsterdam from the Dutch, and renaming it New York, is an indication that he had no idea of its great importance. The Dutch lost their foothold in North America, and it became a valuable link between the New England provinces and Virginia.

¶ *Charles to Minette*

Whitehall, 24 October 1664[25]

I writt to you yesterday, by the Comte de Gramont but I beleeve this letter will come sooner to your handes for he goes by the way of Diepe with his wife and family, and now that I have named her, I cannot choose but again desire you to be kinde to her, for besides the meritt her family has, on both sides, she is as good a creature as ever lived. I beleeve she will passe for a handsome woman in France, though she has not yett, since her lying in, recovered that good shape she had before, and I am affraide never will. I have nothing to say more to you, upon our publique businesse, till I have an answer from you, of my last letter by the post, only that I expect with impatiency to know your mindes there, and then you shall finde me as forward to a strict frindship with the King, my brother, as you can wish. You will have heard of our takeing of New Amsterdame, which lies just by New England. 'Tis a place of great importance to trade, and a very good towne. It did belong to England heeretofore, but the Duch by degrees drove our people out of it, and built a very good towne, but we have gott the better of it, and 'tis now called New Yorke. He that took it, and is now there, is Nicols, my brother's servant, who you know very well. I am yours. C.R.

Minette now has another definite offer to make to Charles from Louis. He will agree to treat the English in France as Frenchmen if Charles will treat Frenchmen in England in a similar way, with one important exception. The tax of fifty sols per tonne on every foreign ship entering a French port will remain. As the Navigation Act of 1660 stated that a five-shilling tax should be levied on all French ships entering a British port, as long as the French shipping tax remained, the status quo was going to stay the same where shipping was concerned. This letter is a reply to Charles's of 17 October, which he asked Minette to have translated into French, so that it could be shown to Louis.

¶ *Minette to Charles*

Paris, 4 November 1664[26]

I have shewn your last letter to the King, who had ordered me to tell you in answer to what you write touching the Dutch, that if you will agree to treat his subjects in England as the English, he consents that the English in France should be treated as French, excepting the fifty sous.

I am not clever enough to know what this means, but these are the King's own words which I repeat to you. If this is what you want, reply as soon as you can, for if you do not quickly end all this, you will not gain time, as you both appear to wish, and this will drag on to infinite lengths! It is so late, and I am so sleepy that I will add nothing more but that I am your very humble servant.

The Queen of France, who was eight months pregnant, was suddenly taken very ill with fever, causing great alarm at the French Court. The Dauphin was a sickly child, and the hope of another, healthier son was of paramount importance to Louis. He was so distressed that he sat up the whole of one night with his wife. Minette despatched a letter to Charles at once, telling him of the gravity of the illness; the letter is lost, but a second one was written a few days later.

¶ *Minette to Charles*

Paris, 12 November 1664[27]

I sent you word by the last post of the Queen's illness, which has much increased since then, owing to the frightful pains in her limbs, which keep the fever high. The King seems much distressed, although we are assured there is no danger at present, either for her or her child. I think you had better send some one to inquire after her, for this is not a little illness which will be over to-day or to-morrow. I have no leisure to say more. I will write more fully by Mr Sidnei, who leaves to-morrow, and will only tell you now that I am your humble servant.

The Queen's illness grew worse. After a night of terrible convulsions, she gave birth to a daughter, who lived for only four weeks. According to Holles's reports and Mademoiselle de Montpensier, the baby was described as looking like a blackamoor. This was ludicrously ascribed to the Queen having been frightened by some negroes at Court just before the birth.

To reinforce the effect of the diplomatic negotiations between brother and sister, Charles decided to send his great friend and confidant, Charles Berkeley, Lord Fitzhardinge, to France as a private envoy. He was a man of great charm but extremely pleasure loving, and many thought him a very unsuitable person to play such an important part in Charles's life and diplomacy. His brief on this trip was to assure Louis of Charles's friendship, and to reiterate the offer of a treaty of mutual defence which would supersede the treaty with Holland.

Charles was well aware that if he was ultimately going to war against the Dutch he needed a very large grant from Parliament to do so. He therefore laid his plans for the forthcoming opening of Parliament very carefully. He was well rewarded. The session opened on 24 November, and the following day a backbencher, with the backing of the Court, suggested a subsidy was granted to him for the fleet of two and a half million pounds. This was the largest sum ever to have been granted to a monarch by Parliament, and continued to be a record until well into the next century.

Fitzhardinge had just returned from his trip to France when Charles wrote this letter, and although he had not had time to make a full report to the King, Charles was well pleased with what he had achieved, and gave him a ring valued at £2,000 for his efforts. Fitzhardinge's speedy return to England was no doubt partly due to the fact that he had very recently been married to

Margot Bagot, a beautiful but penniless Maid of Honour to the Duchess of York. Charles as a further mark of his approval of the Fitzhardinges immediately made her a Lady of the Bedchamber to his wife.

¶ *Charles to Minette*

Whitehall, 21 November 1664[28]

The Parlament being to meet on thursday next gives me so much businesse to put all thinges in a good way at there first comming together, as I have only time to tell you that C. Berkley arrived heere late last night, so as yett I have not had full time to receave an account of the successe of his negotiation. I shall only tell you now the great satisfaction I receave in the obligeing reception he had from the King my brother, which I am sure I will returne with all imaginable kindnesse, and I hope there will not be many steps more before the intier frindeship be made betweene us. Pray tell Monsieur I am as sensible of his frindeship and kindnesse as I ought to be, but that I have not now time to tell him in writing till the next post, for your selfe I am too much obliged to you to say any thing of it in so short a letter nor indeed can I ever diserve it from you. You have my hart and I cannot give you more. C.

Not satisfied with the information he was getting from England from his Ambassador, Comminges, Louis sent Henri de Massue, Marquis de Ruvigny, over to England to try and discover what the political situation really was with regard to France and the Dutch. Minette entrusted the following letter to his care. With deep feeling she begs Charles to consider a secret treaty with France as the best solution to Louis' dilemma of wanting to stick to his agreement with Holland and still remain on friendly terms with England.

¶ *Minette to Charles*

Paris, 28 November 1664[29]

I could not let Ruvigny start without this letter, to assure you again, what he will also tell you, how much your friendship is wished for here, and how necessary it is to France. Profit by this, in God's name, and lose no time in obtaining a promise from the King not to help the Dutch. You understand that he cannot bind himself publicly, owing to his engagements with them, although we all know these are only worth what he chooses to make them. For, as with everything else in this world, it is necessary to keep up a good appearance. You must, therefore, content yourself with a private agreement, which is likely in fact to be more lasting, and I promise to see that this is done in good faith, for I fear the contrary so much, in anything that I am mixed up with, that I will have nothing to do with it, unless I see that this is the case. Tell Ruvigny, I beg, how well I have spoken of him to you, for he is the most honest of men, I do not think you need me to tell you this, nor yet that I am your very humble servant.

The Queen slowly recovered from her severe illness and the birth of her daughter, but the child herself became extremely ill with convulsions, and her life was despaired of. Minette warns Charles that he may have to send condolences on her death rather than the congratulations which were due on her birth.

Monsieur was in favour of the English at this time, and wrote to congratulate Charles on a victory his sailors had over the Dutch in Guinea. Minette wonders if the report is actually true, as Charles had not mentioned it to her.

¶ *Minette to Charles*

Paris, 30 November–10 December 1664[30]

It is said here that your fleet has taken forty Dutch ships, but, as you do not mention it, I fear it may not be true. I gave your letter to the King, who showed it to me. I also gave him the messages that you sent. He receives all your advances so well that I doubt not but he will respond to them in course of time, The Queen is much better, but as for the little Madame, she has suffered from such violent convulsions during the last ten days that her death is hourly expected, so the congratulations you are going to send on her birth will, I fear, have to be changed to condolences for her death which is all that your humble servant has to say for the present.

The Comte de Guiche had returned to Court from Nancy, and had been trying, in vain, to get in touch with Minette to tell her of de Vardes' treachery against them both, which had ended in his three-year posting abroad. A masked ball, given by the Duchesse de Vieuville, gave him his opportunity. Minette and her husband decided to go in disguise, in a hired carriage and without servants. On arrival Monsieur gave his hand to an unknown lady, and Minette was taken into the ballroom by a masked cavalier. They recognized each other, de Guiche by the distinctive perfume that Minette used on her hair, and she by his injured hand, with several fingers missing, a result of a battle injury. De Guiche was at last able to tell Minette of the extent of de Vardes' perfidy. Monsieur, becoming suspicious of Minette's deep conversation with the stranger, came over to take her home. As she left the ballroom she tripped down some stairs and would have had a bad fall if de Guiche had not caught her in his arms. Shortly afterwards, in the Queen's apartments, de Vardes spoke in an extremely disparaging way about Minette to the Chevalier de Lorraine, a friend of Monsieur, who was in love with one of Minette's ladies. He told him in a loud voice, for all to hear, that he should not bother about the maid when he could have the mistress any time he liked.

Minette was outraged, and went straight to the King and told him of de Vardes' latest attack against her, and begged him to punish him severely. At the same time she wrote the following letter to Charles, asking him for his assistance, and a long one to her mother telling her all the details of the affair.

Much to the amusement of his friends, de Vardes took himself off to the Bastille, where he stayed only a short time.

¶ *Minette to Charles*

Paris, 17 December 1664[31]

I have begged the ambassador to send you this courier, that he may inform you truly of the affair which has happened about Vardes, but having written it to the Queen, my mother, you will allow me to refer you to her letter, for the whole story. Here I will only say that the thing is so serious, I feel that it will influence all the rest of my life. If I cannot obtain my object, it will be a disgrace to feel that a private individual has been able to insult me with impunity, and if I do, it will be a warning to all the world in future, how they dare to attack me. I know that you were angry that he was not punished for the first affair, which makes me ask you this time to write a letter to the King, saying that although you feel sure he will give me every possible satisfaction, and finish as well as he has begun – for it will never do for us to let him see that we are displeased with him – yet, out of love for me you cannot help asking him to do so (if you do not think this expression too strong), and that if it had not been one of his own servants who is in fault you would not have asked him for justice, but would have done it yourself. But you will judge better than I what to say, for, as I have already told you, it is a business which may have terrible consequences if this man is not exiled. All France is interested in the result, so I am obliged to stand up for my honour, and leave you to judge what might happen. I hope that the consideration in which you are held here may settle all this. It will not be the first debt that I shall have owed you, nor the one for which I shall be the least grateful, since it will enable me to obtain justice in future. I end by assuring you that I am your most humble servant.

De Vardes very foolishly encouraged his friends to spread the news that in spite of Minette asking for his banishment, he only stayed in the Bastille a very short time. This was too much even for Louis and he was banished to Aigues-Mortes.

Minette, having successfully achieved the removal of de Vardes, still had the treacherous Comtesse de Soissons to deal with. The dangerous woman had always blamed her for the loss of de Vardes as a lover and was still looking for her revenge. Her latest attack on her was to tell the King that the Comte de Guiche had advised Madame to take possession of Dunkirk in Charles's name, and that he had put the Regiment of Guards at her disposal. Minette's excellent relationship now with Louis stood her in good stead. Louis completely believed Minette when she hotly denied such an outrageous story. He decided once and for all to rid his Court of all these damaging intrigues. The Comte and Comtesse de Soissons were banished from Court, and de Vardes was put in jail in Montpelier for two years, and remained away from Court for nineteen years.

It was remarked that the removal of de Vardes and the Comtesse de Soissons from her circle had a profound effect on Minette and helped her to settle down. In her memoirs, Charlotte Elizabeth of Bavaria, Monsieur's second wife, wrote of Minette at this time, 'I think that Madame had more misfortunes than faults. She had to do with wicked people, about whose conduct I could tell a great deal if I chose. Madame was very young, beautiful, agreeable, full of grace and charm. From the time of her marriage, she was surrounded by the greatest coquettes and most intriguing women in the world, who were the mistresses of her enemies. I think people have been very unjust to her.'

Madame de Motteville also said of her that once de Vardes was banished, Madame seemed to wish to alter her behaviour. She wrote:

> She lived on better terms with the Queen, her mother-in-law, and took her part in the necessary diversions of the Court, with no wish but to make herself pleasant to all. As she had much genius and penetration, and could talk well on every subject, those who had the honour of knowing her best, noticed that she was beginning to recognize, by her experience, how little the pleasures she had sought so eagerly, were capable of satisfying the human heart, but she hardly grasped the truth in all its fulness; as yet she only saw it dimly and from afar . . .

The Maréchal de Gramont, father of de Guiche, decided that to avoid any more scandal, his son should be posted abroad again. Determined to see Minette just once more before he departed for Holland, de Guiche dressed up in the livery of one of de La Vallière's servants, and waited in the courtyard of the Palais Royal to see Minette pass in her sedan chair, on her way to the Louvre. As she reached him he stepped forward to speak to her for the last time. He was obviously very unwell, and collapsed at her feet. Having had a few words with him, she ordered him to be carried into the Palais. She never saw him again. Those closest to Minette always looked upon the affair of the Comte de Guiche as a romantic flirtation, rather than a serious liaison between lovers, and it is highly unlikely that she ever became his mistress.

Minette's next letter to Charles was brought to him by her Master of the Horse, M. de Bonnefond, whom she was sending to England to buy some horses. English horses were much sought after in France, and were considered to be some of the finest in the world. She speaks very much as a mouthpiece for Louis in his letter, making it quite clear that he will not publicly repudiate the treaty with Holland, and begging Charles yet again to come to a private agreement between the two countries.

England was drifting inevitably towards war with Holland, and on 18 December the members of the Privy Council, with the exception of Clarendon, issued a general order to English ships to prey on the Dutch shipping in lieu of compensation for losses to their merchantmen. At the same time the news from West Africa was disastrous. The Dutch had swept the waters around Guinea free of British ships and garrisons, ruining the credit of the Royal Africa Company. At the end of this letter Minette thanks Charles for agreeing to be the godfather of her little son, the Duc de Valois.

¶ *Minette to Charles*

19 December 1664[32]

I have sent Bonnefond, who is my Master of the Horse, to buy some horses. Be so good as to give him the necessary passport.

I must tell you that my Lord Hollis has informed me of the articles which you wish to uphold. The first I think very reasonable, but as regards the second, in which you ask that past treaties may be cancelled, the King cannot in honour do this, and if you wish for some pledge of this kind, it must be of a private nature between you and him, for it would be unjust to demand it in any other way. I think you know the Dutch are sending a man here. I tell you this, as I know these comings and goings concern you, and will let you know if I hear any more particulars. I tell the Queen all the news, which she will no doubt give you, and so I will only ask your pardon for not having thanked you before this for the honour you do my son, in promising to be his godfather, and remain your very humble servant.

Charles was always a keen astronomer, and the sightings of the brilliant comet, described by a French writer as having a head as large as a plate, bristling all over with nails, and with a tail as long as three arms, turned now east, now west, caused great interest in both England and France. Pepys spent several nights sitting up to see it, but only spotted it when it was on the wane, and was therefore rather disappointed. Charles, always an optimist, thought it was a portent for good in his forthcoming war against the Dutch. It was sighted in Germany, and heralded the defeat of the Turks in the battle of St Gotthard.

¶ *Charles to Minette*

15 December 1664[33]

I wish very much that the treaty of commerce were finished, that then we might enter into that of the stricte alliance which I am very impatient of, for I assure you my owne inclination carryes me to it, and I am confident we shall finde both our accounts in it. I beleeve my friendship to France is and will be more considerable then that of the Hollanders in many respects, and you may have it, if you will. The house of Commons hath this day settled the severall rates upon the countyes for the raysing of the five and twenty hundred thousand pounds, and there is a bill preparing for that purpose, so as that matter is as good as done. Since my last to you, we have taken many more Dutch ships; the truth is, hardly any escapes us that passe through the chanell. I beleeve we have taken already above fouer-score, and every day there comes in more. They brag very much that they will eate us up in the Spring, and so they did some two monthes agoe, but as yett we are all alive. By the letters from Paris, I perceeve that the blazing starr hath been seen there likewise, I hope it will have the same effect heere as that in Germany had, and then we shall beate our neighbouring Turks, as well as they beate theres. I will say no more at this time, but that I am intierly yours. C.R.

Charles appears to have had two letters from Minette, one carried by Lord Rochester, and one by Silvanus, both of which are missing. We have no direct answer from Charles to her distressed letter of 17 December on the de Vardes affair. It is unthinkable that he did not answer it immediately. His mention of a request of hers in these two letters might well have been over the de Vardes crisis. The presence of the Dutch Ambassador, Van Benninghen, in Paris was a serious blow to Charles, and he now puts his position over Holland into print, as a last recourse. In spite of his worries, his interest in the comet continues, and the rest of his letter concentrates on it.

¶ *Charles to Minette*

Whitehall, 26 December 1664[34]

I have receaved yours by my Ld Rochester but yesterday, Silvius haveing given me your other three dayes before, and will not faile upon the first occasion, to do what you desire with the precaution you wish.

I send you heere a printed paper, which will clearly informe you of the state of the quarrell between me and Holland, by which you will see that they are the agressors and the breakers of the peace, and not we: I pray reade it with care that you may be fully instructed, for I do not dout but Van Benninghen will use all sortes of artes to make us seeme the agressors, and I would be glad that you might be able to answer anything that may be objected in that matter. We have seen heere the Comett, but the wether has been so cloudy, as I never saw it but once. It was very low and had a taile that stood upwards, it is now above twelve days since I saw it, but upon Christmas eve and the night before, there was another seene very much higher than the former. I saw it both nights and it lookes much lesser than the first, but none of the Astronimers can tell whether it be a new one or the old one growne lesse and got up higher, but all conclude it to be no ordinary starr. Pray inquire of the skillfull men, and lett me know whether it has been seen at Paris. This new one was seen heere, the 23rd and 24th of this month, old style, and had a little taile which stood north-east. I have no more to trouble you with, but that I am yours. C.R.

Chapter 6

War

Charles was justified in fearing the Dutch Ambassador in Paris, Van Benninghen. An extremely clever diplomat, he had negotiated the treaty between France and Holland in 1662, and was therefore particularly interested in its being kept. Charles knew that the only hope of France repudiating it was if England could prove that Holland was the aggressor. To prove this he always maintained, rather with his tongue in his cheek, that Holmes had acted against the Dutch in Guinea and New England without his permission, and promised he would imprison him on his return to England. De Ruyter, the Dutch admiral, on the other hand, had always acted under direct orders from his government. In fact it was almost impossible to decide who had been the original aggressor, and Louis XIV was not the man to attempt it.

From this letter it appears that Charles still had enormous faith in the negotiating powers of Charles Berkeley, and an ever increasing dislike of the French Ambassador, Comminges. His pride was beginning to be deeply hurt as it became more and more obvious that Louis preferred to keep his word to the Dutch than to make an alliance with England. Anxious for Minette's sake to be on good terms with France, it was becoming apparent that Charles felt that he had gone as far as he could to keep the friendship going.

¶ *Charles to Minette*

5 January 1665[1]

I have little to say to you at this time, expecting that the Treaty of commerce will be finished, that then we might enter upon the strict alliance. I perceive that Van Benninghen does use all possible artes and trickes, to make me appeare the aggressour, but if you have read over the printed paper I sent you, you will clearly finde the contrary, and that 'tis the Dutch hath begun with us, which now playnly appeares by what de Rutter hath done in Guiny, and I am sure there is nothing in the King of France's treaty that oblieges him to second them, if they be the attaquers, so that except he has a minde to helpe them, he is in no wayes oblieged to it by treaty. For, by the Treaty, he is only to defend them in case they be attaqued, and they are now the attacquers, so that we only defend our-selves. I say this to you, because the Ambassadour heere, came to me by order from his master, and sayd many thinges to me, from him, upon the subject of Holland, a little too pressing, and not in the stile Charles Berkeley was spoken to, in that matter when he was there, and I cannot chuse but observe that Monsieur de Comminges is much more eloquent when there is anything to be said that lookes not so kinde towards me, than when there is any kindnesse to be expressed. I wish with all my hart that there were a good occasion for Charles Berkeley to make another voyage to you, for my inclinations are to give my frindship to France, but if that cannot be had, I am not so inconsiderable but that I can make very consider-able frindships elsewhere. The truth of it is I am presst at this time very much, and am offered very advantageous conditions, but I preferr the frindship with France in the first place, in case I can have it, and I assure you one of the great reasons why I do so, is because you are there. I write all this only to your selfe, though you may make what use of it you please, so as you do not use my name, for I would not be thought to seeke and bodys frindship, who is not ready to meet me halfe way. The wether is so colde, as I can hardly hold a penn in my hand, which you may perceeve by my scribbling, and I am affraide you will hardly reade this letter, my dearest sister, I am intierly yours. C.R.

In a letter to Charles, now missing, which was written to him just before she received his of 26 December, she asked him if the comet had been seen in England. Her next letter, which is enchanting for its humour, tells Charles of the learned investigations into the comet which were in progress at the Jesuit Observatory in Paris. She enjoyed poking fun at them with that delightful irony which was so much part of her character, a quality she shared with Charles. She also shared Charles's devotion and trust in Lord Fitzhardinge as a negotiator between himself and Louis.

¶ *Minette to Charles*

12–22 January 1665[2]

I have read the paper you send me very regularly, and am glad to hear what is happening, in order to know what I am to reply. I tell my Lord Fitzhardinge the reason why there are many things I cannot speak of now, but I expect this will not last, and you will find it out first. The last time I wrote, I begged you to tell me what people think of the comet in England, and, two hours afterwards, I received yours, in which you asked me the same question. I must tell you then, that assemblies have been held at the Jesuits' Observatory, to which all the wise men went and all the foolish ones too. They disputed according to their belief, but no two of them think alike! Some say it is the same star that has come back, and others that it is an altogether new one, and as one would have to go there to find out the truth, I suppose the question must remain undecided, as well as the stuff of which it is made, which is also a matter of great dispute. This is all that my ignorance permits me to tell you, but I daresay it is enough to satisfy your curiosity, since Messieurs les savants are no doubt everyone of them fools, or nearly so, which is all that will be told you to-day by your very humble servant.

The following letter to Minette is on very similar lines to the one Charles wrote her on 5 January. Having sent Holmes to the Tower on 9 January for taking action against the Dutch at Cape Verde without proper authority, Charles felt he was in a stronger position to accuse the Dutch of being the original aggressors, de Ruyter having acted under the direct authority of his government.

The winter of 1665 was bitterly cold, and Charles seems to have suffered from it very much, and complains of it several times. Madame de Comminges, who was a very much more amusing person than her husband, and a woman of great beauty, had married her husband in 1643, but had only spent a short time in England. Her return to France was delayed by the terrible conditions of the roads. Unfortunately she had sent her wardrobe on ahead of her, so was still in England with only her travelling clothes, and had to stay in her apartment for two weeks until the weather broke.

Ruvigny had arrived in France by the time Charles wrote his next letter. Although still hoping for some kind of alliance with Louis, Charles seems well set on a course for war with the Dutch, sending Lord Sandwich with eighteen ships to intercept a Dutch squadron that had been sighted on the north coast.

The King had commissioned Minette to lay on a ballet at the Palais Royal, 'La Naissance de Venus', in which Minette played the part of Venus. The enormous amount of effort she put into it made her ill, but after a few days it was discovered that the real cause of her indisposition was that she was pregnant. Charles in his delightful way darts from serious talk of war to the birth of her next child, and his great hopes that it will be another son. Much to his disgust the Duchess of York had just given birth to a daughter, the future Queen Anne. In spite of Charles's warning that the birth of a son to her, with her slight figure, might be more difficult, he must have forgotten that her previous child, the Duke of Valois, was in fact born very easily.

¶ *Charles to Minette*

9 February 1665[3]

I must, in the first place, aske you pardon for haveing mist so many posts, the truth of it is, which betweene businesse and the little mascarades we have had, and besides the little businesse I had to write, with the helpe of the cold wether, I did not think it worth your trouble and my owne to freeze my fingers for nothing, haveing sayd all to Ruvigny that was upon my harte. I am very glad to find by yours that you are well satisfied with what he brings, it lies wholy on your part now to answer the advances I have made, and if all be not as you wish, the faute is not on my side, I was this morning at the parlament house, to passe the Bill for the five and twenty hundered thousand pounds, and the commissioners are going into there several countryes, for the raysing of it according to the Act. We are useing all possible diligence in the setting out the fleete for the spring. My Ld Sandwich sett saile two dayes since, with 18 good ships, to seeke out a squadron of the Duch fleete, wch we heare was seene upon the north coast of England, and if he had the good fortune to meete with them, I hope he will give a good accounte of them. I am very glad to heere that your indisposition of health is turned into a greate belly, I hope you will have better lucke with it then the Duchesse heere had, who was brought to bed, monday last, of a girle. One part I shall wish you to have, which is that you may have as easy a labour, for shee dispatched her businesse in little more than an houer. I am afraide your shape is not so advantageously made for that convenience as hers is, however a boy will recompense two grunts more, and so good night, for feare I fall into naturale philosophy, before I thinke of it. I am Yours. C.R.

With the return of Ruvigny, Louis felt that it was extremely important to send two more ambassadors to England to join Comminges in trying to avert an open war between the English and the Dutch. He chose his uncle, the Duc de Verneuil, and Honoré de Courtin. He told them that he wished the balance of power between the English and Dutch fleets to be maintained, but wished to make the point that in European waters he felt that the English were the aggressors. In this letter, Minette's reference to a commission of Charles's may be to the one for a French waistcoat which she mentions in a letter of 8 April, having heard of it from Madame Fiennes. The request from Lord Fitzhardinge and the Queen to Charles is also a mystery, and one which appears to be delaying the Ambassador's departure.

¶ *Minette to Charles*

20 February 1665[4]

Madame de Cominges has arrived so well and fat that, if I had no other reason for desiring to go to England, this would make me wish it with my whole heart. Even Mirabeau [Madame de Fiennes] says, she should hang herself, if she did not hope to go back there some day! She has tried to execute your commission, which agreed so well with the style of a letter that you sent me, that I have spared her the trouble. The Ambassadors are very busy preparing to start. Do not forgot to reply to the request which has been addressed to you by the Queen and Lord Fitzhardinge, for they only await your answer to set out. Tomorrow there is to be a ball here, although it is Lent, to bid them farewell.

Lord Holles, always looking for trouble, had reported to Louis an incident that had happened at Bordeaux. Apparently, in a street quarrel between a Dutchman and an Englishman, the Dutchman had made some extremely offensive remarks about King Charles and the Duke of York. Louis had felt bound to take some action, but Minette thought that the whole episode was no more than street tittle-tattle, and suggests to her brother that it is not worth bothering about.

¶ *Minette to Charles*

Paris, 21 February–3 March 1665[5]

The King has ordered me to tell you of a thing which has happened at Bordeaux, and in which my Lord Hollis has asked for justice. You must know then that three or four persons, walking in the port, began to discuss the Dutch war. One of them, an Englishman, said you would never make peace, unless you received compensation for the expenses of the war. They then asked the opinion of a Dutchman, who said his country was not rich enough for that, and you ought to be paid in something that does not sound nice. He also said something of the same kind about the Duke of York. My Lord Hollis insists that this is a point attacking your honour, although no one as a rule cares for what people say in the streets. All the same, the King begs me to tell you, that if you wish it, the men shall be sought out and punished in any way you desire. M. de Verneuil has been rather unwell, but I do not think this will retard his journey. I will tell him the honour you do him, and end this letter is assuring you that I am your very humble servant.

Charles's quick, sharp, slightly bawdy reply to Minette's letter on the Bordeaux affair is delightfully typical of him. His brushing aside of the incident annoyed Lord Holles, who complained bitterly about it to Bennet, shortly to become Lord Arlington.

¶ *Charles to Minette*

Whitehall, 27 February 1665[6]

I am sorry they my L[d] Hollis has asked justice upon a point of honour that I should never have thought of; you know the old saying in England, the more a T. is stirr'd, the more it stinkes, and I do not care a T. for anything a Duch man sayes of me, and so I thinke you have enough upon this dirty subject, which nothing but a stinking Duch man could have been the cause of, but pray thanke the King, my brother, and desire him not to take any kinde of notice of it, for such idle discourses are not worth his anger or myne. I have been all this day at Hamton-court, and it is so long since I have been a-horse back, as with this smale dayes journey I am weary enough to beg your pardon if I say no more now, but that I am yours. C.R.

Rumour and counter-rumour were doing great damage to any hopes of peace with the Dutch, and an alliance with France. Stories of terrible atrocities committed by the Dutch in Guinea proved to be quite false, the invention of a Dutchman pretending to be a Swede. He was severely punished.

Another story concerning torture of French sailors by the crew of an English frigate proved, alas, to be true. Any ships that had any Dutchmen on board, or which were carrying merchandise to or from Holland were considered fair game by the English men-of-war. The unfortunate French ship concerned was the *St Pierre*, of Rouen. She was captured by an English frigate and towed into

Dover. There she was completely stripped of her cargo and the wretched sailors tortured by having their hands and feet burned, to make them admit that their merchandise was for Holland. Minette was naturally appalled when she heard the rumour, and begged Charles either to refute it or severely punish the offenders. The outcome was that the crew were publicly flogged in front of the fleet, the Captain cashiered, and the cargo returned to the owners.

¶ *Minette to Charles*

Paris, 1–11 March 1665[7]

I have heard of the cruelty of the Dutch in Guinea, which is frightful, if it is true. It is also reported that your people have made some Frenchmen prisoners, and tortured them cruelly, to make them confess they were going to Holland, but I maintain that this cannot be true, or at least that it is done without your approval, and that so generous a soul as yours would never allow such treatment of your enemies, far less of Frenchmen who are your friends. Write me word, I beg, of what has happened and whether, if this is true, you have taken care it should not happen again, since nothing is more worthy of you than to use your power to make yourself at once beloved and feared, and to prevent all the horrors which too often accompany war. I end by assuring you that I am your most humble servant.

Charles's next letter to Minette sets her mind at rest over the Guinea affair, but confirms her worst fears about the appalling torture of the French sailors at Dover, a matter that caused Charles great concern.

On 4 March, two days before this letter, Charles officially declared war on Holland, two finely dressed Heralds proclaiming it at the 'Change' in London, followed by similar proclamations in the provinces. This precipitate action on Charles's part was a rebuff to Louis' attempts at mediation, and although Louis still sent his Ambassadors Extraordinary to London in April, he knew that their negotiations had no chance of succeeding.

¶ *Charles to Minette*

26 March 1665[8]

There is no such thing as that newes you heard of Guiny; at first it looked like truth, for a seaman, pretending to be a Swede, came to me, and made a very particular relation of it, and afterwards took his oath of it before the Admiralty, but upon some contradictions, he gave him selfe in examining, we found him to be a Duch man, who thought by this invention to gett some money, but at last he was founde out, and has been whiped through Cheapside for his periury. I could wish that what you write to me, concerning the treatment of some French sea men by ours, were as false. I have receaved a memoriall this day about it from the french Ambassadour, and have given orders that, if it be founde to be true, it be severely punished. I do assure you I am extreamly troubled at it, there shall be very seveare justice done. I am going to Portmouth tomorrow, for 4 or 5 dayes, for the ordering of some thinges there, and have no more time lefte me now, only to assure you that I am intierly yours. C.R.

The following extremely important letter from Minette starts in a delightfully informal way, and moves abruptly from a discussion of the fancy waistcoats she was sending Charles, which had already been alluded to in a letter of 20 February, to the more detailed suggestions for a private treaty, which obviously come from Louis. Owing to the grave illness and imminent death of his father-in-law, King Philip IV of Spain, Louis was most anxious on his wife's behalf to lay claim to certain territory in Flanders, which would be much against the wishes of the Dutch. William Coventry had produced a document where he stated that if Charles and Louis joined against the Dutch, Louis could make himself master of Flanders, while Charles secured some coastal towns and made himself master of the sea.[9] Such a plan was evidently being discussed in Admiralty circles, as Pepys mentions it in an entry in his diary for 8 April 1665, the same date as this letter.

Minette's references to her enemies refer to her husband, who was so deeply jealous of being excluded from her confidential discussions with the King.

¶ *Minette to Charles*

8 April 1665[10]

Madame de Fiennes having told me that you would be glad to see a pattern of the vests that are worn here, I take the liberty of sending you one, and am sure that on your fine figure it will look very well. M. de Verneuil will arrive so soon after this letter, and as I do not think he will succeed in making peace with Holland, and that I do not think it desirable for the King to take their parts, I beg of you to consider if some secret treaty could not be arranged, by which you could make sure of this, by giving a pledge on your part that you would help in the business he will soon have in Flanders, now the King of Spain is ill, and which will certainly be opposed by the Dutch, but will not be contrary to your interests. Think this over well, I beg of you, but never let anyone know that I was the first to mention it to you, only remember there is no one in the world who would so willingly serve you, or who wishes for your welfare as heartily as I do. My enemies here look so suspiciously on all I do, that soon I shall hardly venture to speak of your affairs! So, when you wish me to say something, send me word, and when I have a message to give from you, I shall have a right to speak on the subject.

Although Minette had spent nearly all her life in France, and was married to a Frenchman, the war with Holland brought out all her passionate love for England and her family. On hearing that the Dutch fleet had at last set sail, she was naturally fearful for her brother, the Duke of York, who was in command of the English navy, and other friends such as Fitzhardinge, now the Earl of Falmouth, who she knew would be in the thick of the battle. The Duke had taken the fleet out a month after the declaration of war, but as there was no sign of the enemy he had returned to port for supplies. Minette had a growing fear at this time that any letters she put in the post were tampered with, and although she never named him, her jealous husband must have been one of her chief suspects.

¶ *Minette to Charles*

27 May 1665[11]

I would not answer the letter which you sent me by M. de Sainton, by the post, because our letters are so often opened. I would perhaps have spoken to the King, as it were on my own account, about all that, but I have been prevented by the prospect of a battle which is sure to be furious, and is likely to change the face of affairs. If he had given me a positive reply, everything might be altered before you received this letter, for by the last news from Holland, we hear that their fleet has left port, and that in consequence a battle is certain. This, I confess, is a thing which makes me tremble. Whatever advantage you may have, it is, after all, Fortune which decides most things in this world. I cannot bear to think that this little handful of miserable creatures should dare to defy you. It is pushing glory rather far, but I cannot help it. Everyone has his private fancy, and mine is to be very much alive to all that concerns you! I hope you will not blame me, and this will show you once more that there is no one who loves you as well as I do.

The Maréchal de Humières, a gallant soldier, and great friend of the Maréchal de Turenne, was also a devoted admirer of Minette. Charles was also very fond of him, and in this letter impresses on his sister what a very loyal friend he is to them both, a friend she can really trust when he returns to France after a visit to England. Charles was well aware that Minette was badly in need of people round her who were loyal to her, in a court where there was so much intrigue against her.

She was seven months pregnant, and deeply worried about the forthcoming battle, and Charles's lighthearted talk about his favourite guitar player, Francesco Corbette, whose music was all the rage at the English Court, was obviously meant to calm her nerves, and was certainly not, as has been suggested, a sign of callousness at a time when his attention should have been on more pressing matters.

¶ *Charles to Minette*

Whitehall, 29 May 1665[12]

By that time this letter comes to your handes, I believe Monr d'Humieres will be with you, and I pray be kinde to him upon my score, for I take him to be very much my frinde, and as worthy a man as I do know; he will informe you how all thinges are heere, and I do not give him the commendation upon an ordinary score of civility, but upon the confidence of his being as good a frinde where he applyes himselfe as ever lived, which, in this age, is no little virtue, there being so few persons in the world worth a frindeship, and I will answer for him that he will not make me ashamed of the good opinion I have of him; he expresses to me, upon all occasions, how much he is your servant, for which you may easily beleeve I do not love him the lesse, and I am confident you cannot finde a man in all France worthyer of your good opinion and trust then himselfe. The Ambassadors have given me this day propositions in writing from the Hollanders, in order to the composing of the differences now betweene us; I have not yett had time to consider them, and to make answer to them, but I hope in a few dayes my brother will meet with there fleete, and make them much more reasonable then they are at present, I have had no letters from my brother this day, but I beleeve he will be ready to sett saile in two or three dayes, and then I beleeve a Battle will follow very quickly. I have heere sent you some lessons for the guittar, which I hope will please you; the Comte de Gramont did carry over with him others, which it may be you have, and as Francesco makes any more that pleases me, I will send them to you, I have no more to-day at present but that I am intierly Yours.

C.R.

Anne of Austria had been suffering from breast cancer for some time, and in the spring her illness had become extremely grave, and her family were warned that it was terminal. The letter from Charles that Minette mentions is missing, but must have concerned the proposals put forward by the two new Ambassadors. He got on extremely well with them on a personal level, but made it quite clear that the forthcoming battle with the Dutch fleet was inevitable. The web of secrecy that was becoming so important to Minette's correspondence with her brother was causing her great concern, and adding to her burden of worry about her mother-in-law's health, the imminent battle, and the birth of her third child.

¶ *Minette to Charles*

St Germain, 30 May 1665[13]

> Although the illness of the Queen, my mother-in-law, is the cause of great distress here, and you will see from my letter to the Queen the state she is in, and understand the general consternation, I will not fail to speak to the King, and urge him to give you a positive answer to your last letter. And at least, if he does not write, I shall be able to get some idea of his sentiments, which is, it seems to me, what you wish most to obtain, in order to know where you are. This is the pleasure of having to do with honest persons! Ever since you have let me into your secrets, I am on thorns when I do not see my way clearly what to report. I hope you will send me some positive orders, when you find a safe messenger.

George Porter, the bearer of this next letter from Charles, one of condolence on the Queen Mother's illness, was a Gentleman of the Privy Chamber to the Queen Consort, a quarrelsome, but very entertaining man, well known to Minette, who was very amused by him. His father, Endymion Porter, had been artistic adviser to her father, and had helped to build up his celebrated collection of paintings.

¶ *Charles to Minette*

1 June 1665[14]

> I send this bearer, George Porter, with no other errand then upon the subject of the Queene mother's indisposition, who I feare, by the nature of her disease, and what I finde by the letters from thence, will not long be in a position to receave any compliments. This bearer will tell you of our fleete being gone to seeke out the Duch, and you know him so well as I

neede say nothing more to you. He will play his owne part, and make you laugh before he returnes, which is all the businesse he has there, except it be to assure you with how much kindnesse I am Yours. C.R.

The Battle of Lowestoft took place on 3 June. The first news of it to arrive in France, probably spread by the pro-Dutch faction, was that the Dutch had had a resounding victory, and that the Duke of York had been blown up with his ship. The shock of hearing this terrible news made Minette extremely ill, and probably was the cause of her producing a stillborn child a few weeks later.

The next posts brought the truth, a great victory for the English over the Dutch. The flagship *Eandragt* with the Admiral Opdam on board was blown up, and 500 men killed. Seventeen ships had either been destroyed or captured. The Duke of York was safe, and after fighting a brilliant battle, went to bed, exhausted, leaving orders that the fleet was to continue to pursue the Dutch. If these orders had been carried out this battle might have ended the war. But Henry Brouncker, a Groom of his Bedchamber, afterwards delivered an order, supposedly from James, to slacken sail, thus allowing the remains of the Dutch fleet to escape.

For Charles and Minette the joy of a great victory at sea was marred by the sad news that their devoted friend, Charles Berkeley, Lord Falmouth, had been blown up while standing on deck beside James, who was bespattered with his blood and brains. The Earl of Marlborough, Lord Muskary and the Earl of Portland were also killed. Charles was too grief-stricken to enjoy the celebrations. Pepys, no lover of Berkeley, mentions Charles's sorrow at the loss of his friend in the entry for 9 June. 'I do not meet any man else that so much wish him alive again, the world conceiving him a man of too much pleasure to do the King any good, or offer any good office to him.' More kindly, he continues, 'But I hear of all hands, he is confessed to be a man of great honour, that did show it in the going with the Duke, the most that any man ever did.' Andrew Marvell wrote, rather cruelly, that the blowing off of his head proved for the first time that he had any brains. Several years later, in August 1668, the Duke of York was to speak kindly of him to Pepys. 'His general good nature, desire of public good, and low thoughts of his own wisdom; his employing his interest in the King to do good offices to all people, without any other fault than the freedom he do learn in France of thinking himself obliged to serve his king in his pleasures.'

As a close friend of Charles and Minette, Berkeley certainly had the ear of Louis XIV, and was therefore a loss to negotiations between England and France. It was not only Berkeley's death that cast a shadow for Charles over the victory of Lowestoft, for within a few weeks, in the blazing June, it was obvious that a great outbreak of the plague had struck the city of London.

¶ *Charles to Minette*

Whitehall, 8 June 1665[15]

I thanke God we have now the certayne newes of a very considerable victory over the Duch; you will see most of the particulars by the relation my Lord Hollis will shew you, though I have had as great a losse as 'tis possible in a good frinde, poore C. Barckely. It troubles me so much, as I hope you will excuse the shortnesse of this letter, haveing receaved the newes of it, but two houers agoe. This great successe does not at all change my inclinations towards France, which you may assure the K., my brother, from me, and that it shall be his faute if we be not very good frindes. There is one come from Dunkerke, who says that there were bonefires made on sonday last for the great victory the Duch had over the English. Methinks Mon^r de Mourpeth might have had a little patience, and then it may his rejoiceing might have been on our side; pray lett me know the meaning of this. My head does so ake, as I can only add that I am entierly Yours. C.R.

The next letter is one of the longest we have from Minette, and also one of the most forceful. Behind her great delight in the victory at Lowestoft, and the safety of her brother, her deep desire for peace makes compelling reading. She and Louis XIV were at one in their conviction that having made his supremacy at sea so obvious, now was the time for Charles to make an honourable peace, rather than continue with a costly, damaging war. The hand of the King of France, as well as her own, is behind her impassioned plea. She expresses her great sorrow at the death of Lord Falmouth, and uses her own knowledge of him and Charles's love for him to enforce her arguments.

The Comte and Comtesse de Gramont were always friendly towards England. The Comtesse's elder brother, James Hamilton, mentioned at the end of the letter, was a Groom of the Bedchamber to Charles, Colonel of a Regiment of Foot, and Ranger of Hyde Park. He did not get the job of the Privy Purse, as recommended by Minette, and was killed in the Dutch war in 1679.

¶ *Minette to Charles*

St Germain, 22 June 1665[16]

We cannot delay any longer, Monsieur and I, to send you this gentleman to congratulate you on your victory, and although I know you will easily believe my joy, I must tell you how much it has been increased, owing to the repeated frights we had received from the false reports of the merchants, who all wish the Dutch well. But, on the other hand, the whole Court and all the nobility appear most anxious to show that your interests are as dear to them as those of their own King. Never has such a crowd been seen here, as Monsieur and I have had to congratulate us on this occasion! And indeed you should be grateful to Monsieur for the interest which he has taken in the whole thing, and for the way in which he stands up for all that concerns you. The Comte de Gramont was the first to bring us the news yesterday. We were at mass, and there was quite a sensation. The King himself called out to his ministers who were in the tribune: 'We must rejoice!' which I must say surprised me not a little, for although at the bottom of his heart he wishes you every possible success, I did not think he would care to declare this in public, owing to his engagements with the Dutch. But I hope that the result of this success will be to give you a second, by enabling you to bring the war to an end in so honourable a way that thirty more such victories would not add to your glory. I assure you this is the opinion of all your friends here, who are very numerous, and also that of common sense, since now you have shown, not only what your power is, and how dangerous it is to have you for an enemy, but have also made your subjects see how well you can defend their interests and greatness; you may now show the world that your true desire is for peace, and triumph by clemency as well as by force. For this is what gains hearts, and is no less remarkable in its way than the other, besides being a surer thing than trusting to the chances of war. And even if the result of a long war were certain, you will never be in a position to derive more advantage from success than you are at present, when you might win over people, who, I can assure you, ardently desire your friendship, and are in despair at feeling that their word is already pledged. I have spoken of this several times, and always find the King most reasonable, and since I do not think your feelings have changed, I have good hopes of such a result as your best friends would desire. But if I am so strongly on the side of peace, do not think that it is from a sense of fear, as is the case with most women. I can assure you I only desire your good, and since you have nothing more to win by force, you must seek glory in another way, and try to secure friends, of whom none can be more important than the King, without entering on a perpetual war of chicanery. This is what I most passionately desire.

I cannot end without expressing my sorrow at the death of poor Lord Falmouth, whom I regret as much for the sake of the friendship you felt for him, and which he so justly deserved, as for his goodness to me. Indeed, I had to weep with all my heart for him, on the very day when the news of your victory gave me the greatest joy. I can assure you, by what I knew of his sentiments, he would have been of my mind as to peace, and now that your honour is satisfied, this must be the right step to take. If I dared, I would recommend the elder Hamilton to you, and you could not give the Privy Purse to anyone who deserves it better. I hope you will tell him that I have recommended him to you. His sister begged me to do this, and is really one of the best women I ever knew in my life. As for the Comte de Gramont he is the most English of men, and shows this every day in a thousand ways. He was mad with joy when the news came. This letter is too long by half. I beg your pardon, but indeed I am so happy, I hardly know what I am about, and I could not help telling you, not only all I have heard, but all I think of as to the future consequences which are likely to spring out of these events.

The worry of the battle, the false rumours that circulated, and the sorrow at the death of Lord Falmouth, all took their toll of Minette's precarious health, and while staying at Versailles with the King, she went into premature labour and gave birth to a stillborn daughter. Lord Holles reported that in spite of her ordeal Minette was well. The baby, who was not named, was buried privately at St Denis. Shortly afterwards, Queen Henrietta Maria arrived, much to the joy of her daughter. Monsieur left her in the care of her mother and went with the rest of the Court to St Germain.

As soon as Minette was sufficiently recovered from the birth of the baby, she and her mother went to Colombes, where they stayed until the end of August, when the Queen set out for the baths at Bourbon. Lord Jermyn, who had accompanied Queen Henrietta Maria from England, reported on how well Minette looked, describing her as 'A most excellent person, very beautiful, full of wit and infinitely considered in the Court.'

A long letter from Minette of 5 July is missing, but Charles's reply to it is one of the finest we have in this collection, showing a masterly grasp of the situation between him and his cousin of France. He is extremely outspoken about the endless delays in the negotiations between the two countries, and Louis' temporizing policy. His great fear is that France will eventually come down on the side of Holland and leave him without allies, hence his great interest in the overtures that were being made to him by Spain, though the prospect of an Anglo-Spanish alliance alarmed Minette. He is well aware that a complete break with France would put Minette in a compromising position between her brother and her brother-in-law. In words of deep affection he tries to comfort her, and prepare for what he now sees as a collapse of negotiations between the two countries.

¶ *Charles to Minette*

Hampton Court, 13 July 1665[17]

My going with the Queene as farr as the mouth of the river, the businesse I mett with there about the fleete, my hasty returne hither, and the dayly trouble I have had with neighbours' collations and the Irish Bill, is the reason you have not heard from me in answer to so many letters, and to congratulate your health after such a misfortune to your childe. But now at last I have sett my selfe downe to give you a full answer to your letter of the 5th, which indeede requires it, and I should be wanting to the care and concernement I have for you, if I should not cleerely lett you know my minde, in the negotiation now depending heere with France, that you may governe your selfe accordingly. You remember very well the severall and pressing advances I made by you, the last yeare, afterwards by Ch. Berkely, and last by Ruvigny, for the perfecting our treaty and entring into a strickter alliance with france then ever, which were all in appearance so well accepted, that I may truly say I lost many oportunityes of strengthening my selfe with other aliances abroade, to be in a state of embracing that, which, upon the comming of the Ambassadores, I looked would have been compleated; instead of which, all I have heard from them (after I had accepted there mediation) hath been ouvertures towards an agreement with Holland, but upon propositions which they who made them to me could not but undervalewe, and declaring themselves tide by a treaty to helpe the Hollanders, who was disowned when the treaty was the first made, and now cannot be produced to be appealed unto. If this be the true state of the case (as I dare say you will agree it to be), where is my faute? would any body advise me to make any advances towards a peace, after all the expense I have been at to support the warre, and such a successe in it, upon such weake invitations; it is most certaine, they who propose it do not thinke I ought to agree to it, and standers by say these Ambassadores are kept here only till France can agree with Holland upon what termes they shall helpe them, on which, if they agree, I shall be necessitated to take part with Spaine, and to your exception thereunto, lett me minde you that, according to the course of the World, those are better frinds who see they have neede of us, then whose prosperity makes them think we have neede of them; and whatever be my fortune in this, I should runne it cheerfully, if my concernement for you did not perplex me, who I know will have a hard part to play, (as you say) betweene your brother and brother-in-Law, and yett methinkes it is to early to dispaire of seeing all thinges well agreed betwixt us, and though that should not happen so quickly, it must be your part to keepe your selfe still in a state of contributing thereunto, and haveing a most principle part therein, which will not be a hard taske to your discretion and good talent; and be assured the kindnesse I have for you, will in all occasions make me mindfull of what I owe you, and of reserving the obliging parts for you, and leaveing the contrary for others if there should be any such. And this would be enough in answer to your long letter, if lookeing it over againe, I did not finde you endeavouring to perswade me the King, my brother, is no way guilty towards me of censuring my actions, I do verily beleeve it and should do so, though I should furnish him occasion for it, that being an action infinitely belowe the opinion and caracter I have alwayes figured to my selfe of him, which may also serve to assure you these reports have never made any impression in me, to the prejudice of our frindship. I will conclude this long letter, assuring you the kindnesse and frindship I have for you is as entire as ever, and that no alteration or change in my affaires shall make any in that. C.R.

The spread of the plague to Kingston brought it dangerously near Hampton Court, and Charles decided to move farther afield, to Salisbury. He does not mention the plague in his letter to Minette, but she must have been well aware of it, from her mother, and from the removal of the Court out of London.

Queen Henrietta Maria now became very active herself in negotiations with Louis, in a last-minute endeavour to prevent a final rupture between England and France. Louis visited Minette and her mother at Colombes, and had lengthy talks with them, from which Lord Holles, much to his disgust, was excluded. He had made himself so deeply unpopular at the French Court, and was still so ready to take and give offence, that his position as Ambassador was practically useless. An incident involving his wife and the precedence of her coach did not improve the situation. In spite of Minette's frantic endeavours to pacify him, he refused to accept an apology.

Charles was very unwell in Salisbury, probably picking up some infection from its unhealthy little canals. Even Pepys mentions that the King, due to his ill health, was much out of humour, which is apparent in this next letter, where he talks scathingly of the armchair naval critics in Paris who criticized the tactics of his navy. They were very near the truth.

The command of the fleet had been taken over by Lord Sandwich, who replaced the Duke of York. Both Charles and his mother thought that, as heir to the throne, he should not be exposed again to the danger he met at Lowestoft. The Dutch East Indian fleet was in the neutral port of Bergen, when the English attacked them. This was not only a grave diplomatic error, putting an end to any possible alliance between Denmark and England, but was also a tactical one. While they were occupied there, the Dutch fleet was able to sail up the Channel unmolested on their way back from America, and return to base.

¶ *Charles to Minette*

Salisbury, 9 September 1665[18]

I finde by yours of the 11 of Sep. that you are very much alarumed with the retreate of the fleete to Soule bay, but when you shall know that the fleete had no other businesse there but to take in some drinke, and to joyne with twenty fresh ships (whereof the Soverine is one), and stayd but seven dayes there. It will in some degree satisfie those able seamen at Paris, who judge so suddenly of our want of conduct in Navall matters, and in all newesses il faut attendre le boiteux. I am confident my L[d] Sandwich is some dayes before this, betweene the duch fleete and home, with a better fleete then that which beate them last time, and, if God will permitt it, I do not dout to send you a good account and conclusion of this summers campaigne. I have been troubled these few dayes past with a collique, but I thanke God I am now perfectly well againe. It hath been almost a general disease in this place. I am goeing to make a little turne into dorset sheere for 8 or 9 days to passe away the time till I go to Oxford, beleeving that this place was the cause of my indisposition. I am very glad that Queene-mother is so well of her brest. Pray make my compliments to her upon it. I do confesse myselfe very fauty in my faileing so many weekes. I will repaire my faute for the time to come, but the truth is I have been some what indisposed ever since my being heere, and consequently out of humour, but I beg of you to be assured that what failings soever I may have, nothing can ever change me in the least degree of that frindship and kindnesse I have for you. Pray returne my compliments to Monsieur, with all imaginable kindnesse. C.R.

The Dutch fleet set out again to escort their East Indian merchantmen from Bergen. The English fleet had now been re-victualled and set out to chase them in the most appalling weather. Some of the Dutch were separated from the main fleet, and Lord Sandwich captured thirty-two vessels before abandoning the pursuit. The gallant little ship *Hector*, mentioned by Charles in this letter, managed to capture the Vice-Admiral of the East Indies before she was sunk. Her captain, Captain Cuttle, and all save twenty-four of her crew were drowned. The episode was described in a letter by Lord Sandwich to the Duke of Albemarle and in Pepys's diary for 10 September 1665.[19] Charles was delighted with the success of his much criticized navy.

¶ *Charles to Minette*

St Giles, 11 September 1665[20]

You will see by the list heere inclosed that my Ld Sandwich did not loose much time in Soule bay, and I hope these prises we have taken will be accompanyed with more considerable ones, though these are very rich and of great losse to the Duch. My Ld Sandwich writes me word that he is in very great hopes to meete with the rest of the fleete who are dispersed by foule wether, and his fleete intierly together, and you may easily beleeve in very good harte by this happy successe. We lost a smale frigatt in this encounter called the hector of 24 gunns, and one Captaine hurte. I could not sleep till I gave you part of this good newes, though I am weary by being a hunting all this afternoone, and the first time I have used this exercise since my indisposition, so I hope you will excuse me if I end heere, hopeing that I shall send you more good newes of this kinde very speedily, I am intierly Yours. C.
For my Dearest sister.

Chapter 7

Unquiet Hours

The Queen Mother of France became desperately ill again at the end of 1665, and was taken in a litter-chair from St Germain to Paris. The severity of her illness did not stop the French Court having its usual Christmas festivities, and Minette and Monsieur, on the eve of Epiphany, 5 January 1666, held a glittering ball at the Palais Royal, Louis appearing in a suit of purple velvet, studded with diamonds and pearls. Molière's *Medecin Malgré Lui* was performed to the great amusement of the Court, especially the King. Four days later Minette gave another great feast for the wedding of her favourite Maid of Honour, Mademoiselle d'Artigny, and the Marquis du Roule.

Minette's next letter to Charles was written as her mother-in-law lay dying. She had never had a close relationship with her, but was constantly seeing her, partly from duty, and partly because of the Queen's great affection and kindness towards her little daughter, Marie Louise, who lived in her household for her education.

Monsieur's letter to Charles was ineffectual and full of high-flown sentiments, and Minette herself seems to have given up all attempts to reconcile France and England over the Dutch war, and concentrates here on the Court gossip about the duel on the Pont-Neuf between two members of the Court, La Feuillade and the Chevalier de Clermont. Her shrewd remarks on the outcome are very typical of her sharp wit.

Henriette Anne d'Orléans in childhood, by Claude Mellan

Charles II, by Sir Godfrey Kneller

36

Aug 27.

108

I should thinke my selfe much to blame if I lett this bearer see you without a letter from me, I know not whether the long time we have been a sunder doth not slacken the kindnesse you had for me, I am sure nether that or any thing else can alter me in the least degree towards you, deare sister be kinde to me, for assure your selfe there is no person living will strive to deserve it more, then him that is and ever will be most truly. &c

Yours

MS letter: Charles II to the Princess Henrietta

55

de St germain le 27 May

il nay pas voulu vous faire
de response par lordinaire a
la lettre que vous maves escrite
par mr de St Au par ce quelle
sont trop sujete a estre ouverte
vous peut estre parle au Roy
comme de moy mesme pre
tout cela sans que la rencontre
present et la dessein dun
combat qui sera sans doute
furieux et qui changera entiere
:mant bien la face de toute
vos affaire man a empeche
par la raison que quand

MS letter: Henrietta, Duchess of Orleans to Charles II

Monsieur: Philippe, Duc d'Orléans, by Jean Nocret

Louis XIV, by Robert Nanteuil, 1664

¶ *Minette to Charles*

Paris, 15 January 1666[1]

Monsieur has sent you a long letter, with a last attempt at mediation. As for me, I confess that I do not care to attempt what is useless, so that I only pray God to guide you in all your actions to do what is best. After this, I must tell you that the Queen, my mother-in-law, is very ill. Her fever has increased very much during the last week, and the doctors are greatly alarmed. A curious adventure has just happened here. La Feuillade and the Chevalier de Clermont fought on the Pont-Neuf, because the latter accused the other of speaking ill of him to the King and Monsieur, saying that he had cheated the Maréchal de Gramont at play. As a matter of fact, La Feuillade had defended him against others who said this, which makes people think there must be more than we know of behind this. Clermont, being the instigator, has been banished as guilty of duelling, and the other is safe, because witnesses say that he only defended himself. As a matter of fact, one is a fool who has ruined himself by gambling, and the other may think himself very fortunate. My Lord St Albans will be sorry for the sake of our friend, M. l'Abbé de Clermont, brother of the Chevalier, who is in despair, and with good reason. This is all your humble servant has to say.

Anne of Austria died on 18 January 1666. Monsieur, who was deeply attached to his mother, remained with her until the end. He was overcome with grief, and he and Minette went at once to St Cloud, without hearing her will read. She left her crucifix and much of her splendid jewellery to Minette, and the bulk of her fortune to her little granddaughter, Marie Louise.

The King and Queen went to Versailles, leaving Minette and Monsieur to be chief mourners at her funerals. Her heart was buried at her Abbey of Val de Grâce, and her body at St Denis. Another requiem was sung in Notre Dame. For these occasions Minette wore an enormous train, seven yards long. Apparently Louis was strongly criticized for not attending his mother's funeral celebrations. He declared war on England a week later. Pepys writes in his diary for 25 January 1666, 'It is now certain that the King of France hath publikly declared war against us, and God knows how little fit we are for it.'

Lord Holles's appointment as Ambassador was terminated, but he was allowed to stay in France for three months. His wife was very ill and he was still a martyr to gout. Lord St Albans was also allowed to stay with Queen Henrietta Maria, and both these men were able to write privately to Charles about his mother and sister.

Charles's declaration of war on France came on 19 February. He seemed in this letter quite reconciled to the situation; his great regret and worry was being cut off from news of his beloved sister. He finishes with very touching words of his lifelong love and devotion to her.

¶ *Charles to Minette*

Hampton Court, 29 January 1666[2]

I did intend to have answered last weeke yours and Monsieur's letters, upon the subject of doing good offices betweene me and France, but that I found, by the letter the Queene writt me of a later date, that mediations of that kinde were not sesonable at this time, France being resolved to declare for Holland, so that I only write now to Monsieur a letter of condolance upon the death of Queene-mother, which I sure you, gave me an equal share in the losse. I have been two dayes in this place, and do intend to go to Whithall this weeke, for to dispatch all my preparations against the spring, which are allready in very good forwardnesse. We had some kinde of an alarum, that the troopes which Mon^r de Turene went to reviewe, were intended to make us a visite heere, but we shall be very ready to bid them welcome, either by sea or land. I have left my wife at Oxford, but hope that in a fortnight or three weekes to send for her to London, where already the Plague is in effect nothing. But our wemen are afraide of the name of Plague, so that they must have a little time to fancy all cleere, I cannot tell what kind of correspondence we must keep with letters, now that France declares war with us; you must derect me in it, and I shall observe what you judge convenient for you, but nothing can make me lessen in the least degree, of that kindnesse I alwayes have had for you, which I assure you is so rooted in my hart, as it will continue to the last moment of my life. C.R.

At this period of her life Minette was badly in need of a sympathetic friend, and she found one in Daniel de Cosnac, Bishop of Valence, who had officiated at her wedding in 1661. He had spent the last four years in his diocese, and had now returned to Court. After the death of the Queen Mother he had followed Monsieur and Minette to St Cloud to tender his condolences. He encouraged Monsieur, who had a great admiration for him, to get on better terms with his brother, with the aid of his wife, and to develop his considerable skill as a soldier. The Bishop became devoted to Minette and wrote vividly of his memories of her:

Madame had a clear and strong intellect. She was full of good sense, and gifted with fine perception. Her soul was great and just. She always knew what she had to do, but did not always act up to her convictions either from natural indolence or else from a certain contempt for ordinary duties, which formed part of her character. Her whole conversation was filled with a sweetness which made her unlike all other royal personages. It was not that she had less majesty, but she was simpler, and touched you more easily, for, in spite of her divine qualities, she was the most human creature in the world. She seemed to lay hold of all hearts, instead of treating them as common property, and this naturally gave rise to the mistaken belief that she wished to please people of all kinds without distinction. As for the features of her countenance, they were exquisite. Her eyes were bright, without being fierce, her mouth was admirable, her nose perfect, a rare thing, since nature, unlike art, does its best in eyes and its worst in noses! Her complexion was white and clear beyond words, her figure slight, and of middle height. The grace of her soul seemed to animate her whole being, down to the tips of her feet, and made her dance better than any woman I ever saw. As for the inexpressible charm which, strange to say, is so often given to persons of no position, 'ce je ne sais quoi', which goes straight to all hearts, I have often heard critics say that in Madame alone this gift was original, and that others only tried to copy her. In short, everyone who approached her agreed in this, that she was the most perfect of women.

Suddenly the ghost of the old scandal over the Comte de Guiche materialized in the form of a libellous pamphlet called *Les Amours du Palais Royal*, written by a friend of the Comte Manicamp, and published in Holland. It was presented to Louis by his Minister, Louvois. The King warned Minette that Monsieur must not see it. She immediately confided her trouble to Cosnac, who sent Gui Patin, a confidential agent, to Holland to buy up the entire edition of 1800 copies, with an order to the States prohibiting any future publication. The copies were brought to Minette by Monsieur's valet Merille, who burnt them in front of her. Apparently the original manuscript survived, and appeared a hundred years later in an edition of Bussy-Rabutin's *Histoires Amoureuses des Gaules*. Minette never forgot the great debt of gratitude she owed Cosnac for his timely intervention.

Queen Henrietta Maria, deeply anxious to get peace between England and Holland, suggested a conference, which was held at St Germain in April. Lord Holles, who was still in Paris, did take part, but the negotiations came to nothing.

The discussion on horses, at the end of this letter, an abrupt switch from talk of war to things personal, is so characteristic of this correspondence.

¶ *Charles to Minette*

Whitehall, 2 May 1666[3]

There are few occasions could be unwelcome to me, when they give you a pretence to make me happy with a letter from you, I do assure you that, if there were no other reason but this constraint which is upon our commerce of letters, I should use all my endeavours to have a good inteligence betweene me and France, but I do feare very much that the desire to peace is not wished for there, as it is on my part, for else my Ld Hollis would not have been stoped so long to so little purpose, there being lesse proposed at the conference then I refused last yeare, which certainly does not shew any great inclination to an agreement, but rather to amuse me, and certainly they must thinke me in a very ill condition to accept of such propositions as were offred to my Ld Hollis, in which I beleeve they will finde themselves mistaken; however, I shall alwaies be very ready to harken to peace, as a good Christian ought to do, which is all I can do to advance it, for I have long since had so ill lucke with the advances I made to that end, as I can now only wish for peace, and leave the rest to God. I am goeing to-morrow to see the fleete, which will be ready very speedily, and I do assure you, tis much better in all respects then it was the last yeare, and the great want the Hollanders have of seamen, we are in no danger of, for we have more and better seamen then we had the last yeare. I will be very carefull of the choice of your horses, my Ld Crafts [Crofts] has promised me two, which he assures me will fitt you, and I will looke out for others, when I can light upon them, for if I had had any good of my owne, you should not have stayd so long but the plague of horses has been in my stable, and I shall have much ado to mounte my selfe with so much as jades for this summer's hunting, the scarsity of good ones is so great at this present. I will say no more, but only to assure you that nothing can alter that passion and tendernesse I have for you, and to beg of you that you will continue your kindnesse to me, for I am truly Yours.

C.R.

There is a gap now in the correspondence, due to the war, which made communications between England and France extremely difficult. This must have been a sad time for Minette, cut off from her brother and also estranged from Louis, who had accused her of taking the Queen's side over the dismissal from Court of de La Vallière – now pregnant with Louis' child.

The English fleet, under the command of Prince Rupert and the Duke of Albemarle, had several naval engagements during the summer. The longest took place in early June, and was known as 'The Four Days' Battle'. It was fairly disastrous for the English, due to incompetence and misunderstanding. Prince Rupert, thinking that the French fleet, under Beaufort, was about to set out for the Channel, went with twenty-four ships to intercept them, leaving the remaining fifty-four ships, under Albemarle, to encounter the Dutch. The French never materialized, and Prince Rupert, realizing his mistake in dividing the fleet, rushed to the aid of

Albemarle against the Dutch, but too late to avoid considerable damage and loss of life. The *Royal Prince* was grounded on the Galloper Sands and burnt. Both fleets, exhausted with the battle, returned to port for a refit, and were again in action by 22 July. This time, in an action off the North Foreland, the English had the victory. De Ruyter's flagship, badly harassed by Prince Rupert's little yacht, *Fan-Fan*, fled to safety. The Dutch lost twenty ships, the English one capital ship, the *Resolution*. The redoubtable Sir Robert Holmes, of Cape Verde fame, followed up the Dutch defeat by attacking the West Friesian islands of Vlieland and Schelling, burning the town of Brandaris.

The French fleet eventually sailed out from La Rochelle, under the command of the Duc de Beaufort, to rendezvous with the Dutch in the Channel. The Dutch, meeting Prince Rupert's squadron, decided that discretion was the better part of valour, and took refuge in St John's Roads, near Boulogne. Extremely bad weather prevented any engagement between the French and English, and the French were able to reach Brest with the loss of only one ship, *Le Rubis*, whose captain, La Roche, was taken prisoner. And so ended the relatively uneventful war at sea between France and England.

Louis obviously had no stomach for it, and sent Lord Jermyn back to England to discuss further peace negotiations with Charles. Charles welcomed these overtures, but in his next letter to his sister makes it clear that he will not put up with the 'general terms' of Louis' proposals; he demands something more concrete.

There is no mention in this letter of the great fire of London, which started on 2 September, and burned for nearly a week. As Charles took such an active part in the operations to bring it under control, his description of what happened would have been fascinating. The rumour mentioned by Pepys in his entry for 7 September, that the fire was started or at least aggravated by the French, may have been the reason for Charles's tactful silence about it.

The Venetian Ambassador in France, reporting back to the Doge and Senate, remarked that the King recognized the fire of London as a stroke of good luck for him. In his view he certainly owed the preservation of his fleet to it. There was considerable talk in France about the fire, and Louis offered to send provisions and food.[4]

¶ *Charles to Minette*

Whitehall, 18 October 1666[5]

It seems to me by that which my Lord St Albans sayes to me, that this commerce may at present begin againe, and continue, even till the next campaigne; it was a great displeasure to me, to finde it forbidden, and by so much the more, that as I do not thinke this to be an eternall warr, I should be very glad that you should have part in all the thinges that may conduce to the ending of it. I was likewise very glad to learne that the King, my brother, makes professions still of haveing as just a sence in this subject as I have, that is to say, beleeving it nether good for him, nor for me, and desireing an end of it, as much as I do; but allowe me to tell you that in this occasion 'tis not enough to speak in generall termes, espetially after haveing given so much place to doute of his intentions, to reestablish the trust, it were very good to speake more particulally what that shall be. You may assure your selfe I shall corresponde on my side as farr as reason ought to guide me; this is all I shall trouble you with at present, only to tell you the joye I have to assure you my selfe with how much tendernesse and kindnesse I am yours. C.R.

Marie Louise had always been a difficult child to manage, and Minette was very happy that she lived in the household of her grandmother. For her son, Philippe Charles, Duc de Valois, she had a deep and passionate love. He was a delightful child, with a sunny disposition, and gave her endless joy. The King, whose only son was a puny, sickly child, was also devoted to him.

In November 1666, while Minette was at St Germain rehearsing for Molière's 'Ballet des Muses', she was urgently summoned back to St Cloud, where the boy was under the care of his nurse, Madame de Saint-Chaumont. He had developed a high fever due to teething problems. After a few days he seemed to recover, and Minette took him to Paris to the Palais Royal. When she thought he had recovered sufficiently, she returned to St Germain for a performance of the ballet on 3 December. She took the part of a shepherdess, and her little spaniel, Mimi, who could never bear to be parted from her, was carried in her arms. The following day, Minette was called back to Paris. The little Duc had caught a cold, and suddenly became gravely ill, with a high fever and convulsions. His father was so alarmed that he insisted on him being fully baptized. Although Valois had been sprinkled with water when he was born, the royal children were not officially baptized until they were twelve. The ceremony, performed on 7 December by the Bishop of Valence, took place in the chapel of the Palais Royal. Going through such an ordeal when he was so ill may have aggravated his condition. He died the following evening. Minette and her husband were beside themselves with grief at the loss of this promising boy. Louis wrote to Charles fifteen days later, the following brief but heartfelt note:

¶ *Louis XIV to Charles II*

St Germain, 23 December

The common loss we have had at the death of my nephew the Duc de Valois touches us both so closely that the only difference in our mutual grief is that mine began a few days sooner than yours.

Louis

There is no known correspondence between Charles and Minette about the death of her son. The boy lay in state for twenty-four hours, and was buried with his ancestors at St Denis. Christmas was spent quietly at St Germain, but after the Queen had given birth to a daughter on 4 January the round of balls and masques started again, and a sorrowing Minette consented to the 'Ballet des Muses' being performed at the Palais Royal on 12 January.

Peace negotiations between England and France, were carried out in great secrecy under the guidance of Queen Henrietta Maria, although Minette was included in the discussions. Charles kept all knowledge of these negotiations from Parliament. Some said that owing to the very grave financial state he was in he might make peace and pocket the grant for the war for himself! A secret treaty signed by Louis and Charles was put into Queen Henrietta's hands at Colombes in April. Under the terms the West Indian Islands were restored to England, and Charles pledged himself not to assist Spain in any way for a year. A conference was arranged to meet at Breda in July, when the treaty would be formally drawn up and ratified.

No sooner had the secret treaty been signed than the French army of 50,000 men, under Turenne, marched to the Flemish frontier. Louis joined them on 16 May, shortly followed by Monsieur. Cosnac had instilled in him a desire to do well as a soldier, and the warlike Bishop accompanied him to the front. He showed great aptitude as a soldier, but unfortunately he soon tired of the life, and on hearing that Minette, pregnant again, was threatened with a miscarriage, used the news to return to Paris. The French met little resistance, and their progress through Flanders was rather like a triumphal procession – so much so that the ladies of the court, including the Queen and de La Vallière, joined them. Minette was extremely ill with this miscarriage, and nearly died. Monsieur returned to Flanders to rejoin the King, and as fate would have it, met the evil Chevalier de Lorraine once more, and fell completely under the spell of his good looks. This infatuation, which was to last for the rest of Minette's life, dominated him, and ruined their marriage.

In spite of the possibility of peace in the near future, the Dutch were determined to take their revenge on the English before a peace treaty was signed. The English fleet was still laid up due to lack of funds. On 27 May the Dutch fleet, under de Witt, set sail, and on 10 July bombarded the fort that commanded the entrance to the Medway. The half-built defences surrendered immediately. Two days later the Dutch sailed up the river, burnt the *Royal James*, the *Oake* and the *London*, and worst of all, captured the *Royal Charles*, the ship that had brought the King home for the Restoration. They then returned to the mouth of the river and blockaded it, their ships being supplied from the sea. Charles reacted swiftly to the crisis, which was causing panic in London. He and his brother supervised sinking ships in the Thames to block it, and planted cannon along the Medway and at Woolwich. The militia was called out, and reinforced by a field army of 9000. This was the greatest defeat ever suffered by the Royal Navy, and the fact that it occurred so near home was a severe blow to morale and to Charles's prestige. Right up to the day the Treaty of Breda was finally ratified on 24 August, the Dutch continued to cruise off the English coast. As promised, the West Indian

Islands were restored to England, and Cayenne and Acadia to France. New Amsterdam remained English, and retained the name of New York.

The next letter from Charles, written two days after the signing of the treaty, hardly comments on it. He is obviously overwhelmed by a crisis in his own love life, which Minette must have commented on in a previous letter, making clear her liking for the lady concerned. She was the much loved Frances Stuart, who never succumbed to the King's advances, and who had secretly married the Duke of Richmond. This, at the moment of writing, seemed to take precedence in Charles's mind over everything else.

¶ *Charles to Minette*

Whitehall, 26 August 1667[6]

I do assure you I am very much troubled that I cannot in everything give you that satisfaction I could wish, especially in this businesse of the duchesse of Richmonde, wherein you may thinke me ill natured, but if you consider how hard a thing 'tis to swallow an injury done by a person I had so much tendernesse for, you will in some degree excuse the resentment I use towards her; you know my good nature enough to beleeve that I could not be so severe, if I had not great provocation, and I assure you her carriage towards me has been as bad as breach of frindship and faith can make it, therfore I hope you will pardon me if I cannot so soon forgett an injury which went so neere my hart. I will not now answer the letter you writt by your watterman who fell sick upon the way, and so I had the letter but some dayes since, but will expect a safer way to write then by the post. I beleeve Ruvigny will be heere in two or three dayes, and the other gentleman whos name I cannot reade in your letter. The peace was proclaimed heere on saturday last, and so I will end my letter, and will only add the assurance of my being intirely yours. C.R.

Clarendon was dismissed from office during the parliamentary session in August. Minette was deeply upset at the downfall of a man who had been such a loyal servant to her father, and her brothers and herself, for so long. Charles, although in awe of him, disliked him for his parsimony, and for his criticisms of the King's private life, and held him directly responsible for the marriage of Frances Stuart to the Duke of Richmond. He only touches on Clarendon's troubles in this next letter. He is most anxious to warn Minette against the charming but disreputable Harry Killigrew, who after publicly insulting his former mistress, the Countess of Shrewsbury, fought her current lover, the Duke of Buckingham. With mounting debts he had decided to leave England, and was making his way to Paris. Charles felt very strongly that he was not a good companion for Minette. The Dowager Duchess of Richmond, who was sister to the Duke of Buckingham and who had been appointed Groom of the Stole and First Lady of the Bedchamber to Queen Henrietta Maria, was travelling to France with a consignment of twelve horses for the Queen's household.

¶ *Charles to Minette*

Whitehall, 17 October 1667[7]

I hope you will pardon the faute I am in towards you, in point of writing to you of late, when you consider the multitude of businesse is now upon my hands by the alteration I have made, and the Parlament now sitting, and though there anger may make them a little forward to particular persons, yett in the end I dout not but they will do what they ought to do towards me. For Harry Killigrew, you may see him as you please, and though I cannot commende my L^dy^ Shrewsbury's conduct in many things, yett Mr Killigrew's carriage towards her has been worse then I will repeate, and for his demele with my L^d^ of Buckingham, he ought not to brag of, for it was in all sorts most abominable. I am glad the poore wrech has gott a meanes of subsistance, but have one caution of him, that you beleeve not one word he sayes of us heere, for he is a most notorious lyar, and does not want witt to sett forth his storyes pleasantly enough. I am very glad that Monsieur is so well recovered. Pray make my compliments to him with all imaginable Kindnesse. I shall write to you by the Duchesse of Richmond, with greater freedome then I am willing to do by the post, for feare of miscarrying, and so will say no more to you now, but the assuring you of the constant tendernesse and kindnesse I have for you. C.R.

Monsieur had returned from the campaign in a poor state of health, but was on the way to recovery when Charles wrote again. Meanwhile Minette herself was taken ill with an unknown disease which gave her terrible headaches, and made her incapable of writing, even to her brother. It was about this time that the Chevalier de Lorraine took up residence permanently in their household, and cast a dark shadow over her life.

Monsieur wrote to Charles on 20 October to tell him of her illness: 'Madame begs me to excuse her to you that she does not write, but for six days she has had headaches so violent that she has had her shutters always closed. She has been bled in the foot, and has tried many other remedies, but they have not relieved her at all.'

Phillip, 2nd Earl of Chesterfield, sent a description of Minette at this time to the Countess of Derby. He called her Armida, and in spite of his flowery language, it is a fascinating sketch of her.

> Armida, whom all the world so much admires, is a princess who, at the first blush, appears to be of the greatest quality, and has something in the looks beside her beauty, so new and unusual that it surprises the beholders. Her stature is rather tall than otherwise, her shape is delicate, her motions graceful, her eyes sparkling and yet compassionate, and do not only penetrate the thoughts of others, but often also express her own, teaching, as it were, a language yet unknown to any but the blessed above. Her breasts seem two little moving worlds of pleasure, which, by the reflection of her eyes, fire the harts of all that see them, and yet so sweet an inocency shines in her composure, that one would think that she neither knew nor had ever heard the name of sin. Her lips do always blush for kissing of the finest teeth that were ever seen, and her complexion is unparralled. The freedom of her carriage and the pleasantness of her discourse would charm an ancorite, yet there is something of majesty so mixed with all the rest that it stifles the breath of any unruly thought, and creates a love mingled with fear, very like that we owe to a deity. Her wit is mostly extolled by all that hear her, for she not only has a peculiar talent in finding apt similitudes, and in the quickness of her repartee, but in the plainest subjects of her discourse, she finds out something new and unex-

> pected which pleases all her auditors. But now as to her mind; although always generous, it is so changeable, as to other things, that it seems incapable of lasting friendship; for she is never long satisfied with herself, or with those who endeavour most to please her.

Chesterfield himself was only a casual acquaintance, and this last sentence about her is completely untrue. Cosnac, and Madame de La Fayette and many other contemporaries say she was the staunchest and loyalest of friends to those who were close to her.

Charles deals more fully with the fall of Clarendon in this next letter. Minette must have written to him of her deep concern for the old Chancellor. Charles had written in detail to his mother about his reasons for allowing Clarendon to be dismissed from office. He and his brother were on very bad terms at this time. James had naturally taken his father-in-law's side. Clarendon's enemies in Parliament, Buckingham, Arlington and Coventry, brought up the sale of Dunkirk as one of the many charges against him, and the general public blamed him for organizing the marriage of the King to his barren Queen. Lord Bristol joined in the ranks against him, and on 20 October Charles agreed to his impeachment. The Houses were deeply divided on the issue and Charles was in despair. Finally the old man bowed to the inevitable, and on 29 November took ship for France. Parliament immediately banished him for life.

It is difficult to understand Charles's attitude to Clarendon. His lack of legitimate heirs put James and his two daughters in a powerful position, and Charles felt threatened by them. He never forgave Clarendon for arranging the marriage of the Duchess of Richmond, who some thought he might have made his Queen, if the opportunity had arisen.

Charles's hope that, having got rid of Clarendon, Parliament would be kindly disposed to helping him over his pressing financial troubles, was not to be fulfilled. They turned their attention to the royal accounts, which were in a terrible state, partly due to Charles's extravagance, and partly to the mismanagement of the war.

¶ *Charles to Minette*

Whitehall, 30 November 1667[8]

If you looke upon our condition heere, as it is reported by common fame, I do confesse you have reason to have those apprehensions you mention in your letter by this bearer; the truth is, the ill conduct of my Ld Clarendon in my affaires has forced me to permitt many inquiryes to be made, which otherwise I would not have suffred the parlament to have done, though I must tell you that in themselves they are but inconvenient apearances, rather than real mischives. There can be nothing advanced in the Parl: for my advantage, till this matter of my Ld Clarendon be over, but after that I shall be able to take my mesures to with them, as you will see the good effects of it; I am sure I will not part with any of my power, nor do I beleeve that they will desire any unreesonable thing, I have written at large to the Queene, in the particular of my Ld Clarendon, which I could not do but by a safe way, and I dout not that you will in that matter, and many others, have informations very farr from the truth. I will add no more, only thanke you for your kindnesse in being so free with me, which I pray continue upon all occasions, and be assured that I am entierly Yours. C.R.

Charles always had a keen sense of the balance of power and he was alarmed by Louis' great success in the Spanish Netherlands. The terms Louis was trying to negotiate with Spain would have given him a dangerously powerful position, and Charles was determined to prevent it. He therefore, with the able assistance of the clever negotiator Sir William Temple, ingratiated himself with his former enemy the Dutch. De Witt and Temple were delighted with each other and what was to be known as the Triple Alliance of Holland, Sweden and England was drawn up, and eventually signed on 13 February 1668. Under this pact France was to be allowed its existing conquests only. At the same time Lord Sandwich concluded a peace between Spain and Portugal. France was not pleased with the alliance, as can be imagined. By this clever diplomacy, her relationship with Holland was ruined, and Louis' hopes of more glittering conquests thwarted. Charles's letter to Minette about the new treaty shows that he is well aware that he has offended France yet again, but justifies what he has done on the grounds that as usual he has been unable to get any co-operation from Louis.

The Duchess of Richmond had returned to Court hoping to be taken back into favour by Charles. The hurt done to him by her secret marriage was not to be so easily healed.

¶ *Charles to Minette*

Whitehall, 23 January 1668[9]

I believe you will be a little surprised at the treaty I have concluded with the States, the effect of it is to bring Spaine to consent to the peace, upon the termes the King of France hath avowed he will be content with, so as I have done nothing to prejudice France in this agreement, and they cannot wonder that I provide for my selfe against any mischifes this warre may produce, and finding my propositions to France receave so cold an answer, which in effect was as good as a refusall, I thought I had no other way but this to secure my selfe. If I finde by the letters that my L^{d} St Albans is come away, I do intend to send somebody else into France, to incline the King to accept of this peace. I give you a thousand thankes for the care you take before hand of James [Duke of Monmouth, who was visiting the French Court], I will answer for him that he will be very obedient in all your commands, and your kindnesse to him obliges me as much as tis possible, for I do confesse I love him very well; he was, I beleeve, with you, before your last letter came to my hands. You were misinformed in your intelligence concerning the D^{esse} of Richmond. If you were as well acquainted with a little fantastical gentleman called Cupide as I am, you would neither wonder, nor take ill, any suden changes which do happen in the affaires of his conducting, but in this matter there is nothing done in it. I do not answer Monsieur's letter by this post, because I have not yett spoken with M. de St Laurens, to whom the letter refers me, so I shall only desire you to remember me very kindly to him, and be assured that I am entierly yours. C.R.

The Duke of Monmouth's visit to France is still uppermost in

Charles's mind in this next letter, and he thanks Minette for all she is doing to make his stay a very happy one, and also his gratitude to her for successfully persuading him not to join the army, particularly during such a delicate stage in his negotiations with Holland.

¶ *Charles to Minette*

Whitehall, 30 January 1668[10]

I cannot thanke you enough for your goodness and kindnesse to James. His letter to me is almost nothing else but telling how much he is obliged to you and Monsieur for your care of him, and since you have taken the trouble of lodging him at the Palais-Royal, I am sure he cannot be better. I am very glad that you have put the thought of going to the army out of his head, for it were not proper that he should apeare in any army, now that I have become a mediataur, by the treaty I have lately made with Holland, and I am now despatching an envoye to the King of france in order to the mediation, which I hope will hinder Monsieur's journey into Catalogna, and save him from a hott campaigne, and this is all I will trouble you with at present, only againe thanke you for your kindnesse to James, and beg of you to be assured that my kindnesse and tendernesse to you is more then I can expresse. C.R.

Louis had done brilliantly in the winter campaign, conquering the whole of Franche Comté from the Spanish. A short note written to Minette at this time, from the front, indicates the deep affection he still had for her.

Dijon, 5 February 1668

If I did not love you so well, I should not write to you, for I have nothing to say, and I have given my brother all the news there is to tell. But I am very glad to be able to assure you once more of what I have already told you, which is that I have as much affection for you as you can possibly desire.

Charles, yet again, in the following letter, impresses on Minette his wish that the Duke of Monmouth should not go into the army. His strong reasons for this, mentioned in a previous letter, are not reiterated here, but apart from the political aspect, Charles's deep concern for the safety of this dearly loved son, and possible heir to the throne, must also have been paramount considerations.

¶ *Charles to Minette*

Whitehall, 4 February 1668[11]

I cannot enough thanke you for your kindnesse to James. I hope he is as sensible of your goodnesse to him as I am. I do not intende to call him yett away from you, except Monsieur should go to the army, but in that case I thinke it will not be decent for him to stay at Paris, when everybody will be in the feilde, and on the other side, as matters stande, it will not be convenient for me that he should goe to the army, for divers reasons, which I will not trouble you with in this letter. But I hope there will be no neede of Monsieur's going thither. I went this day to the parlament, to acquaint them with the League I had latly made, and to put them in minde of my debts I had contracted in this last warr, and to give me some mony at this present. They have put of the consideration of it till friday, and then I hope they will behave themselves as they ought to do. I have dispatched Mon^r de St Laurans this day to you, who I finde as much an honeste homme as you tould me he was, so I have not any more to say to you now, but to assure that I am intierly yours. C.R.

A letter from Minette of 7 March is missing, but the contents of it can be gathered from Charles's long reply.

Sir John Trevor had made a bad impression on her on his arrival in France. Once again the choice of an envoy to France was not a happy one. He was a dour Protestant and Charles makes it fairly obvious that he did not like the man much himself.

Minette not only chided Charles for his extravagance, but like many others she was very worried about the influence upon him of the debauched Duke of Buckingham. In fact Buckingham never became a Minister. The only office he held was Master of the Horse, and he took no part in the secret diplomacy of 1668–70.

Charles probably kept him near him as a foil to the clever Arlington, and as Charles himself said, reporting on him to the French Ambassador, he was useless in power but dangerous out of it.

Charles blames Clarendon, now living in France, for Minette's strictures. His personal dislike of the former Lord Chancellor tends to make him lay all the ills of his country at the poor man's door. Captain La Roche, who had been captured when his ship, *Le Rubis*, had been taken by the English in the only encounter between the French and English navies, was very much at large again, in charge of two French men-of-war. He blatantly defied all the rules of international law by following the *Sainte Marie* from Ostende to Torbay, seizing her ammunition and tackle, which had been hidden in a private house, and making off with it. He behaved in a similar fashion in the Cowes roads, taking four British sailors prisoner. Charles was outraged, and instructed Trevor to inform Louis, and ask him to punish the man. Meanwhile Sir Thomas Allen had searched him out, retaken the *Sainte Marie* and released the prisoners.

A very delicate diplomatic situation arose. Louis was furious at the high-handed action of Allen, and the Duke of York replied to him in a very truculent fashion, causing fears for another outbreak of hostilities between the two countries. Pepys, in his entry for 29 February, writes of the incident, 'Everybody to think a war will follow; and then in what a case we shall be for want of money, nobody knows.'

¶ *Charles to Minette*

5 March 1668[12]

I am extreamly troubled that Trevor carried himselfe so like an Asse to you. I have sent him a chideing for it. I can say nothing for him, but that it was a faute for want of good breeding, which is a disease very much spread over this country. I receaved your long letter of the 7th inst. now, wherein I perceave you are very much alarmed at my condition, and at the caballs which are growing heere. I do take your concerne for me very kindly, and thanke you for the councell you give me, but I do not thinke you have so much cause to feare, as you seeme to do, in your letter. There is no doute but a house of Commons will be extravagant enough when there is neede of them, and 'tis not much to be wondred at, that I should be in debt, after so expencefull a warr as I have had, which undoubtedly will give me some trouble before I gett out of it. I will not deny but that naturally I am more lazy then I ought to be, but you are very ill informed if you do not know that my Treasury, and in deede all my other affaires, are in as good a methode as our understandings can put them into. And I thinke the peace [13 February 1668] I have made betweene Spaine and portugal and the defensive league [23 January 1668] I have made with Holland, should give some testimony to the world that we thinke of our interest heere. I do assure you that I neglect nothing for want of paines. If we faile for want of understanding, there is no helpe for it. The gentleman by mistake gave hamilton's letter to my Ld Arlington, who read it, without looking upon the superscription, and so brought it to me. I assure you that my L^{d} of Buckingham does not governe affaires heere. I do not doute by my Ld Clarendon, and some of his friends heere, will discreditt me and my affaires as much as they can, but I shall say no more upon that subject, for, if you knew how ill a servant he has been to me, you would not doute but he would be glad things should not go on smouthly, now he is out of affaires, and most of the vexation and trouble I have at present in my affaires I owe to him. The Parlament have voted me three hundred thousand pounds for the setting out of a fleete, and are now finding out the meanes of raising it. You will heare great complaints from La Roche, who was taken in the ship called the Ruby last yeare, but Trevor will lett you know the truth, and then you will see that I have reason to complaine. I will add no more to this long letter, only againe thanke you for your good councell, which I take very kindly from you, as a marke of your concerne for me, but pray do not be alarumed so soone by politique coxcombes, who thinke all wisdome lies in finding faute, and be assured that I have all the kindnesse and tendernesse for you imaginable. C.R.

The next few letters from Charles are full of Court gossip and tittle-tattle, written to amuse Minette. Charles was deeply worried about her health at this time. As she was not pregnant, it is possible that the cause was an internal disorder, a grim forewarning of her future fate.

Henry Killigrew, mentioned by Charles in his letter of 17 October 1667, was still in France after his hasty exit over his affair with the Countess of Shrewsbury, the current mistress of the Duke of Buckingham, and his manifold debts. He wanted to return to England, and through Minette had appealed to the Duke of Buckingham over the matter. Although Charles was always anxious to indulge his sister, he would not give in on this point, and insisted that Killigrew remain in France for the time being.

¶ *Charles to Minette*

March 1668[13]

I am very sorry that your health obliges you to go to bourbon, but undoutedly 'tis the best course you can take to establish your health againe, which is that which you ought to thinke of in the first place. I am sure I am more concerned for it then for anything in this world, and if I had no other reason but gratitude, I ought to love more than I can expresse. My L^d^ of Buckingham is so affraide, that you should thinke that he is the cause that Killigrew does not return hither, since you have desired him to forgive what is past, as he has againe desired me to tell you, there is nothing of what relates to him in the case; as in truth there is not, but he has offended so many of the Ladyes relations in what concernes her, as it would not be convenient for him to shew his face heere. The Truth is, both for his owne sake and oure quiett heere, it will be no inconvenience for him to have a little pacience in other countries. The parlament goes on very slowly in there mony, but they advance something every day. How ever I am prepareing my ships to goe to sea for the summer guarde; we expect Don John every day heere, in his way to Flanders. I hope his only businesse will be for the conclusion of the peace, which I wish may have a happy conclusion for many reasons. This bearer, Tom Howard, will lett you know of all things heere, so I shall not add any more, but to assure you that I am with all imaginable kindnesse, Yours.

C.R.

Continuing with Court gossip, Charles in this letter replies to a query about the Duchess of Richmond's health. She had been stricken with a bad attack of smallpox. Pepys in his entry of 26 March 1668 says of her illness, 'She is mighty full of smallpox, by which all do conclude that she will be wholly spoiled, which is the greatest instance of the uncertainty of beauty that can be in this age, but when she hath had the benefit of it to be first married, and to have kept it so long, under the greatest temptation in the world from a king, and yet without the least imputation.'

Charles continues with his worry about Minette's health. From this letter it would appear that she certainly had some form of intestinal obstruction. He disapproved of her current doctor and sent over his own personal physician, Dr Alexander Fraizer, who had treated the Princess Royal in her last illness in 1660, and had successfully superintended the trepanning of Prince Rupert's skull in 1666.

¶ *Charles to Minette*

Whitehall, 4 April 1668[14]

I send this expresse back againe, with the returne of what he brought from Trevor and Van Benninghen, the particulars of which he will acquainte you with, so as I will only add upon that matter, that I hope the peace will follow. I receaved yours of the sixth since the post went, so as I could not say anything to you then. I cannot tell whether the duchesse of Richmond will be much marked with the small pox, she has many, and I feare they will at least do her no good; for her husband, he cannot alter from what he is, lett her be never so much changed! But to turne my discourse to a matter which I am more concerned with than anything in this world, I see by your letter to James Hamilton that you are consulting your health with a Physisian, which I have a very ill opinion of in that affaire, which is your selfe. I must confesse I have not much better opinion of those you were governed by before, not beleeving they understood the disease you have so well as they do heere. I have therefore sent Doctor Fraser to you, who I will dispatch to-morrow, who is well-acquainted with the constitution of your body, and I beleeve is better verst in those kind of diseases, than any man in Paris, for those kinde of obstructions are much

> more heere than in France, and this is all I shall trouble you with at this time, but that I am intierly yours. C.R.

It is obvious from the following letter that Charles was still infatuated with the beautiful Duchess of Richmond, who was living in great splendour in Somerset House, the dower house of Queen Henrietta Maria. He was so deeply concerned with her illness that he had neglected writing to Minette. Pepys has a delightful account of Charles's passion for the Duchess in his entry of 19 May 1668.

> The King sups every night with great pleasure with the Queen, and yet it seems he is mighty hot upon the Duchess of Richmond; insomuch that, upon Sunday was se'nnight, at night, after he had ordered his guards and coach to be ready to carry him to the Park, he did on a sudden, take a pair of oars and a sculler, and all alone, or but with one with him, so to Somerset House, and there, the garden door not being open, himself clambered over the wall to make a visit to her, which is a horrid shame!

His attentions to the Queen were partly, at least, because there were hopes of her being pregnant at last. But in spite of the great care that was taken of her, assisted by medicine sent from France by Minette, she miscarried. But at least hopes were revived that she might ultimately bear a child.

The problem of Lord Sandwich that Charles mentions must have been the usual irritating one that bedevilled all his Ambassadors – that of precedence. Sandwich was Ambassador to Spain at the time. Trevor, who was out of favour with Minette just after his arrival, seems to have improved his standing with her considerably by assisting her in her efforts to stop Lord Clarendon from being expelled from France.

Sir Theodore Mayerne, who was sent to the Queen by Charles I before the birth of Minette, was a very distinguished physician, deeply respected in the royal family, in spite of his lack of courtly manners. Born in France, he graduated in medicine at Montpelier, and was called to London in 1611, when he was appointed physician to King James I. He died in 1655, but his skilful remedies were still being used, and Minette's remarkable recovery from her illness was due to some pills that he had invented.

The Duke of Monmouth, like his father, was not such a diligent correspondent as Minette, and in this letter Charles apologizes for his idleness.

¶ *Charles to Minette*

Whitehall, 7 May 1668[15]

I have so often asked your pardon for omitting writing to you, as I am almost ashamed to do it now, the truth is, the last weeke I absolutely forgott it till it was to late, for I was at the Duchesse of Richmond's who, you know, I have not seene this twelve monthes, and shee put it out of my heade that it was post day. She is not much marked with the smale pox, and I must confesse this last affliction made me pardon all that is past, and cannot hinder myselfe from wishing her very well, and I hope shee will not be much changed, as soone as her eye is well, for she has a very great defluction in it, and even some danger of haveing a blemish in it, but now I beleeve the worst is past. I did receave your letter by FitzGerald the same day that the physisians were doing the very prescriptions you advise in your letter, but now that matter is over, for my wife misscaried this morning, and though I am troubled at it, yett I am glad that 'tis evident she was with childe, which I will not deny to you; till now, I did feare she was not capable of. The Physisians do intend to put her into a course of physique, which they are confident will make her holde faster next time. Ruvigny did tell me some dayes since of that matter concerning my Ld Sandwich, which I can say nothing to, till I heare from hence, only, if he has done what you are informed of, I am sure he is inexcusable, and shall answer for it severely when he comes home, for I never did nor never will permitt my ambassadore to give the place to any whatsoever. I am very glad you are so well pleased with Trevor, for I have a very good opinion of him, not only of his ability to serve me, but likewise of his inclination and faithfullnesse to do it; he shall know the obligation he has to you, and when 'tis a fitt season, the effects of it also. I will not go about to decide the dispute betweene Mam's masses or Mr de Mayerne's pills, but I am sure the suddenesse of your recovery is as neere a miracle as anything can be, and though you finde your selfe very well now, for God's sake have a care of your diett, and beleeve the planer your diett is the better health you will have. Above all, have a care of strong brothes and gravy in the morning. I aske your pardon for forgetting to deliver your message to James [the Duke of Monmouth], but I have done it now; he shall answer for him selfe, and I am sure he has no excuse, for I have often put him in minde to acknowledge, upon all occasions, the great obligations he has to you for your goodnesse to him, which I assure you he expresses every day heere. If he does faile in writting, I feare he takes a little after his father, and so I will end this long trouble with the assureing you that I cannot expresse the kindnesse and tendernesse I have for you. C.R.

On 8 May the Duchess of Monmouth had sprained her thigh while dancing. It turned out to be a serious fracture, and was set. On 12 May it had to be reset, an agonizing performance for the poor girl. The result was not satisfactory, and she was lame for the rest of her life.

The Marquis de Montbrun and his daughter, the Marquise de Morangle, were obviously butts for Charles's wit, and he enjoyed joking about them with Minette. The Marquis had come to England to try, probably unsuccessfully, to get the repayment of a £100,000 debt from Charles. His daughter was apparently not the paragon of virtue that her father led everyone to believe.

In Charles's letters at this time, politics seem to have been put aside, and Court gossip predominates.

¶ *Charles to Minette*

Whitehall, 14 May 1668[16]

Trevor was very much in the right to assure you that I would not take it ill that you did that part of charite for my Ld Clarendon, for my displeasure does not follow him to that degree as to wish him any where but out of England. I see Monbrun does not change his humour; he allwayes tould every lady heere that his daughter was not painted, as was beleeved as much as he is in france; for her two other qualities, I can only say that if she be as truly his daughter as I am confident she was honest heere, he may be beleeved, for I am very confident no lady heere tooke the paines to aske her an indecent question. The truth is, James did maintaine for some time that she was not painted, but he was quickly laffed out of it. I am sorry to finde that cucolds in France grow so troublesome. They have been inconvenient in all countries this last yeare. I have been in great trouble for James his wife, her thigh being as we thought sett very well, for three dayes together. At last we found it was still out, so that the day before yesterday it was sett, with all the torture imaginable; she is now pretty well, and I hope will not be lame. I have been to sea, and am but newly returned, so as I have not time to add any more, but that I am entierly Yours.

C.R.

The Duke of Monmouth had enjoyed his first visit to Versailles so much that as soon as his wife was sufficiently recovered from her accident he decided to return, in the company of James Hamilton, bringing this next letter with him. Apparently the admiring ladies in the French Court and his father thought he looked better without his perriwig!

There is more gossip in this letter, primarily about the goings-on of the beautiful Hortense Mancini, Duchess of Mazarin, the great Cardinal's niece. Charles had met her in France, and had contemplated marriage with her, but the Cardinal forbade any thoughts of it, and she had married an elderly admirer, the Marquis de la Meilleraye. On the understanding that they changed their name to Mazarin he left his niece a large part of his fortune. The marriage was a disaster, and she eventually fled to her sister, Marie Colonna, in Italy, taking her jewellery with her. Charles was wrong in thinking she had stolen it from her husband. She was to come to England in 1675, captivating Charles again, and becoming his mistress until 1677.

French fears of the Triple Alliance, and the re-emergence of the English fleet coming out in force against them, were put to rest by Charles. The Treaty of Aix-la-Chapelle in May 1668 between France and Spain had removed fears of another war with France.

Although often accused of idleness, Charles was an astute diplomat and far from idle where foreign policy was concerned. His wandering in Europe before his restoration had given him a deep insight into the workings of the minds of the foreign diplomats he had to deal with, in a way that his forebears had not possessed.

¶ *Charles to Minette*

Whitehall, 14 June 1668[17]

The bearer and James Hamilton will tell you all that passes heere. The suden retreate of Madame Mazarin is as extraordinaire an action as I have heard. She has exceeded my Lady Shrewsbury in point of discretion, by robbing her husband! I see wives do not love devoute husbands, which reason this woman had, besides many more, as I heare, to be rid of her husband, upon any tearmes, and so I wish her a good journey. I finde, by the letters from Trevor, that they are allarumed in france, that I intende something against Denmarke, with the fleete that I am now setting out. I do assure you there never was any such intention, for I am now sending most of the great ships into harbour, which are now only a charge, the peace at Aix being concluded, and I shall have this summer at sea only the ordinary summer guarde. I shall say no more to you now, only desire you to have the same goodnesse for James you had the last time, and to chide him soundly when he does not that he should do. He intendes to put on a perriwig againe, when he comes to Paris, but I beleeve you will thinke him better farr, as I do, with his short haire, and so I am intierly yours. C.R.

Charles had been well aware of the sorry state of Minette's marriage for some time. The evil influence of the parasitic Chevalier de Lorraine over her husband was making him intolerable to live with. For some time, as well as having a homosexual relationship with Monsieur, the Chevalier had been carrying on a passionate liaison with Mademoiselle Fiennes, one of Minette's Maids of Honour. When he discovered about the liaison, Monsieur went into a jealous rage, and without consulting his wife, sent Mademoiselle Fiennes to a convent. Minette was understandably extremely upset at his high-handed behaviour. She managed to get hold of a casket of letters belonging to Mademoiselle Fiennes, and discovered that it contained a lengthy correspondence between the lovers. Some of the letters were extremely derogatory about her and her husband. Cosnac, Bishop of Valence, and devoted friend of Minette, saw a chance here of ridding the household of the Chevalier. Selecting the most damaging of the letters, he showed them to the King and Monsieur. He had reckoned without the cunning Chevalier. His mistress warned him that the letters were missing, and he managed to turn Monsieur against the Bishop, who was told to sell his appointment as Grand Almoner to Monsieur's household, and return to his diocese.

Minette was heartbroken to lose her old friend, and appealed to the King, but Louis, who had little love for the Bishop, refused to intervene. This was the 'just trouble' to which Charles refers in this letter.

Minette had also warned Charles of her husband's jealousy of the young Duke of Monmouth. Charles dismisses this as 'ridiculous fancy', but Minette found it yet another cause for stress. Monsieur's second wife, in her memoirs, mentions that there was gossip that Minette did have an affair with Monmouth. This would have amounted to incest, and was highly unlikely.

The brother and sister had been longing for a meeting, and now the war was over, Monmouth had been entrusted with the task of making preliminary negotiations for this.

¶ *Charles to Minette*

Whitehall, 22 June 1668[18]

I did not receave your letter by Church till yesterday, and am very sorry that the occasion of your just trouble continues. Ruvigny was gone before I receaved your letter, so as I could not say anything to him; therfore you must give me new directions what I am to do. I understand your letter of the 26, and by it perseave the ridiculous fancy that comes in to some people's head, but I cannot chuse but be troubled at it, when I consider what small occasions furnish matter to give you unquiett howers. I did order James to speake with you about one part of the commands you layd upon Trevor, which, if we can bring to passe, will be the greatest happynesse to me imaginable. I have had but little time yett to speake with Trevor, so, as for publique affaires, I deferr speaking of till I returne from sheerenesse, where I am going this afternoone, and shall not be heere againe till the end of the weeke, which is all I shall say at this time, only to assure you that I am, with all the kindnesse imaginable, Yours. C.R.

After the Treaty of Aix-la-Chapelle, Louis was again anxious to come to closer terms with England, and Charles, who always felt politically and emotionally nearer to France than to the Low Countries, was again anxious to use Minette as a go-between. Trevor, after a successful term in France, had returned to England with good news of Louis' intentions, and the arrival of the new French Ambassador, Colbert de Croissy, was awaited eagerly by Charles.

Minette had written to Charles pouring out her troubles over the Chevalier de Lorraine, and his devastating effect on her household and Monsieur, and Charles mentions her trouble in this letter, but has decided to wait until he has a safer carrier for a letter than the post before he enlarges on it.

The entertainment at Versailles that he mentions took place on 18 July. Ostensibly it was given by Louis to celebrate the Treaty of Aix-la-Chapelle, but in fact was given in honour of his new mistress, Madame de Montespan. The new gardens at Versailles were opened to the public for the first time. Molière's new play, *Georges Dandin*, was performed in the Central Vestibule, and was followed by a magnificent banquet and firework display. As the Duke of Monmouth was due to return to England on the following day, Charles was looking forward to a firsthand account of it all from him.

¶ *Charles to Minette*

Whitehall, 8 July 1668[19]

I cannot say much to you yett, in answer to the letters you have writt to me, concerning the good correspondence you desire there should be betweene the King of France and me. I am very glad to find, by your letters as well as Trevor's relations, the inclinations there is to meete with the constante desire I have allwayes had, to make a stricter alliance with France then there has hitherto been, and pray say all to the king you ought to say from me, in returne of the kindnesse he expresses towards me, and when M. de Colbert comes, I hope he will have those powers as will finish what we all desire, and be assured that whatsoever negociation there is betweene France and me, you shall alwayes have that part in it as they shall see the valew and kindnesse I have for you. One thing I desire you to take as much as you can out of the king of France' head, that my ministers are any thing but what I will have them, and that they have no parciallity but to my interest and the good of England.

I shall not say any thing upon the letter you writt to me by Mon^r de Boisiolly, till I have a more sure way to write then by the post, only I cannot chuse but say that I am sorry there can be so much impertinence in the world, as I see upon that subject. We are heere in great expectation of the relation of the entertainment of Versailles, I hope James will be the first messenger that will bring it, and so I am yours. C.R.

There is now a gap of three weeks in Charles's correspondence with Minette, and the following brief note apologizes to her for this, and blames it on an excess of stag hunting.

¶ *Charles to Minette*

Whitehall, 27 July 1668[20]

I have been so faulty to you in matter of writing, as it is impudence to expect pardon from you. The truth is, I am gotten into such a vaine of hunting and the game lies so farr from this towne, as I must spende one day intirely to kill one stagg, and then the other dayes I have a great deale of businesse, so that all this, with my lazynesse towards writing, has been the cause of my faulte towards you. I am but just now come from hunting, and am very weary, but I am resolved for the future to be very punctuall in writing to you so that in time I hope to merritt your pardon, for though I am fauty to you in letters, I am sure there is nothing can love an other so well as I do you. C.R.

Minette and Louis had always been suspicious of Buckingham and Arlington's influence on Charles, and once more, in the following letter, he tries to set their minds at rest, insisting that he is master in his own house. Two months later, Pepys wrote in his entry for 30 October, 'The King is made a child of by Buckingham and Arlington, to the lessening of the Duke of York, who they cannot suffer to be great, for the fear of my Lord Chancellor which therefore they make the King violent against.' Even such close observers as Pepys always underestimated Charles's strength and determination to get his own way. His outward air of good humour and indolence concealed a man of great political acumen, one who having waited so long to come into his own was not prepared to let the strings of government pass from his hands. Once again, at the end of this letter, Charles's subtlety reminds Minette that France is 'The country where she is', not her native home.

¶ *Charles to Minette*

Whitehall, 3 August 1668[21]

I have received so many letters of yours by James and the company, as you will not expect a punctuall answer to all the particulars by this post, and besides, there are many thinges which I will expect to answer by a surer way then the post. I am very glad to finde by you, and what James sayes to me, the inclination and intention the king, my brother, has to enter into a stricter frindeship with me. I am sure I have all the inclinations towards it, and ether he or you can desire in that matter, and when Mon[r] Colbert comes, he shall find nothing wanting on my part. I wish with all my hart, that the propositions which Ruvigny sent, long since when he was heere, had receaved that answer which I might reasonably have expected. They would have then seene, that whatsoever opinion my ministers had been of, I would and do alwayes follow my owne judgement, and if they take any other mesures then that, they will see themselves mistaken in the end. I will say no more to you now, but expect Mon[r] Colbert, and I assure you the kindnesse I have for you will always make me do all I can to have a very good understanding with the country where you are, for there is nothing more at my hart then the letting you see, by all the wayes I can, how truly I love you. C.R.

Charles evidently thought he could trust the bearer of this next letter. It is the first time in his surviving correspondence that he discusses openly the problem of the friendship between the Chevalier de Lorraine and Monsieur and its effect on Minette's married life. Clearly the relationship between her and her husband had slightly improved, and Charles was anxious to give her his advice on how to keep the situation in control. Given the outrageous character of the Chevalier, he was more than likely to destroy himself, though Charles also suggests that if Minette saw a chance to rid the household of him, it should be taken.

Charles seems well pleased with his first impressions of Colbert de Croissy, the newly-arrived French Ambassador.

¶ *Charles to Minette*

Whitehall, 9 August 1668[22]

I take the occasion of this bearer to say some thinges to you, which I would not send by the post, and to tell you that I am very glad that Mon^r begins to be ashamed of his ridiculous fancyes; you ought undoutedly to over see what is past, so that, for the future, he will leave being of those fantasticall humours, and I thinke the lesse eclairecissement there is upon such kind of matters, the better for his frind the Chevalier. I thinke you have taken a very good resolution not to live so with him, but that, when there offers a good occasion, you may ease your selfe of such a rival, and by the carracter I have of him, there is hopes he will find out the occasion himselfe, which, for M^r's sake, I wish may be quickly. Mr Colbert is come, and I saw him in privat last night, we only discoursed in generall termes about what he comes, so as I can only tell you that I sayd those thinges concerning you as I beleeve he will acquaint his master with by to-morrow post, by which you will perceave the valew and kindnesse I have for you. I shall write to-morrow, to you, by the post, so I will add no more, but that upon all occasions, you may be most assured, that I will lett you see how truly I am Yours. C.R.

Chapter 8

Something of Majesty

The arrival of Colbert de Croissy was a significant boost to good diplomatic relations between England and France. Charles, while holding fast to the Triple Alliance as a protective measure against France, still hoped to arrange a firm treaty between England and France – one with commercial advantages to both sides. After the humiliations of the Dutch naval war, his main concern was for the supremacy of his navy and merchant ships at sea. As an island, trade was the life blood of his country's well-being, and supremacy at sea was vital for her security.

¶ *Charles to Minette*

Whitehall, 14 September 1668[1]

At my returne from Portsmouth, I found two of yours, one by the post, and the other by Mr Lambert, with the gloves, for which I thanke you extreamely. They are as good as is possible to smell, and in the other letter, you assure me most justly for my failing towards you, which I do ingeniously confesse, as most people do, to their gostly father, and as offten fall into the same sinn againe. I hope I shall not be so fauty for the time to come, haveing now done stag hunting for this yeare, which now and then made me so weary, as with the naturall lazinesse I have towards writting, gave me occasion to misse offtener than otherwise I would have done. The reason why I begin with the treaty of commerce is because I must enter first upon those matters which will render the rest more plausible heere, for you know that the thing which is neerest the harte of the Nation is trade and all that belongs to it. But I shall not enter farther upon this matter now, because I have done it fully by de Chapelles, who will be with you before this time. And, you may be sure, that I will continue my care to lett them see the power you have over me, and how much my kindnesse to you adds to my inclination to live allwayes very well with France. . . . I do intend to go to Newmarkett the last day of this month, at which place, and at Audely End, I shall stay neere a month. My wife goes to the latter of these places at the same time, which is all I will trouble with at this time, but to assure you that 'tis impossible to have more kindnesse and tendernesse then I have for you. C.R.

Charles preferred discussing diplomatic problems in private, often in his wife's bedroom, and encouraged by Buckingham and Arlington he issued an Order in Council that he would only discuss public affairs with Ambassadors if they sought a formal audience. Hence Colbert de Croissy came to rely more and more on second-hand information, some from one of Buckingham's henchmen, Sir Ellis Leighton. Described by Pepys as a 'mad frieking fellow',[2] he sounds an unsuitable man for coping with diplomatic affairs. Nevertheless Buckingham sent him to France with letters to Minette, Queen Henrietta Maria, and Lord Jermyn (St Albans). Charles was well aware of this journey, in spite of Buckingham not consulting him in this matter; indeed he took a malicious delight in watching the political flounderings of Buckingham, and pretended to be very annoyed when he heard of this visit through the French Ambassador.

This next letter from Minette is the longest letter we have of hers, and the most impressive. It shows her masterly grasp of the political situation between France and England, and fully justifies the great trust in her opinions and intellect of her brother and her brother-in-law, the two Kings. Few women as young as Minette have ever had the confidence and love of two Heads of State, and the power to use it for good or evil. Many argue that Minette's influence over Charles was extremely dangerous, and not only threatened the internal peace of England but threatened to plunge

Europe into another war. Whatever the opinions may be, there is no doubt that her intentions were excellent. Her love for her own country, which she had only visited once for a few weeks since her escape as a child of two; her deep desire to see England return to the Roman Catholic Church, led by her brother, were all matters dearest to her heart. Her knowledge of her native country seen mostly through the eyes of her mother, Queen Henrietta Maria, and through those of English courtiers, was faulty. But Charles himself had come a long way since those days before the Restoration, when he looked upon the possible conversion to Catholicism of his young brother the Duke of Gloucester as a major disaster, and a threat to his chances of regaining the throne. Eight years on, his natural inclination towards the Roman Church, his love of France and his sister, as well as his great need for financial support from Louis to maintain his beloved navy, had made him change his course. The treaty with France set out by Minette in this next letter was very attractive to him.

There is much argument about the date of this letter. Was it 1668 or 1669? Cyril Hughes Hartman favoured the 1669 date, largely on the grounds that at the end of the letter Minette states that as it was so long she is afraid to send it to him directly; Hartman believes it was sent through Lord Arlington, to whom she wrote from St Cloud three days before. Certainly the letter she wrote to Arlington mentions a long letter she has written to Charles which she is enclosing with his.

The argument for this letter having been written on 21 September 1668 is much more convincing, and was well set out by Keith Feiling in the *English Historical Review* of October 1932. If the date of 1669 was correct it would mean that this *tour de force* was written by Minette when she was still recovering from the disappointment of giving birth on 27 August to her second daughter, rather than to the son for which she had hoped; it would also have been written only eleven days after her mother's death on 10 September. It is well known that Minette was absolutely devastated by Henrietta Maria's death, and it is almost beyond belief that she would have written a letter of this calibre under these circumstances, let alone without any reference to these two deeply emotional events in her life.

The other strong argument for ascribing the letter to 1668 is the fact that she sets out, as if for the first time, the outline for the treaty, and the possibility of war against Holland and the conversion of England occurring simultaneously. By 1669 the main details of the treaty had already been decided, and the war was certainly seen by Minette as preceding Charles's public conversion and the return of England to the Catholic Church. The letter also coincides with the arrival of the new French Ambassador. I am therefore placing it here on 21 September 1668, where I think it rightly belongs.

¶ *Minette to Charles*

St Cloud, 21 September 1668[3]

Following the promise I made to you to let you know my opinion and what I have been able to see in this important business I will tell you that the order into which the King has put his finances has greatly increased his power and has put him more than ever in a position to make attacks on his neighbours, but so long as England and Holland are united they have nothing to fear from that quarter, and they can even protect their neighbours as they have been seen to do at the time of the last war in Flanders, when they became allied because they were indirectly interested in the preservation of that country. It is not surprising then that the majority of people who do not know the inside of things judge that the safest part you can play would be not to enter into any alliance against Holland. But the matter takes on a different aspect, firstly because you have need of France to ensure the success of the design about R. [religion], and there is very little likelihood of your obtaining what you desire from the King except on condition that you enter into a league with him against Holland. I think you must take this resolution, and when you have thought it well over you will find that besides the intention of R. your glory and your profit will coincide in this design. Indeed what is there more glorious and more profitable than to extend the confines of your kingdom beyond the sea and to become supreme in commerce, which is what your people most passionately desire and what will probably never occur so long as the Republic of Holland exists?

It is true that by establishing your dominion on the ruins of that of Holland you will also contribute towards increasing that of the King, who aspires perhaps not less than yourself to becoming supreme in commerce; but the situation of your Kingdom, the number, the extent, and the order of your ports which are suitable for the biggest vessels, the natural disposition of your subjects, and the convenience you possess for building vessels remarkable for the manner of their construction and their power of endurance are advantages which France cannot possess; and to these advantages you can add that of reserving for yourself, in the division you will make, the most important maritime towns, whose commerce will depend entirely on the laws which you choose to impose upon them for the benefit of your kingdom and yourself. I know well that there are some people who think that after France has increased her power by bringing about the downfall of Holland she would endeavour to take away from you your share of the conquests you will have made; but besides the ease with which you could hold the towns near to you it is easy to see that this opinion is not well-founded when one considers that by the division of the conquests of the territories which the Dutch possess in Europe the King will become more than ever a near neighbour of Flanders and of several German States, which, as well as Spain, would have an interest in combining to take measures to assure you your conquests. For it is certain that after having deprived you of them France would not spare them; and it would even be in the King's own interests to remain allied with you, because if he should separate himself from you his conquests would be in greater danger than yours; since, judging from all appearances, he would have much trouble in finding anyone to form a league with him against you, and you would easily find amongst these neighbours, and amongst others as well, plenty disposed to join you against him. And as for the countries which the Dutch possess outside Europe, you could take and keep what you will have agreed to take as your share with all the more ease in that you already possess considerable settlements in various parts which are near to them. And so it appears that you should easily enough be able to make your Parliament agreeable to your alliance with France; and if you foresee that you cannot at first obtain from them all the money of which you are in need to fit yourself out for war, you can oblige the King to make you a considerable advance, which will serve as a pledge of the sincerity of his procedure. And when the war has begun your Parliament will take care not to let you want for what you will require for the successful outcome of an enterprise on which will depend not only the glory and profit but even the security of the whole Kingdom. This war is not likely to be of long duration if the right measures are taken, and far from injuring the design you have touching R. it will perhaps give you the means of executing it with greater certainty and ease. But if you wish to begin by the execution of this design you will perhaps encounter obstacles which will prevent you from being able to think of anything else and cause you to miss the opportunity of profiting by all the advantages that you can hope for in agreeing at once to what the King desires of you. Up to now I have only spoken of your interest joined to that of your kingdom; but it is easy to see that the execution of the design which is being proposed to you would be the veritable foundation of your own greatness, because, having a pretext for keeping up troops outside your kingdom to protect your conquests, the thought alone of these troops, which for greater safety could be composed of foreigners and would be practically in sight of England, could keep it in check and render Parliament more amenable than it has been accustomed to be. As for your design to oblige the King to be the first to declare himself against the Dutch, it seems to me that since England has engaged herself to help them by the League of Defence she has made with them, it would not be so honest on your part to fail in this engagement and abandon them in order to ally yourself with France, as to break with them first yourself on any of those grounds which you agree can spring up any day out of the jealousy between the two nations and their commercial rivalry. If you should be the first to declare yourself it would not be necessary for you to begin the war save in conjunction with France who would declare immediately afterwards; but if France should declare herself first, and the English Parliament – on the conduct of which it is only possible to make very uncertain conjectures – were to insist on maintaining the defensive League between England and Holland and on granting money only on this condition, France would find herself engaged to make war without the help of England to whom this inconvenience could not happen if she declares herself first, because the execution of the King of France's will depends upon himself alone. I think, therefore, that if it suits you to be the first to break with Holland, the two designs, that is to say that of R. and that of the Dutch war, could be executed at the same time. And you would find in it this advantage: that at the same time as the King sends you troops you could send him such as you judge suitable to do and give the command of them to persons whose presence in England might be embarrassing to you.

So far as the Pope is concerned it seems to me that it would be useless and even dangerous to confide your design to him at the present moment; since he will have no part in its execution and there would be danger that the secret might be discovered. It is true that the present Pope is a man whose mind and intentions are very honourable; but he may perhaps not live until the time when he will actually be needed; and there is a great likelihood that his successor, whoever he may be, will not fail to furnish every possible facility in order that his Pontificate may be honoured by the reconciliation of England to the Church of Rome.

I have become engaged in such a long discussion and my zeal has carried me so far that I no longer dare to direct this letter to you. I only venture to assure you that the same tenderness which leads me into arguments more serious than are becoming to me will always cause me to act in such a manner as to make you admit that there is no one who loves you so much as I.

Charles, in this next letter, suggests that owing to the highly secret nature of the negotiations, he will send a cipher for Minette to use in future. The letter received by Charles from Minette at this time was brought back from France by Leighton.

¶ *Charles to Minette*

Whitehall, 14 December 1668[4]

He that came last, and delivered me your letter of the 9th, has given me a full account of what he was charged with and I am very well pleased with what he tells me. I will answer the other letter he brought to me very quickly. I am sure it shall not be my faute if all be not as you can wish. I will send you a cypher by the first safe occasion, and you shall then know the way I thinke most proper to proceede in the whole matter, which I hope will not displease you. I will say no more by the post upon this businesse, for you know 'tis not very sure.

I do intende to prorogue the Parliament till October next, before which time I shall have sett my affaires in that posture as there will not be so many miscarriages to be hunted after, as in the last sessions. I beg your pardon for forgetting, in my last, to thanke you for the petticote you sent me, 'tis the finest I ever saw, and thanke you a thousand times for it. I can say no more to you now, for I am calld to goe to the Play, and so I am intierly yours. C.R.

Once again in this next letter Charles impresses on Minette the paramount importance of keeping the negotiations of the new treaty absolutely secret. But personal worries about her health and happiness are to the forefront of his mind.

The Chevalier de Rohan, a handsome firebrand at the French Court, had decided to take up Minette's cause against the hated Chevalier de Lorraine by challenging him to a duel. Louis' hatred of duelling was well known, and Minette was horrified of the scandal such a fight would create, and appealed to Louis to intervene. The Duc de Noailles was told to investigate the matter, and de Rohan was duly reprimanded.

Charles was not pleased to hear from Minette that she was pregnant again, partly on the grounds of further danger to her health, and partly because it put a stop to his plans to arrange a visit by her to England in the near future.

¶ *Charles to Minette*

Whitehall, 27 December 1668[5]

You must yett expect a day or two for an answer to what Leighton brought, because I send it by a safe way, and you know how much secrecy is necessary for the carrying on of the businesse, and I assure you that nobody does, nor shall, know anything of it heere, but my selfe and that one person more, till it be fitt to be publique, which will not be till all matters are agreed upon. In the meane time, I must tell you that I receaved yours of 26th of this month, and the 2 of Jan: just now, and am very glad that the Chevalier de Rohan has that mortification put upon him, by your desire, for it will make others have a care of their behaviour towards you . . . I must confesse, I would rather have had you stayd some monthes before you had been with childe, for reasons you will know shortly, but I hope it will be for your advantage, and then I shall be glad of it. I shall say no more now, only wish you a good new yeare, which, if it proove as happy to you as I wish, you will have no reason to complayne. C.R.

The enigmatic side to Charles II is one of the many facets of his character that make him such a fascinating person. This quality in him was never more clearly shown than in his attitude to the Roman Catholic Church. Fifteen years earlier, when he was a King in exile, he had been deeply troubled by his mother's attempts to convert the young Duke of Gloucester to her faith. The consternation it had caused in the royal family, even causing anguish to the little Minette, was an indication of how strongly he felt then that Roman Catholicism was a damaging religion for the Stuart family to embrace, and one quite unacceptable to his English subjects. Now, nearly ten years after his restoration, he is prepared to make a public declaration of his conversion to the faith, and the return of England to Catholicism as a vital part of his new treaty with France.

His affection and respect for his mother played their part, but on the deeper level his profound love of Minette and knowledge that his conversion to her faith was the dearest wish of her life, must have been a highly important factor. Above all there was his instinctive attraction towards Catholicism and his natural dislike of all things Protestant, his love of France and his dislike of the Dutch.

At a meeting at the Duke of York's house in 1659 he spoke publicly to Lord Arundel and Sir Thomas Clifford, telling them and the Duke of his conversion. As for Minette, she had always considered herself to be her brother's Ambassador in France, and partly because she had so little knowledge at first hand of her native country, she could not see that the conversion of her beloved brother to her faith, and the return of England to Catholicism, could spell disaster for Charles and risk plunging England into civil war again. From now until her death, the religious terms of the Treaty of Dover were to dominate her thoughts and hopes.

Charles was well aware of the dangerous ground he was treading on, and insisted on the religious side of the treaty being kept absolutely secret between himself, Minette and Louis. He tells her in this next letter of his decision to write in cipher to her on these matters, and sends her the key for future correspondence. He also used a numbers code, numbers being substituted for names, and most of the last letters from him use it.

He again mentions in this letter how disappointed he is that she is pregnant again, making it impossible for her to come to England. Charles's warning to Louis not to attack the Duke of Lorraine was evidently heeded.

¶ *Charles to Minette*

Whitehall, 20 January 1669[6]

You will see, by the letter which I have written to the King, my brother, the desire I have to enter into a personall frindship with him, and to unite our interests so, for the future, as there may never be any jealousys betweene us. The only thing which can give any impediment to what we both desire is the matter of the Sea, which is so essenciall a point to us heere, as an union upon any other security can never be lasting, nor can I be answerable to my kingdomes, if I should enter into an alliance, wherein there present and future security were not fully provided for. I must confesse, I was not very glad to heare you were with childe, because I had a thought by your making a journey hither, all things might have been adjusted, without any suspicion, and as I shall be very just to the King, my brother, in never mentioning what has past betweene us, in case this negociation does not succeede as I desire so I expect the same justice and generosity from him, that no advances which I make out of the desire I have to obtaine a true frindship between us, may ever turne to my prejudice.... I thinke Mr de Lorraine

> deserves to be punished for his unquiett humour, but I wish the King, my brother, do not proceede too farr in that matter, least he gives a jealousy to his neighbours, that he intends a farther progresse than what he declared at first, which might be very prejudiciall to what you and I wish and endeavour to compasse. And you shall not want, upon all occasions, full informations necessary, but we must have a great care what we write by the post, least it fall into hands which may hinder our design, for I must againe conjure you, that the whole matter be an absolut secrett, other wise we shall never compasse the end we aime at. I send you heere a cypher, which is very easy and secure, the first side is the single cypher, and within such names I could thinke of necessary to our purpose. I have no more to add, but that I am entierly Yours. C.R.

The next letter is the first one that we have in which Charles uses the code which he sent to Minette on 20 January.

James Hamilton was never a popular figure with Ralph Montagu, the Ambassador in Paris, although Minette was fond of him. He was considered to be a meddler and gossip. Although Buckingham was never aware of the religious side of the secret treaty with France, he did have considerable influence at court, and it was largely due to him that the faithful and distinguished Lord Ormonde was removed from his post as Deputy Governor of Ireland. Also by taunting Sir William Coventry into challenging him to a duel, Buckingham put an end to his career. Charles stripped him of his posts, and put him in the Tower. He was soon pardoned, but never returned to public life, and lived in retirement in Minster Lovell in Oxfordshire. The Abbé Pregnany was a fascinating character, part spy, part courier, and part astrologer. Charles, although very amused by him, was never taken in by such people, unlike his cousins in France. He warns Minette against getting carried away with astrology, telling her that it is better not to know the future, either for good or for evil.

¶ *Charles to Minette*

Whitehall, 7 March 1669[7]

I am to go tomorrow morning to newmarkett at three a clocke. . . . I have dispatched this night n.z.m.p.s.e.b.s.w.o.e.f.m. [m.y.l.o.r.d.a.r.u.n.d.e.l.] to 103. [Madame] who is fully instructed as you can wish. You will see by him the reason why I desired you to write to no body heere of the businesse of 271. [France] but to my selfe. He has some privat businesse of his owne to dispatch before he leaves this towne, but he will certaynely sett out this weeke. But pray take no notice of his haveing any commission from me, for he pretends to go only upon his owne score to attend the Queene. You need not feare any thing concerning hamilton for there is nobody are like to burne there fingers but those who medle in businesse and he does not come in that trap. But I see you are misse informed if you thinke I trust my L^d^ of Ormond lesse then I did; there are other considerations which makes me send my Ld Roberts into Irland which are to long for a letter. I am not sorry that Sir Will: Coventry has given me this good occasion, by sending my L^d^ of Buckingham a chalenge, to turne him out of the councell. I do intend to turne him allso out of the tresury. The truth of it is he has been a troublesome man in both places and I am well rid of him. You may be sure that I will keepe the secrett of your profett, I give little creditt to such kinde of cattle and the lesse you do it the better, for if they could tell any thing tis inconvenient to know ones fortune before hand whether good or bad, and so my dearest sister good night for tis late, and I have not above three howers to sleepe this night. C.

I had almost forgott to tell you that I find your frind l'abbé pregnany a man very ingenious in all things I have talked with him upon, and I find him to have a great deale of witt, but you may be sure I will enter no farther with him then according to your carrecter. C.

The next letter from Charles to Minette is purely social, written from Newmarket, where the King had gone to race and hunt. Although he does not mention the episode to Minette, for fear of worrying her, he and the Duke of Monmouth, the Duke of York, and Prince Rupert had a bad coach accident on the way. They left Whitehall at three in the morning on 8 March, all travelling in the same vehicle, when it was overturned at the King's Gate, Holborn, tipping the occupants out into the road. According to Pepys, the King was 'dirty but unharmed'. He gives the reason for the accident as lack of adequate lighting. Or was it a sinister attack on the Stuart dynasty which went wrong, involving the King, his natural son, his only brother and his cousin?

¶ *Charles to Minette*

Newmarket, 12 March 1669[8]

I have had very good sport heere since Monday last, both by hunting and horse-races. L'Abbé Pregnany is heere, and wonders very much at the pleasure everybody takes at the races, he was so weary with riding from Audly End hither, to see the foot-match, as he is scarce recovered yett. I have been a fox hunting this day and am very weary, yett the wether is so good, as my brother has perswaded me to see his fox-hounds runn to-morrow, and at night I am to lye at Saxum [Lord Crofts'], where I shall stay Sunday, and so come hither gaine, and not returne to London, till the latter end of next weeke. This bearer, my L[d] Rochester, has a minde to make a little journy to Paris, and would not kiss your hands without a letter from me; pray use him as one I have a very good opinion of; you will find him not to want witt, and did behave him selfe, in all the duch warr, as well as anybody, as a volunteer. I have no more to add, but that I am intierly yours. C.R.

On his return from racing to Whitehall, Charles again refers to his amusement over the predictions of the Abbé Pregnany. His tips for the races were all wrong. Charles was too clever to take any notice of him, but the Duke of Monmouth lost a lot of money. He makes it very clear to her that Buckingham is to be kept out of any of the treaty negotiations that touch on the King's conversion to Catholicism. The Duke of York, on the other hand, who had recently announced his conversion to the faith, was of course to be included in the secret discussions.

The sick priest he refers to is his wife's Almoner, an Irishman, Father Patrick Maggin. He was very fond of him. His attitude to Henrietta Maria's messenger, Mercer, is less kindly. Bearing a present for him from his mother, the unfortunate man was drowned. Charles's reference to the ill luck of his mother's messenger may half jokingly refer to her notorious ill fortune with anything connected with the sea.

¶ *Charles to Minette*

Whitehall, 22 March 1669[9]

I came from Newmarkett the day before yesterday where we had as fine wether as we could wish, which added much both to the horse matches as well as to hunting. L'abbé pregnani was there most part of the time and I beleeve will give you some account of it, but not that he lost his mony upon confidence that the Starrs could tell which horse would winn, for he had the ill luck to foretell three times wrong together, and James beleeved him so much as he lost his mony upon the same score. I had not my cypher at Newmarkett when I receaved yours of the 16 so as I could say nothing to you in answer to it till now, and before this comes to your hands you will cleerly see upon what score 363. [the Duke of York] is come into the businesse and for what reason I desired you not to write to any body upon the businesse of 271. [France]. 341. [Buckingham] knowes nothing of 360. [Charles II] intentions towards 290.315. [Catholic religion] nor the person 334. [Charles II] sends to 100. [Louis XIV] and you need not feare that 341. [Buckingham] will take it ill that 103. [Madame] does not write to him, for I have toald him that I have forbid 129 [Madame] to do it for feare of intercepting of letters, nor indeed is there much use in our writing much upon this subject because letters may miscarry and you are before this time so fully acquainted with all as there is nothing more to be added till my mesenger comes back.... I had not time to write to you by father Paterique for he tooke the resolution of going to france but the night before I left this place, but now I desire you to be kinde to the poore man, for he is as honest a man as lives, and pray derect your phesisian to have a care of him, for I should really be troubled if he should not do well. What you sent by Mercer is lost, for there are letters come that informes of his setting saile from havre in an open shalloupe with intention to come portsmouth, and we have never heard of him sence, so as he is undoutedly drownd. I heare Mam sent me a present by him wch I beleeve brought him the ill lucke, so as she aught in consience to be at the charges of praying for his soule, for tis her fortune has made the man miscarry. And so my dearest sister I am yours with all the kindnesse and tendernesse imaginable. C.

From the opening of this next letter it is obvious that Lord St Albans, a close confidant of Queen Henrietta Maria, strongly suspects that negotiations for a new treaty with France are going on behind his back. Ralph Montagu, the newly appointed Ambassador to France, and Colbert de Croissy, newly appointed French Ambassador in London, were both unaware of the negotiations. The charming Montagu, who was Master of the Horse to Queen Catherine, had been appointed in February, but did not take up his post until the spring. He was accompanied on his journey to France by Father Patrick Maggin, mentioned by Charles in the last letter, whose health improved rapidly on the journey. There was the usual palaver about precedence at the new Ambassador's entry and as usual Minette's tactful advice solved the problem. She suggested that as Master of the Horse he was entitled to put Queen Catherine's arms on his coach, driving directly behind the King. Lord St Albans in his day had wanted to precede Louis – not a popular suggestion.

It was the devoutly Catholic Lord Arundel who was entrusted with the secret negotiations over religion. Later he was able to persuade the King to stop his programme of building new warships for a year. He was Master of the Horse to Queen Henrietta Maria, and was therefore able to travel to and fro from France without arousing suspicion. Lord Arlington was a gifted courtier, assiduous and subtle. He was haughty with those who posed a threat to him, but pleasant and ingratiating with those he wished to please. He was always pro-Catholic, but like Charles he was not received into the Church until his deathbed. He was a close friend of Clifford, but there was great animosity between him and Buckingham. Although Buckingham appeared to be at the height of his power at court at this time, Charles was adamant that he should be kept in absolute ignorance of the secret negotiations. That he was successful in this is an indication of what a master of intrigue and politics Charles could be, if he put his mind to it. He rather enjoyed the game of pretending to Buckingham that he was completely in the know about the content of the treaty, and asked Minette to continue her correspondence with him to keep him happy. Minette of course co-operated in the deception, writing to him and Lord Arlington frequently. Finally, it was Arlington and Clifford who signed the treaty, Buckingham still being safely excluded from it.

Macaulay, assessing Minette's part in the Treaty of Dover, wrote, 'She lived in an intolerant land at an intolerant time, and she had in her the fatal strain of Catholic zeal that was common to most of her family, a strain brought to them, perhaps, by Mary of Guise, who married James V of Scotland.' The Treaty of Dover came to be named, not surprisingly, the Treaty of Madame, as it took its momentum from her, and lost it on her death.

She was well advanced in her pregnancy at this time, so great concern was felt for her and the child when she had a bad fall. Charles as always shows his love and concern for her health at the end of this letter.

¶ *Charles to Minette*

Whitehall, 25 April 1669[10]

I find by 405. [Lord St Albans] that he does beleeve there is some businesse with 271. [France] which he knowes nothing of; he tould 341. [Buckingham] that I had forbiden you to write to him by which he beleeved there was some mistery in the matter, but 341. [Buckingham] was not at all alarumed at it because it was by his owne desire that I writt that to you; but how 379. [Lord St Albans] comes to know that I cannot tell. It will be good that you write some times to 393. [Buckingham] in generall termes that he may not suspect that there is farther negociations then what he knowes of, but pray have a care you do not say any thing to him which may make him thinke that I have imployed any body to 152. [Louis XIV] which he is to know nothing of, because by the messenger he may suspect that there is something of 290.315. [Catholic religion] interest in the case, which is a matter he must not be acquainted with, therfore you must have a great care not to say the least thing that may make him suspect any thing of it. I had writt thus farr before I had heard of your fall which puts me in great paine for you, and shall not be out of it till I know that you have receaved no preiudice by it. I go tomorrow to Newmarkett for 6 dayes, and shall be in the meane time very impacient to heare from you, for I can be at no rest when you are not well, and so my dearest sister have a care of your selfe as you have any kindnesse for me.

For my Dearest Sister.
C.

In spite of Ralph Montagu's efforts, Minette and the French Court still had a strong distrust of Arlington and his foreign policies, aggravated, perhaps, by the fact that his wife Isabella van Beverweert was Dutch, and a kinswoman of the Prince of Orange. Charles had great confidence in him, and the more he discussed the French treaty with him, the more Arlington came round in its favour. Charles in this letter is still persuading Minette to change her attitude towards him. Lord St Albans, who was a close confidant of both Courts, suddenly returned to England at this time, giving rise to wild rumours that it was more than a commercial treaty between France and England that was at stake. The more Charles tried to suppress all knowledge of his secret plans to become a Catholic and bring England into that Church with him, the more afraid he became that the real truth might be disclosed. Pepys, in his diary entries of 21 and 28 April 1669, has obviously heard strong rumours that Charles is negotiating for a large sum of money from Louis to help him against the Dutch.

One of Minette's complaints against Arlington was that he never answered her letters. Charles promised that this fault would be rectified.

Charles's affection for the colourful Abbé Pregnany is obvious, and he asks Minette not to think harshly of him for failing to impress the English Court with his fortune-telling.

Hopes that Queen Catherine was pregnant at last are mentioned at the end of this letter. How different the history of England might have been if they had been realized.

¶ *Charles to Minette*

Whitehall, 6 May 1669[11]

You cannot imagine what a noise Lord St Albans' comming has made heere, as if he had great propositions from 152 [the King of France], which I beate down as much as I can. It being preiudiciall, at this time, to have it thought that 360 [Charles II] had any other commerce with 126 [Louis XIV] but that of 280 [the Treaty of Commerce], and in order to that, I have directed some of the councill to meat with 112 [Colbert], which in time will bring on the whole matter, as we can wish, and pray lett there be great caution used on the side of 271 [France] concerning 386 [Charles II's] intentions towards 126 [Louis XIV] which would not only be preiudiciall to the carrying on of the matters with 270 [Holland], but also to our farther designes abroade, and this opinion I am sure you must be of, if you consider well the whole matter. I beleeve Mr Montagu has, before this, in some degree satisfied you concerning my Ld Arlington, and done him that justice to assure you that nobody is more your servant than he, for he cannot be so intierly myne as he is, and be wanting to you in the least degree, and I will be answerable for him in what he owes you. I finde the poore Abbé Pregnany very much troubled, for feare that the railleries about fore-telling the horse matches may have done him some prejudice with you, which I hope it has not done, for he was only trying new trickes, which he had read of in bookes, and gave as little creditt to them as we did. Pray continue to be his frind so much as to hinder all you can any prejudice that may come to him upon that score, for the man has witt enough, and is as much your servant as is possible, which makes me love him. My wife has been a little indisposed some few dayes, and there is hopes that it will prove a disease not displeasing to me. I should not have been so forward in saying thus much without more certainty, but that I beleeve to you, you should not want whole sheetes of paper with nothing but that, but I hope you have the iustice to beleeve me, more then I can expresse, intierly Yours. C.R.

The beginning of the next letter is full of highly important information about the position of the English fleet, and is not in cipher. This would have been dangerous information to fall into the wrong hands. The messenger was the Chevalier de Hillière, a man whom Charles must have trusted implicitly.

He continues, also not in cipher, to hint very strongly at the position of church lands, in the event of England reverting to Roman Catholicism, another piece of information that could be extremely damaging if it went astray. Continuing the letter in code, Charles yet again tries to persuade Minette to think more kindly of Arlington, impressing on her Arlington's complete loyalty to him and his wishes over the new treaty with France. He speaks of his readiness to assist Louis in an attack on Holland.

When Colbert de Croissy arrived in England as Ambassador, Charles took a great liking to him, and seemed to be delighted with the appointment. But as time went on, the relationship soured, and by the time of this letter he is deeply worried at Louis' suggestion that the Ambassador should be included in the secret negotiations. Arlington also had taken a great dislike to him, and wrote to Ralph Montagu in Paris to try to get him recalled, with the assistance of Minette. Montagu put the matter to Lionne, the French Foreign Minister, but made no headway at all. On being told how unsuccessful Colbert was as Ambassador in London, Lionne replied, 'Il est bon homme notre Ambassadeur, et ne songe point à malice; il le faut corriger mais je ne scay pas comment le changer.'[12]

¶ *Charles to Minette*

Whitehall, 6 June 1669[13]

The oportunity of this bearers going into france gives me a good occasion to answer your letters by my Ld Alinton, and in the first place to tell you that I am secureing all the principall portes of this countery not only by fortifying them as they ought to be but likewise the keeping them in such handes as I am sure will be faithfull to me upon all occasions. And this will secure the fleete because the cheefe places where the ships lye are chattam and portsmouth the first of which is fortifying with all speede and will be finished this yeare; the other is in good condition already but not so good as I desire, for it will coste some mony and time to make the place as I have designed it, and I will not have lesse care both in Scotland and Ireland. As for that which concernes those who have church lands there will be easy wayes found out to secure them and put them out of all aprehension. There is all the reason in the worlde to joyne profitt with honour, when it may be done honestly, and the King will finde me as forward to do 299 [Holland] a good turne as he can desire, and we shall, I dout not, agree very well in the point, for that country has used us both very scurvily, and I am sure we shall never be satisfied till we have had our revenge, and I am very willing to enter into an agreement upon that matter whensoever the King pleases. I will answer for 346 [Arlington] that he will be as forward in that matter as I am, and farther assurance you cannot expect from an honest man in his post, nor ought you to trust him, if he should make any other professions then to be for what his master is for. I say this to you, because I undertooke to answer that part of the letter you writt to him upon this subject, and I hope this will be full satisfaction as to him in the future, that there may be no doute, since I do answer for him: I had writt thus farr when I receaved yours by Ellwies, by which I perceave the inclination there still is of trusting 112 [Colbert] with the maine business, which I must confess, for many reasons, I am very unwilling to, and if there were no other reason than his understanding, which, to tell you the truth, I have not so great an esteeme for, as to be willing to trust him with that which is of so much concerne. There will be a time when both he and 342 [Montagu] may have a share in part of the matter, but for the great secrett, if it be not kept so till all things be ready to begin, we shall never go through with it, and destroy the whole businesse. I have seen your letter to 341 [Buckingham] and what you write to him is as it ought to be. He shall be brought into all the businesse before he can suspect anything, except that which concernes 263 [Charles II], which he must not be trusted with. You will do well to writ but seldome to him, for feare something may slip from your penn which may make him jealous that there is something more then what he knows of. I do long to heare from 340 [Arundel] or to see him heere, for till I see the paper you mention which comes from 113 [Lionne] I cannot say more then I have done. And now I shall only add one word of this bearer, Mons[r] de la hilliere, who I have founde by my acquaintance with him since his being heere, to have both witt and judgement, and a very honest man, and pray lett him know that I am very much his frind, and if att any time you can give him a good word to the King of France, I shall be very glad of it. I will end this with desireing you to beleeve that I have nothing so much at my harte as to be able to acknowledge the kindnesse you have for me. If I thought that making many compliments upon that matter would persuade you more of the sincerity of my kindnesse to you, you should not want whole sheetes of paper with nothing but that, but I hope you have the iustice to beleeve me, more then I can expresse, intierly Yours. C.R.

A brief extract from a letter written by Arlington to Minette at this time gives us a good idea of the courageous character of the man, who is not afraid to speak out in his own defence even to the King's sister: 'If your Royal Highness complains of the general terms in which my letter is written, I have, with submission, much more reason to complain of the particular terms of yours; and assuredly your correspondents in this court must have given a false description of me to your Royal Highness, otherwise you would never have thought of treating me in this way. I have been all my life a good servant to the King my master, and such I will die, by the Grace of God, and I will not, for all the wealth of the world, act any other part than that of a good Englishman.'

The next letter was written the day after the previous one, and in it Charles continues on the theme of how unsuitable a man Colbert is to be included in the secret diplomacy of the French treaty. He is, on the other hand, against him being replaced at this stage. He awaits eagerly the return of Lord Arundel, with the news of Louis' real intentions over a war with Holland.

Charles, realizing that rumours of a close relationship again between France and England would be unpopular with Parliament, begs that if Colbert is told the non-secret parts of the treaty, he must not speak of it in England. He does not want to jeopardize in any way his chances of getting money out of Parliament at the next session.

The sad news for Minette at the end of this letter is the Queen's miscarriage, dashing hopes of a legitimate heir for Charles. The general opinion then and since is that this time Catherine was pregnant, probably for the first and last time.

¶ *Charles to Minette*

7 June 1669[14]

I writt to you yesterday by Mr de La hilliere upon that important point, whether 112 [Colbert de Croissy] ought to be acquainted with our secrett, and the more I thinke of it, the more I am perplexed, reflecting upon his insufficiency, I cannot thinke him fitt for it, and therefore could wish some other fitter man in his station, but because the attempting of that might disoblige 137 [Colbert, the French minister], I can by no meanes advise it; upon the whole matter I see no kinde of necessity of telling 112 [Colbert de Croissy] of the secrett now, nor indeede till 270 [Charles II] is in a better redinesse to make use of 297 [France] towards the great businesse. Methinkes, it will be enough that 164 [Colbert de Croissy] be made acquainted with 360 [Charles II's] security in 100 [the King of France's] frindship, without knowing the reason of it. To conclude, remember how much the secrett in this matter importes, and take care that no new body be acquainted with it, till I see what 340 [Arundel] brings 334 [Charles II] in answer to his propositions, and till you have my consent that 164 [Colbert de Croissy], or anybody else, have there share in that matter. I would faine know (which I cannot do but by 366 [Arundel]) how ready 323 [France] is to breake with 299 [Holland]. That is the game that would, as I conceive, most accomodate the interests both of 270 [England] and 207 [France]. As for 324 [Spain], he is sufficiently undoing himselfe to neede any helpe from 271 [France], nay, I am perswaded the medling with him would unite and make his councells stronger; the sooner you dispatch 340 [Arundel], the more cleerly we shall be able to judge of the whole matter. One caution more, I had like to have forgotten, that when it shall be fitt to acquainte 138 [Colbert de Croissy] with 386 [Charles II's] security in 152 [the King's] frindship, he must not say any thing of it in 270 [England], and pray lett the ministers in 297 [France] speake lesse confidently of our frindship then I heare they do, for it will infinitely discompose 269 [Parliament] when they meete with 334 [Charles II] to beleeve that 386 [Charles II] is tied so fast with 271 [France], and make 321 [Parliament] have a thousand jealousies upon it. I have no more to add, but to tell you that my wife, after all our hopes, has miscarried againe, without any visible accident. The physicians are divided whether it were a false conception or a good one, and so good night, for 'tis late. I am intierly yours. C.R.

In the following brief letter Charles speaks yet again of his eagerness for Arundel to return from France, and again of his total trust and confidence in Arlington. In a manner so typical of the man he switches from grave political concerns to apologies for cutting this letter short as he is off to a new play. And thus abruptly and without warning this fascinating correspondence comes to an end.

¶ *Charles to Minette*

Whitehall, 24 June 1669[15]

It will be very difficulte for me to say anything to you upon the propositions till 340 [Arundel] returne hither, and if he makes many objections, which it may be are not alltogether reasonable, you must not wonder at it, for, as he is not a man much versed in affaires of state, so there are many scruples he may have, which will not be so heere, and I am confident, when we have heard the reasons of all sides we shall not differ in the maine, haveing the same interest and inclinations. And for 372 [Arlington] I can say no more for him than I have already done, only that I thinke, being upon the place, and observing every body as well as I can, I am the best judge of his fidelity to me, and what his inclinations are, and, if I should be deceived in the opinion I have of them, I am sure I should smarte for it most. I shall write to you to-morrow by l'Abbé Pregnany, so I shall add no more now, and, in truth, I am just now going to a new play that I heare very much commended, and so I am Yours. C.R.

Chapter 9

The Treaty of Madame

The sudden end of this correspondence between Charles and Minette is a great loss. Fortunately we have some wonderful letters written by Minette to her friends, in particular Madame de Saint-Chaumont, and Daniel de Cosnac, which throw not only a strong light on these last few months of her life, but also show us a quality of writing that we have seldom seen from her in her earlier letters. It is inconceivable that only at this stage of her life did she feel that she could open her heart in a letter, and one can only assume that she either wrote many such intimate letters to her brother which he felt had to be destroyed, or her fear of her correspondence falling into the wrong hands acted as a strong restraint on her when she wrote to him.

For the last few weeks of her pregnancy Minette stayed quietly at St Cloud. On 23 August Queen Henrietta Maria, whose health was failing rapidly, paid a last visit to her before her confinement, and on 27 August at midnight Minette gave birth to another daughter, Anne Marie. Her hopes for a son thus dashed, she became very depressed, and she had hardly recovered from the disappointment when Monsieur brought her the tragic news on 10 September that her mother had died.

Queen Henrietta Maria had been suffering from bad insomnia, and much against her will, and the former advice of her old friend Dr Maynard, who had always advised her to avoid narcotics, she took a dose of opium to make her sleep. She never woke up.

Once again the French doctors had blundered, although to have such a peaceful end to what was a terminal illness must have been a blessing.

Henrietta Maria's death greatly aggravated Minette's post-natal depression. Seeing how acutely distressed she was, Monsieur immediately wanted to take steps to get hold of the dead Queen's effects for his wife, but Minette would have none of it, and insisted that nothing should be done about the estate without Charles's consent. Louis XIV took over her possessions until Charles's wishes were known. Was it at this time that all Minette's very personal correspondence with her mother vanished? As the Queen had died without a will, Charles was her sole heir. He immediately gave the house and contents of Colombes to his sister, as well as the wonderful set of pearls that belonged to her mother. Two commissioners were appointed, Dr Jenkins and Sir Thomas Bond, to take over the remains of her possessions, and organize their safe return to England. These included most of the dead Queen's jewellery and some magnificent paintings.

To console Minette for the loss of her mother, Madame de Lafayette suggested that they resumed the task of writing the memoirs of her early marriage, which they had started in 1665. The hours spent together in this pastime proved a good antidote for Minette's grief, and she became very involved in it again, to the extent of doing some of the writing herself.

The Duke of York's little daughter Anne, who had come to France for treatment for an eye complaint, had been staying with her grandmother at Colombes at the time of her death. Minette's daughter Marie Louise had also spent a great deal of her time with the late Queen. On her death, both little girls returned to Minette's nursery to be brought up together, until Anne returned to England at the end of her treatment.

The Abbé Bossuet preached a magnificent oration at Queen Henrietta's funeral at Chaillot on 16 November. He started visiting Minette frequently at St Cloud, and their meetings developed into a deep friendship. The serious side of Minette's complex character developed under the guidance of this brilliant scholar, and no doubt helped prepare her to face the painful and sudden ordeal of her fatal illness with such fortitude.

There is only one extant letter which Minette signed with her

Christian names. This is to Cardinal de Retz, who had rescued her and her mother from cold and starvation in the Louvre during those dark days of the battle of the Fronde. He wrote her a letter of condolence on the death of her mother, and she replied as follows:

¶ *Minette to Cardinal de Retz*

St Cloud, 2 October 1669[1]

Mon cousin, even if you had not all the reasons that you give me for the concern that you show in my recent loss, I am too glad to believe that consideration for me alone would have prompted your kind words. These are my feelings, little as I know you. You can imagine what they would be if all the merit, of which Madame de La Fayette tells me daily, were better known to me. It will not be my fault if we are not better friends before long. Meanwhile, I value your kindness as it deserves, and hope that you are persuaded of my regard for you and believe me to be, my cousin, yours very affectionately.

Henrietta Anne

Minette was in contact by letter with her great friend Daniel de Cosnac, now banished to his bishopric, and was constantly trying to get his return to Court. She had long discussions with Madame de Saint-Chaumont about his future. Her dream was that once Charles had become a Catholic he could use his influence with the Pope to get Cosnac a Cardinal's hat. The idea amused the bishop very much and the first letter to him on the subject was written as far back as June 1669. Although sworn to secrecy about England's return to Rome and Charles's conversion, she mentions it in the letter to the Bishop.

¶ *Minette to Daniel de Cosnac*

St Cloud, 10 June 1669[2]

In your grief for the injuries which you have received, it might well add to your sorrow, if your friends did not seek for consolations to help you bear your misfortunes. Madame de Saint-Chaumont and I have resolved that the best thing we can do, is to get you a Cardinal's hat. This idea may, I understand well, appear visionary to you at first, since the authorities on whom these favours depend, seemed so little inclined to show you any good. But, to explain this enigma, you must know that among an infinite number of affairs, which are now in course of arrangement between France and England, the last-named country is likely, before long, to become of such importance in the eyes of Rome, and there will be so great a readiness to oblige the King, my brother, in whatever he may wish, that I am quite certain nothing that he asks will be refused. I have already begged him, without mentioning names, to ask for a Cardinal's hat, and he has promised me to do this. The hat will be for you, so you can reckon upon it. If only I could have obtained your return to Court, we could have taken means to facilitate the business, but however far off you may be, I will not cease to work for this end, and shall be glad to hear your ideas on the subject, and to find out the best way of making the thing acceptable here. I leave Madame de Saint-Chaumont to tell you the rest, and only ask you to believe, that as I have undertaken this joyfully for your benefit, so I shall persevere in the design, with all the resolution necessary to bring it to a happy conclusion.

A second letter written to Cosnac on 19 September reveals openly for the first time Minette's fear and dislike of the Chevalier de Lorraine and his friends, and the grave mischief he has caused between her and her husband. She also speaks of the faults of her husband, which she has tried so hard to ignore but which continue to cause her so much distress. The fact that this letter, like so many of hers, is almost illegible, leaves some doubt about which particular plot against her she is referring to. She mentions again the prospect of a Cardinal's hat for the Bishop.

¶ *Minette to Daniel de Cosnac*

19 September 1669[3]

I see, by your letter, that you have been informed of the strange treatment which I have met with in this State, where it was hitherto supposed that it was dangerous to harm others, but

> ordinary rules do not apply to those persons. One proof of this lies in their eagerness to disown their designs against me, which would in itself be a sufficient revenge to gratify me, were it not that Monsieur is mixed up in the thing. This distresses me as much as it has always done, and I cannot bear to recognize his faults, although he has so many that by this time I ought to be used to it. As for the business which I mentioned to you, I mean the affair of the hat, all is progressing according to my desire. I have received fresh assurances from the person on whom it depends, and I see nothing to hinder it now, unless it is your ill-luck. But I hardly think even this can be bad enough to make the person who has made me this promise break his word. I only wish it were as easy to bring you here for the Assembly of Clergy. Your friends agree with me that, till then, it would be useless to make any further efforts for your return. But I continually beg M. le Coadjuteur de Reims [Le Tellier, a son of the minister] to induce his father to approach the King on this subject. He promised me an answer, but the death of the Queen, my mother, has prevented me from seeing him. The loss of your brother has grieved me very much for your sake and you will always find me as grateful to you as I ought to be.

Knowing her brother's desire for her to improve her relationship with Lord Arlington, Minette made a great effort by carrying on a friendly correspondence with him. In this next letter she answers one from him condoling with her on her disappointment on the birth of a daughter.

For some time Minette's relationship with Louis XIV had been strained, the probable reason being that he felt that all her affections and loyalty over the treaty negotiations were with her brother in England rather than with France. At a time when she had lost so many friends the added coolness of the French King towards her was another cause for distress, and she speaks of this to Arlington. We can tell by this letter that Arlington was almost paranoiac in his distrust of Clarendon, and she tries to put his fears at rest.

It would appear that Minette had so lost confidence in herself under the constant ill treatment she suffered from her husband and his minions that she was even afraid to send Charles a long letter in case it annoyed him, sending it to Arlington instead.

¶ *Minette to Lord Arlington*

c. 21 September 1669[4]

I am infinitely obliged to you for the wish you express that I may have a son. And I shall be so too if you will take it upon yourself to remind the King of a request I made him in favour of Lord Bockurs, who desires to have the post of First Gentleman of the Bedchamber. You know well that his merit entitles him to hope for this favour, and I know also that your help can contribute much to it. I hope that you will accord it to him, and I am informing the King that I have asked you to make this request.

As for the suspicions I had, they were founded on reasons of which I informed the King some time ago by a Page of the Backstairs to the Queen. He may have told you of them and I gave some credence to them, because at the same time I had perceived a coldness in the feelings of the King of France for me, which made me think that, fearing that I might discover that he was not acting in good faith, he wished to remove me from the business, for fear that I might warn the King my brother of it, as assuredly I should have done. But as for my Lord Clarendon I do not think that he is concerned in it.

It is not on your suspicion alone that I am trying to discover if there is any foundation. I will not repeat to you those I had to cause me the feelings of mistrust which were apparent to you: ask the King for them. But I may tell you that the last paper that was sent me has so convinced the King here of the King my brother's sincerity that, as he has so rightly judged, the rectitude of his proceedings has made others have it. I venture to answer for this now, and if my Lord Arundel is sent back here to complete this affair, nothing will pass of which I shall not be well informed, nor anything against the interests of the King my brother.

I will confess to you that if I had known that a promise would be made to undertake to assist France in the just pretensions she may have against Spain, I would have begged the King my brother not to do it so soon but to wait till something has happened to procure more advantages from it than the thanks he has been given. But this cannot be remedied now, and after all it is not a great misfortune. But you must see that, even in the smallest thing, I think of furthering the interests of the King my brother. I wrote him this long letter, but finding it too long I have not dared to direct it to him; show it to him when you judge that he will not be importuned by it.

Such are the reflections which the solitude of St Cloud gives me the leisure to make. There remains nothing more for me to add to this save compliments to M. d'Arundel. The doubt I am in as to whether he has left prevents me from writing to him. Assure Father Patrick also of my friendship and ask him for the continuance of his.

The King has informed me that he loves me dearly, and, though I am persuaded of it, this confirmation has not failed to be very agreeable to make. He will be very glad to see so good an understanding between us, you and me. For this was one of the things he seemed to hope for most. I can answer that it will endure; at least I will contribute to it by all the sincerity and regularity that a friend should have.

Minette had a great longing to see her old friend Cosnac and discuss her manifold problems with him, and rather unwisely she begged him to come to Paris to see her. She felt the death of her mother acutely, and her isolation in her own household was unbearable. Having been forbidden by both Kings to discuss the treaty with her husband, the wise counsels of the Bishop were an urgent need for her. In a letter to him she wrote: 'You no longer care for me, dear Bishop, since you refuse to give me consolation which I cannot do without.'

He was deeply touched by her pathetic words, and decided to risk the journey. He arranged to meet Minette in a friend's house at St Denis after her mother's funeral, and decided to travel in disguise. As luck would have it he fell ill and was taken to a poor lodging in the Rue St Denis. He sent his nephew to the Palais Royal to give the vital papers he carried to Madame de Saint-Chaumont, to be delivered safely to Minette. The police, finding his movements suspicious, arrested him and he was forced to reveal his true identity by producing his bishop's crozier, which he had hidden under his pillows. He was taken to the Fort d'Eveque, and from there was sent into exile to l'Isle-Jourdain.

Monsieur was delighted to be able to break the news to her that her old friend had been arrested and sent into exile. She was horrified to hear of his fate, and blamed herself bitterly for it.

Worse was to follow. Although the Bishop thought he had destroyed all the letters he had on him from Minette, one from Madame de Saint-Chaumont was overlooked, and fell into the hands of the police. Louis, feeling that some intrigue was afoot between the Bishop and the governess, sent Turenne to Minette, ordering Saint-Chaumont's instant dismissal. To lose such a dear companion, who had nursed all her children and was her nearest confidante, was intolerable. Madame de Saint-Chaumont retired to the country, and on Minette's death entered a Carmelite convent. Actually Minette's terrible loss has been our gain, as from now until her death Minette kept up a constant correspondence with her ex-governess, and the letters written to her are among the most fascinating that she wrote. Her final humiliation was that she was not allowed to appoint her next governess. Her choice would have been Madame de Lafayette. But instead Monsieur appointed Madame de Clerembault, a worthy woman who did her duties well, but who was no substitute for her predecessor.

The odious Lorraine boasted openly that he and Monsieur had been responsible for the removal of all Minette's closest friends. Minette at last decided to appeal to her brother to intervene on her behalf to Louis XIV. Ralph Montagu wrote of her at this time:

> You may give credit to Madame's intelligence; some of the most understanding people of France apply themselves to Madame, having a great opinion of her discretion and judgement, and tell her all they know; and it is not without reason they have that opinion of her, for she has them both in great perfection; besides in England you ought not to slight any advance that comes from her, because she is so truly, compassionately concerned for the King her brother.[5]

As ambassador, Montagu was appalled at her treatment and decided to intervene. He first wrote to Arlington informing him that it was time her brother acted on her behalf. This was followed by a moving, strongly worded letter to Charles himself, begging him to protect his sister from further grief and indignities. The letter speaks for itself.

¶ *Ralph Montagu to Charles II*[6]

I suppose your Majesty has, by Madame's own letter, as well as by what I writ to my Lord Arlington, had an account of the disgrace of Madame de St Chaumont, which has been done with so many unkind circumstances, and so little consideration of whose daughter and whose sister she is, that I do not see how your Majesty can avoid doing something that may show the world that you both intend to own her and right her when occasion shall serve, which will make them here for the future use her at another rate, when they see that your Majesty lays her concerns and interests to heart. By all the observation that I have made since I have been in this country, nobody can live with more discretion than Madame does both towards the King and Monsieur, and the rest of the world; but she is so greatly esteemed by everybody that I look upon that as partly the occasion of her being so ill used both by the King and her husband. To remedy this, I would humbly propose to your Majesty what Madame has already discoursed to me of, which is, that your Majesty would tell the French Ambassador in England, that you know the Chevalier de Lorraine is the occasion of all the ill that your sister suffers, and that she is one that you are so tender of that you cannot think the French King your friend, whilst he suffers such a man about his brother, by whose counsels he doth every day so many things to Madame's dissatisfaction.

The King here is sufficiently convinced of all the impertinencies and insolencies of the Chevalier de Lorraine, and doth at this time both desire and stand in need so much of your friendship that I believe in a little time he may be brought to remove him from about Monsieur, if he sees it is a thing your Majesty really insists upon. If, Sir, you shall ever think fit to say this to the French Ambassador, at the same time a letter from you to the King here would be very necessary, with some instruction to me to speak to him in it too.

In case your Majesty doth not approve of this way, nothing could be more for Madame's comfort, as well as credit, than

> that your Majesty should desire to have her make a journey to you into England in the spring. I think there needs not many arguments to persuade your Majesty towards the seeing of one that you love so well. If you shall think this improper too, Madame would then desire that you would let fall to the French Ambassador that you are informed how unkindly she is used here, but that she has desired you to take no notice of it, but only, if you please, not live so freely, nor do the French Ambassador so much honour, as you use to do.
>
> Your Majesty may perhaps think me very impertinent for writing of this, but I assure you, Sir, not only all the French, but the Dutch, the Swedish, and Spanish Ministers are in expectation of what your Majesty will do in this business, for they all know Madame is the thing in the world that is dearest to you; and they whose interest it is to have your Majesty and the King here be upon ill terms, are very glad that he has done a thing which they think will anger you. I believe the King is now sorry that he has done this, though he be of a humour not to own it. This is a conjuncture of that consequence for the quiet and happiness of the rest of Madame's life, that I thought I should be wanting both in the duty I owe your Majesty and the zeal I have for her service, if I did not give you the best account I could of what concerns her, which I hope you will pardon.

Montagu's letter to Arlington reached Charles before the one written directly to him, and this normally easy-going man was enraged at the appalling insults his sister was suffering from her husband and the Chevalier, and also extremely angry at Louis for dismissing her governess. He immediately summoned Colbert de Croissy, the French Ambassador, and in forthright terms told him of his great displeasure at his sister's treatment, and demanded instant recompense to her for Louis' high-handed dismissal of her governess, and the despicable behaviour of her husband. Arlington added his voice to the King's, insisting that the complaints had not come directly from Minette, but the French Court in general, and the English Ambassador. De Croissy immediately communicated the King of England's feelings to his master, and Louis, who was already getting very impatient with the behaviour of Lorraine, made up his mind to remove him from Court at the earliest opportunity.

Monsieur, hearing of the communications about his favourite from the English Court, was deeply anxious for Lorraine's safety. Taking advantage of Minette's increased piety, he tried to persuade her through her confessor, Father Pierre Zoccoli, that she should be kinder to Lorraine, and threatened to refuse to sleep with her unless she complied with his wishes.

In this next letter to Bishop Cosnac, condoling with him on the failure of his mission, and subsequent exile, she pours out her heart to him over her domestic troubles. But at least there is now an underlying hope in the letter that the days of the Chevalier in her household are numbered.

¶ *Minette to Cosnac*

St Germain, 28 December 1669[7]

If I had not heard of you from your friends, who told me of your letter, I should be very anxious about you, fearing the journey would injure your health, but, from what I hear of its improvement, I see, as I have often found myself, that bodily health does not always depend upon peace of mind. If this were the case, I should hardly be alive now, after the grief I have had in losing you, and your strength would not have resisted the effects of so much fatigue, at the worst season of the year, and of all the trials to which you have been exposed. Madame de Fiennes showed Monsieur your letter, but I cannot say that it moved him as it ought to have done. He has long since lost the use of his native tongue, and can only speak in the language which has been taught him by the Chevalier de Lorraine, whose will he follows blindly, and the worst is, I have no hope that he will ever mend his ways. You will understand how happy this certainty is likely to make me, and what hours I spend in bitter reflections! If the King keeps the promises which he daily repeats to me, I shall in future have less cause for annoyance, but you know how little I have learnt to trust such words, from a personage who is so obstinate in refusing to forgive you, and who is able to do what he wills. As for good Père Zoccoli [Madame's Capuchin confessor], he implores me every day to be kind to the Chevalier de Lorraine, and blames me for refusing to receive his insincere advances. I tell him that, in order to like a man who is the cause of all my sorrows, past and present, I ought at least to have some esteem for him, or else owe him some debt of gratitude, both of which are absolutely impossible, after the way in which he has behaved. Yet Monsieur refused to communicate at Christmas, unless I would promise him, not to drive his favourite away. I did this to satisfy him, but at the same time, I had the pleasure of letting him know, how much wrong this intimacy did me, and what grief I felt at seeing how little he cared for me. Farewell, nothing can ever diminish the esteem that I have for you.

The Chevalier seemed to be oblivious of the storm that was about to crash about him, and continued to boast of his great influence with Monsieur, and the possibility that Monsieur might separate from, and even divorce his wife. Monsieur, as besotted as ever, was foolish enough to offer him the revenue of two vacant abbeys in the Orléans' gift. He was shattered when Louis categorically refused to give his consent, stating that among other reasons for his action was the fact that the life of the Chevalier made him quite unsuitable for an income from a church benefice! Monsieur was very angry, and his favourite openly spoke slanderously of the King. As soon as his words reached Louis he seized the opportunity to have him arrested at St Germain, and imprisoned in Pierre-Encise. Monsieur fainted away at the shock, and raged at his wife for being the cause of his minion's downfall.

Minette immediately wrote off to Madame de Saint-Chaumont with the news, with a typical touch of irony and kindness, so characteristic of her, and of her brother.

¶ *Minette to Madame de Saint-Chaumont*

Paris, 30 January 1670[8]

You will need all your piety to enable you to resist the temptation, which the arrest of the Chevalier will arouse in you, to rejoice at the evil which has befallen your neighbour! You will soon hear how violently Monsieur has acted, and I am sure you will pity him in spite of the ill-treatment which you have received at his hands. But, even if I had time to tell you all that has happened, I would prefer to speak of the injustice that you do me, in ever thinking that I can forget you. I love you, and you must, I am sure, know this. I have never tried so hard to help anyone as I have tried to help you, and, as often as ever you wish, I am ready to tell you that I care more for you than for any of my friends. After this, do not judge what I wish to do by what I can do, and believe that my only wish is to find out how I can best please you. Time will show you the truth of my words, and you may rest assured that nothing can ever change the tenderness that I feel for you.

Vowing that he would never return until the Chevalier had been released, Monsieur dragged his wife off to Villers-Cotterêts. Before leaving she just had time to send a short note to her friend Maréchal Turenne.

¶ *Minette to Maréchal Turenne*

Paris, 31 January 1670[9]

I only write to bid you farewell, for things have come to such a pass that, unless the King detains us by much affection and a little force, we go to-day to Villers-Cotterêts, to return I know not when. You will understand what pain I feel from the step which Monsieur has taken, and how little compared with this I mind the weariness of the place, the unpleasantness of his company in his present mood, and a thousand other things of which I might complain. My only real cause of regret is having to leave my friends, and the fear I feel that the King may forget me. I know he will never have to complain of me, and all I ask him is to love me as well in my absence as if I were present with him. With that, I shall rest quite content, as far as he is concerned. As for you, I will not let you off so easily. I pretend to be regretted by you, without counting the 100 pistoles which you lose by my absence, and, to speak seriously, you would be very wrong not to miss me, since no one is so truly your friend as I am.

Minette had to stay in the gloom of Villers-Cotterêts for a month, in the depth of winter, which could not have done her precarious health much good. Monsieur wrote to Colbert protesting at the treatment of his favourite, and refusing to return to Court until the Chevalier had been released from prison. Louis was extremely annoyed by his obstinacy, and had the Chevalier removed to the grim Château d'If at Marseilles, where he was forbidden any communication with his friends.

The row between the two royal brothers was the talk of both the French and English Courts, with deep sympathy for Minette and sorrow at her absence from Court being widespread in the palaces of Paris. In his rage against Minette, Monsieur refused to sleep with her, the ultimate sanction against her, a situation that had not happened in their marriage before. It is difficult in these days to understand that in spite of Minette's disgust with Monsieur's sexual behaviour with his minions, they were still very much a married couple. All the outward panoply of being the second lady in France, married to the King's brother, was carried out to the full for the public to see. The couple's deep desire for another son, and the in-built sense of duty in a royal princess to produce children, was a very strong reason for the marriage remaining intact. Unlike some modern royal marriages, this one was still very much a marriage. Hence Louis XIV's disgust and anger with the Chevalier de Lorraine for his malicious gossip that the couple were about to separate, or even be divorced.

Monsieur, with all his faults, could be excellent company, and in these last letters Minette shows a certain compassion for him in the loss of his friend, and a desire to please which is very touching. Like all marriages, hers to Monsieur had its good moments. The malignant influence of Lorraine was the overwhelming reason for the unhappiness between them. It is interesting to note that Monsieur's second wife, Charlotte Elizabeth, the Princess Palatine, who was married to Monsieur for thirty years, although of a completely different temperament, suffered from him and his minion in the same way. For most of that time the Chevalier was living in their household and in her memoirs she admits that it was only in the last three years of their marriage, before Monsieur's death, when her husband had at last got bored with him, and realized to the full how he had been abused by him and his friends, that the marriage was comparatively happy. Made of stern,

Lutheran stock, with a strong sense of humour and a violent temper, the second Madame was able to survive the horrible conditions in her household in a way which the more sensitive, delicate Minette was unable to do. The damage to her health and spirits was incalculable, and too late her brother took steps to ease her burden.

The impending Treaty of Dover was a paramount reason why Louis felt that this quarrel between him and his brother should be resolved and that he and his wife should return to Court. Secret plans were already afoot for Minette, under cover of a visit to her brother, to take the treaty to England for his signature. The fact that such plans were kept from her husband aroused his deep jealousy when he eventually heard of them. To understand Monsieur's jealous feelings, which were so damaging to the marriage and may even have caused Minette's death, it must be understood that she threatened the two dominating passions of his life, his deep love for his brother and his infatuation with the Chevalier de Lorraine. Minette's 'affair' with Louis XIV in the early days of their marriage was an early blow to any chance of happiness, not because Monsieur minded his wife having an affair, but because he felt that he was being ousted from his brother's affections by it. Although he was bisexual to the point of being able to father children, those closest to him felt that, except for a few weeks before his marriage, he was not capable of falling in love with a woman. Thus from Minette's point of view he was not a demanding husband. The second Madame, in a bawdy way, describes how Monsieur was in the habit of masturbating with the medals of his rosary, and making love with gloves on!

Letters passed between Colbert de Croissy and Louis XIV suggesting that the journey to England should be made when the Court were visiting Flanders to inspect the province handed over to the French by Spain at the Treaty of Aix-la-Chapelle. They would be near enough for Minette to use it as an excuse to cross the Channel to visit her brother. Lord Falconbridge, who had been appointed Ambassador to Venice, Florence and Savoy, stopped on his way at St Germain to hand over letters officially requesting that Minette should visit England in the spring. Finding that the Orléans household had gone to Villers-Cotterêts, he sent his secretary, Doddington, to Minette to find out what the position was. Doddington's account of his interview with her follows.

> Madame received me with all imaginable kindness, much beyond what a man of my figure could pretend to, and did me the honour to give me a full hour's private discourse with her, and, perceiving that I was not unacquainted with her affairs, and flattering herself that I had address enough, or, at least, inclination, to serve her, she was pleased to tell me she had designed to see the King, her brother, at Dover, as this Court passeth by Calais to Flanders; that this King had received the motion with all kindness, and conceived the ways of inducing Monsieur to accomplish it, which was that both her brothers and my Lord of St Albans should write to Monsieur to that effect, which they had done; but the letters, coming hither a day or two after the Chevalier de Lorraine's disgrace, Monsieur fell into so ill a humour with Madame, even to parting of beds, that the King of France had commanded the letters should not be delivered to Monsieur, until he was better prepared to receive such a motion. That, since his coming to Villers-Cotterêts, he began to come to himself, and that she thought, if the King of France approved of it, that the letters might now be delivered, in order to which Her Highness gave one of these three letters into my hand, and desired that my Lord Ambassador Montagu would, presently on my return, dispatch away one to St Germain, to get the King's permission that my Lord Falconbridge might bring them with him to Villers-Cotterêts, and deliver them to Monsieur. The King of France is extraordinary kind to Madame, and hath signified it sufficiently in all this affair of the Chevalier de Lorraine, who he disgraced on her account, and on hers also it is that Monsieur is now invited to Court, although he seems not to take notice of it. She is even adored by all here, and, questionlesse, hath more spirit and conduct than even her mother had, and certainly is capable of the greatest matters.[10]

Monsieur had always outwardly shown friendship to the English ambassador, and had kept up a stream of superficial correspondence with his English cousins. He was therefore pleased to see Ralph Montagu, and Doddington, and by the time of Colbert's second visit, Lord Falconbridge had also arrived. He wrote a despatch after his interview with Minette.

¶ *Monsieur to Lord Falconbridge*

25 February 1670[11]

Madame's reception was obliging beyond expression. She has something of particular in all she says or does that is very surprising. I found by her that, although Monsieur were at that time in better humour than he had of late been, yet he still lies apart from her; that she wanted not hopes of inducing his consent to her seeing of the King, my master, at Dover or Canterbury this spring, as this Court passes into Flanders, nor is this King unwilling to second her desires in that particular; and, to say the truth, I find she has a very great influence in this Court, where they all adore her, as she deserves, being a princess of extraordinary address and conduct.

Colbert arrived the following day with a magnificent set of presents for Minette from Louis, which he said she had won at the annual lottery. Jewellery, perfume, laces, diamond garters (which were all the rage), gloves, and 2000 louis d'or, all helped to lighten the spirits of Monsieur and his wife. Colbert told Monsieur that Lorraine had been released from the Château d'If, and was being sent to Italy, and that correspondence between them would be allowed, but no return to Court. Monsieur was satisfied with this climb-down of his brother, and decided to return to Paris the following day, with Colbert and the ambassadors.

Although on the surface the relationship between Minette and her husband had been patched up, his treatment of her was still appalling, and Mademoiselle felt forced to remonstrate with him, and remind him that Minette was the mother of his children and should be treated with greater respect. Many people remarked on how thin and ill she looked on her return from Villers-Cotterêts, but put it down to her misery and depression while she was incarcerated there with a hostile husband. On 10 March she wrote again to her governess, Madame de Saint-Chaumont.

¶ *Minette to Madame de Saint-Chaumont*

St Germain, 10 March 1670[12]

I did not write to you from Villers-Cotterêts, because I had no safe means of conveyance, and the post is too dangerous to be trusted with anything but mere compliments. While I was there, I received your answer to the letter in which I informed you of the Chevalier de Lorraine's disgrace, and am not surprised to find how calmly you take this revenge, which le bon Dieu has so promptly granted you. Monsieur still persists in believing that it is all my doing, and forms part of the promises which I made you. That is an honour of which I am unworthy, excepting so far as wishes go, and I was not guilty in this respect, if indeed it can be called guilt, to desire the ruin of a man, who has been the cause of all my troubles. In your piety, you seem even to have ceased to wish for vengeance. That is a pitch of perfection to which I confess I cannot attain, and I am glad to see a man, who had never done justice to anyone, get his deserts. The bad impression which he left on Monsieur's mind still lasts, and he never sees me without reproaches. The King has reconciled us, but since Monsieur cannot at present give the Chevalier the pensions which he desires, he sulks in my presence, and hopes that, by ill-treating me, he will make me wish for the Chevalier's return. I have told him that this kind of conduct will never answer. He replies with those airs of his which you know well. I fear the King is still displeased with you. Let us hope that he will one day recognize your innocence, and repent of the way in which you have been treated. But alas! it is too late already, for your place is filled, and Monsieur is so conscious, and so much ashamed of the injustice which he has done you, that he will, I fear, never forgive you. Another day, I will answer the letter which you wrote before your last one, and will only now reproach you for ever dreaming that I could forget to defend you. I forget nothing which concerns you, and you will always find me the most constant and tenderest of friends.

Minette's longed-for visit to her brother hung in the balance. In a letter Lionne wrote to Colbert from St Germain, dated 22 March 1670, he writes, 'When he [Louis] proposed to Monsieur a journey to England for Madame, whom his Britannic Majesty has a great desire to see, Monsieur replied in as contrary manner as possible, and with a violent fit of rage, saying that he would not even let

Madame take the journey into Flanders.' Louis continued with his persuasions, and in a letter to Colbert de Croissy a week later, wrote that he thought some progress was being made, only to be met with Monsieur's insistence that he accompany his wife on the trip, an exchange visit, according to protocol, with one to be made at the same time by the Duke of York coming to France.

Minette was extremely alarmed at this turn of events. Monsieur was still ignorant of the secret terms of the treaty, and his presence in England would cause deep embarrassment, and ruin any pleasure Minette would have in seeing her brother again. Charles was horrified at the idea, and saw his way out of the impasse by saying that it was impossible to spare the Duke at this time, and that it would be quite improper for Monsieur to come to England without a reciprocal visit from his brother to France. He sent Lord Godolphin over to Paris to talk to Monsieur, with promises that Minette would be received with precedence over all the other ladies at Court, bar the Queen. Monsieur still hesitated, whereupon Louis' patience was exhausted, and he gave him a stern warning that it was of the utmost national importance that his wife went to England, and that he would not stand for any more prevarication. Monsieur unwillingly relented, but stated that the visit must be for only three days, and under no circumstances must she go to London. Minette was made very unhappy by such opposition to a visit that she had hoped for for so long, and wrote the two following letters to Madame de Saint-Chaumont, telling of the objectionable new favourites Monsieur had put in the place of the absent Chevalier de Lorraine.

In the midst of all her troubles, Minette writes to comfort her banished governess, and tells her of her endeavours to get her her freedom.

¶ *Minette to Madame de Saint-Chaumont*

St Germain, 26 March 1670[13]

It seems as if all the peace of my life had departed with you, and as if the wrong which had been done you, had left neither quiet nor repose of mind to those who were its cause. It is true that I too have had to suffer, who am certainly not answerable for this, but the truth is, all that Monsieur does, concerns me so nearly, that it is impossible his actions should not fall back upon me. He has been very angry at the wish which the King, my brother, has expressed that I should go and see him. This has driven him to lengths which you would hardly believe, for, regardless of what the world may say, in his wrath against me, he declares aloud that I reproached him for the life he led with his favourite, and many other things of the kind, which have been very edifying hearing for our charitable neighbours. The King has worked hard to bring him to reason, but all in vain, for his only object in treating me so ill is to force me to ask favours for the Chevalier, and I am determined not to give in to blows [coups de batons]. This state of things does not admit of any reconciliation, and Monsieur now refuses to come near me, and hardly ever speaks to me, which, in all the quarrels we have had, has never happened before. But the gift of some additional revenues from the King has now softened his anger a little, and I hope that by Easter, all may yet be well. I am, on the whole, content with what the King has hitherto done, but I see that, from the ashes of Monsieur's love for the Chevalier, as from the dragon's teeth, a whole brood of fresh favourites are likely to spring up to vex me. Monsieur now puts his trust in the little Marsan [another prince of the house of Lorraine] and the Chevalier de Beuvron, not to speak of the false face of the Marquis de Villeroy, who prides himself on being his friend, and only seeks his own interests, regardless of those of Monsieur, or of the Chevalier. All I can do, is to spend the rest of my life in trying to undo the mischief which these gentlemen have done, without much hope of remedying the true evil that lies at the root of all. You will understand how much patience I shall need for this, and I am quite surprised to find that I have any left, for the task is a very hard one. As for my journey to England, I do not despair that it may yet take place. If it does, it will be a great happiness for me. All these affairs have prevented me from mentioning your business, but not from thinking of you. Nothing in the world can ever hinder me from showing you fresh marks of my remembrance and tenderness. But, as you know, there are moments when all one can do is to hold one's peace and wait for a better chance. This alone is the reason why I will say nothing about your affairs, but, as I have already told you, no one could love you more tenderly than I do.

This letter was written from the Palais Royal where Minette had gone to spend Holy Week and Easter. Bossuet visited her here often, encouraging her in her course of serious reading and religious instruction. 'I am afraid,' she said to him, 'I have thought too little of my soul. If it is not too late, help me to find the way to salvation.'

Monsieur, having had to capitulate over giving permission for the journey, as a last ditch means of stopping her going, decided to sleep with her every day, in the hopes of making her pregnant – if the report from the Marquis de St Maurice to the Duke of Savoy can be believed. Before she left for England, she ordered an emerald ring from her jeweller to be made for Bossuet as a token of her great gratitude to him for all his help in a very difficult time.

¶ *Minette to Madame de Saint-Chaumont*

Palais Royal, 6 April 1670[14]

As for my reconciliation with Monsieur, you will see that the news which you heard respecting my journey is one of those too favourable judgements with which the world is kind enough to honour me, from time to time; unfortunately absolutely without foundation. I have indeed wished to see the King, my brother, but there has been no question of the Chevalier's return in all Monsieur's opposition to my journey. Only he still declares that he cannot love me, unless his favourite is allowed to form a third in our union. Since then, I have made him understand that, however much I might desire the Chevalier's return, it would be impossible to obtain it, and he has given up the idea, but, by making a noise about my journey to England, he hopes to show that he is master, and can treat me as ill in the Chevalier's absence as in his presence. This being his policy, he began to speak openly of our quarrels, refused to enter my room, and pretended to show that he could revenge himself for having been left in ignorance of these affairs, and make me suffer for what he calls the faults of the two Kings. However, after all this noise, he has thought fit to relent, and said he would make peace if I would make the first advances. This I have done gladly enough, through the Princesse Palatine [Anne de Gonzague]. He accused me of saying a thousand extravagant things, which I should have been mad ever to dream of saying! I told him that he had been misinformed, but that I was ready to beg his pardon, even for what I had not said. Finally he became more tractable, and after many promises to forget the past, and live more happily in future, without even mentioning the Chevalier's name, he not only agreed that I should go to England, but proposed that he should go there too. I wrote at once to my brother, to make this proposal, but as yet I have had no answer, and none of this news has yet been made public. Every one talks according to his own ideas. All the world knows that I am going, but no one imagines that Monsieur wishes to accompany me, after all that he has said against the King, my brother, and his repeated declarations that he would never let me go, in order to have his revenge. You will confess that the version of matters which you had heard, is altogether contrary to the true state of things. Once for all, you may be certain that I shall never do such an extravagant thing as to ask for the Chevalier's return, even if this depended upon me, which is not the case. As for your affairs, I have spent the last week in Paris, and have, therefore, been unable to speak to the King. But do not imagine for a moment that I consider the permission which you ask, to stay within three days' journey of Paris, is to be held in the light of a favour. I shall only ask for this as a sign of your respect for the King, and as a thing which cannot be refused, since the promise was made before you left. It is to be hoped that, once this first step has been taken, you will no longer be honoured with the importance of being treated as a dangerous person, but will be able to go wherever you like, whether for your affairs, or for your health. You see that I agree with you on all of these subjects, and will do everything that I can. You know this is not always what I should like to do, and I will own to you that, however fair things appear outwardly, I do not always see the kindness which I hope for in certain quarters. When you would think me happiest, I often meet with terrible disappointments, of which I tell no one, because it is of no use to complain, and, besides, I have no one whom I can speak to now. I have lately wished for you back again, a thousand times a day, and although you used formerly to reproach me with not telling you what I felt, but I am sure I should have spoken this time, if only I could have had you. But that, alas! is a pleasure which I cannot hope for now. Be sure, at least, that I shall always feel your loss, and shall never forget what you have suffered for my sake, and what I owe to my love for you.

On 8 April Minette's little daughter, Anne Marie, Mademoiselle de Valois, was baptized in the chapel of the Palais Royal. Plans for the journey, including the choice of who was to accompany her, were going ahead and Louis gave Minette 200,000 crowns for her expenses.

In her next letter Minette openly criticizes him, in what was a dangerously indiscreet manner. She does say that she feels that she can speak freely as the messenger employed by the Bishop of Valence to carry her letters is trustworthy. There is a suggestion that Minette felt that her life would be in danger if the Chevalier returned to Court. Although she appears to make the remark half in jest, like all such remarks it has an underlying truth to it, which should not be overlooked.

The Marquis d'Effiat, whom she mentions as being slightly better than most of her husband's friends, was in fact the one who was suspected of being involved in the attempt to poison her.

¶ *Minette to Madame de Saint-Chaumont*

St Germain, 14 April 1670[15]

I was hoping for an opportunity of asking the King to give you the liberty of going where you like, but my good intentions have been hindered by some bad offices which have been done you. The King sent for your brother [the Maréchal de Gramont] and told him that he heard you were in Paris, and that he knew I meant to intercede for you, but begged I would do nothing of the kind, since it grieved him to be compelled to give me a refusal. Your brother replied, with the utmost earnestness, that these were all unkind inventions, which fell heavily on innocent persons, but that he would certainly beg me not to think of interfering on your behalf, so that I have said nothing, fearing that I should do more harm than good. It grieves me to feel that I can do nothing for you. This is one of my worst sorrows, and I cannot be happy until you are free to go where you will, and there seems to be a hope that I may once more have you with me. The Marechale has been ill; never before have I so earnestly wished for any one's recovery as I have for hers. If she had died, I have no doubt Monsieur would insist on giving her place to the daughter-in law [probably a member of the Lorraine faction], and all the fuss we had at Saint-Cloud on the subject would begin again. But, thank God! she has recovered, and I still flatter myself with the hope that one day you may succeed her, although La Comtesse remains his favourite, and is one of those respectable characters with whom Monsieur is always anxious to surround me. I have not spoken to you of the state of affairs, because of the insecurity of the post, and all the couriers are in M. de Louvois' service. Also, you know that Monsieur's sole complaint against you is that you knew too many of my secrets. So I have waited to reply to the letter which I received at Villers-Cotterêts, but now that M. de Valence has sent me a trustworthy messenger, I must tell you that all is finally settled between the two Kings, and that there is very little left for me to do in England. From this, you would imagine that I might do whatever I liked! But although the King has been exceedingly good to me in some ways, I often find him very troublesome. He makes a thousand mistakes, and commits inconceivable follies, without the least intending it. For instance, I had begged him to allow Monsieur to grant certain pensions to the Chevalier, so as to put him into a good humour. He refused, saying that I only asked for this because I was so anxious to go to England, and that I need not distress myself on that score, for I should certainly go, since my presence there was necessary to him. He spoke to Monsieur, who was furious, as you know, and made all this noise about the journey. Meanwhile, the King, after promising me he would do nothing for the Chevalier, excepting at my request, releases Monsieur's favourite to appease him, and promises him these pensions on his return from his journey, providing I agree, and all this without saying a word to me. You will confess that a naturally honest mind finds all this very surprising, and that it becomes difficult to know how to act in these circumstances. I had asked the King to allow me to give Monsieur . . . [the words are effaced in the original]. He refused, saying people would think that Monsieur's bad temper had been rewarded. Two days afterwards, he gives him more than I had ever asked for, and allows Monsieur himself to go to England, without reflecting what embarrassment this will cause my brother, who would never consent to discuss affairs with him. Naturally, when this proposal was made, he met it with a decided refusal, saying that my brother, the Duke of York, could not come to Calais while Monsieur was at Dover, and that one visit should not take place without the other. This refusal has renewed Monsieur's irritation. He complains that all the honour will be mine, and consents to my journey with a very bad grace. At present, his chief friends are M. de Marsan, the Marquis de Villeroy and the Chevalier de Beuvron. The Marquis d'Effiat is the only one of the troop who is perhaps a little less of a rogue, but he is not clever enough to manage Monsieur, and the three others do all they can to make me miserable until the Chevalier returns. Although Monsieur is somewhat softened, he still tells me there is only one way in which I can show my love for him. Such a remedy, you know, would be followed by certain death! Besides, the King has pledged his word that the Chevalier shall not return for eight years, by which time it is to be hoped Monsieur will either be cured of his passion, or else enlightened as to his favourite's true character. He may then see what faults this man has made him commit, and live to hate him as much as once he loved him. This is my only hope, although, even then, I may still be unhappy. Monsieur's jealous nature and his constant fear that I should be loved and esteemed will always be the cause of trouble, and the King does not make people happy, even when he means to treat them well. We see how even his mistresses have to suffer three or four rebuffs a week. What then must his friends expect?

The Comtesse de Gramont will accompany me to Dover, as well as her brother, M. d'Hamilton. Everyone in France wants to follow me, but the King, my brother, will not allow this, and Monsieur is delighted to hear only a few persons are to accompany me, fearing too much honour should be paid me. I will see on my journey what can be done for this poor M. de Valence, as to his Cardinalate. You may be sure that I long to help him more than ever. I am going to ask the King once more to-day if he may return to his diocese, but I know not if I shall succeed. Perhaps the bearer of this will be able to inform you if I have not time to tell you myself. I hardly know how I have managed to write such a long letter. I will finish by assuring you that I cannot console myself for your absence, and that I am always saying, what I will repeat once more, that I can never be happy without you.

The royal party at last set out for Flanders on 28 April. Just before her departure, Minette wrote a quick letter to her beloved ex-governess.

¶ *Minette to Madame de Saint-Chaumont*

28 April 1670[16]

I should not think my journey could prosper if I began it without bidding you farewell. Never has anything been more wrangled over, and even now Monsieur refuses to let me stay more than three days with the King, my brother. This is better than nothing, but it is a very short time for all which two people, who love one another as well as he and I do, have to say. Monsieur is still very angry with me, and I know that I shall have to expect many troubles, on my return. You will believe this, when you recollect how I foretold all that would happen after my last accouchement, although I knew that there was nothing to be done. The same thing will happen now. Monsieur vows that, if I do not procure the Chevalier's return, he will treat me as badly as the meanest of creatures. Before his arrest he advised Monsieur to find means to obtain a separation from me. I told the King, who laughed at me, but since then he has owned that I was right, and that Monsieur had actually proposed this to him. So I told him that he must see the necessity of never allowing the return of this man, who would only do far worse in the future. I have no time to say any more, and can only assure you that nothing will ever diminish my tenderness for you.

The royal party consisted of the King and Queen, Monsieur and Minette, Mademoiselle de Montpensier, Madame de Montespan, and a large number of ladies and courtiers, and an army of 30,000 men. Although all the trappings of royalty travelled with them, including the gold and silver plate, the food was vile, and the conditions under which they lived, appalling. The poor roads were waterlogged by the incessant rain, and made almost impassable by the huge extra body of traffic. When they reached the River Sambre, they found it had overflowed its banks, and destroyed the only bridge. After many hours waiting in the coaches, Louis decided they would all have to sleep on the floor in a two-roomed farmhouse just outside Landrecies. The Queen by this time was hysterical, and at first refused to leave her coach. Minette was in a state of collapse with exhaustion, having been unable to take any food except milk. The royal party spent the night together on mattresses. One remark of Madame de Thianges', recorded by Mademoiselle de Montpensier, made even the Queen laugh: on hearing cattle lowing outside the window, she said the noise made her feel religious as it reminded her of the birth of Our Lord.

Monsieur's rudeness to Minette on this trying journey disgusted the royal party, particularly the Queen and Mademoiselle, who remonstrated with him. He even told her that an astrologer had told him that he would have several wives, and that as she looked so ill, she would not be his for much longer.

At Courtray, the English envoy who met them told Minette that Charles was waiting for her at Dover, and begged her to embark at Dunkirk where the fleet under the command of Lord Sandwich was standing off, ready to take her to England.

Monsieur's loud protests that she was not to go, as he had changed his mind, were ignored by Louis. As she said farewell to the royal family, in spite of her excitement at seeing her brother, Monsieur's unkindness even then reduced her to tears. Her escort included the enchanting Louise de Kéroualle who was to become a much-loved mistress of Charles after Minette's death, Maréchal de Plessis, the Comte and Comtesse de Gramont, the Bishop of Tournay, and Anthony Hamilton.

M. de Pomponne, who was the French Envoy at The Hague, accompanied her from Courtray to Lille, and had a chance to discuss the political situation with her. He was astonished at her grasp of affairs and wrote: 'From what the King has said to me in general about the hope which he had of bringing back the King of England into his interests, and from what was confirmed to me by Madame, it was easy to guess that the voyage of this Princess to London was not confined to the simple pleasures of seeing the King, her brother.'[17]

Charles, the Duke of York, the Duke of Monmouth and Prince Rupert had been waiting impatiently for her at Dover. As soon as the fleet was sighted on 16 May they set out in the Royal Barge to row to meet her. It was nine years since Charles and Minette had met. Her joy at being reunited with him and her brother, cousin and nephew must have been overwhelming.

Dover was not the ideal place for such a large party to stay. The royal family were accommodated in the Castle, but many of the entourage had to stay in surrounding cottages, as Dover at that time was little more than a village.

The Duke of York had to return almost immediately to London to quell a disturbance, and as Minette's stay was thought then to be not more than three days, the final business of the Secret Treaty was set in motion at once. Although she had been at the heart of the secret correspondence between the two Kings, the intricacies of the individual clauses had in the final weeks been determined on the one hand by Charles, the Duke of York and the English Commission, and on the other by Colbert de Croissy and Lionne, acting for Louis XIV.

Minette's main concern was of course Charles's public announcement of his conversion to Catholicism. As a highly intelligent woman, she must have been aware of the hostility such an action would arouse against her brother. The timing of the conversion was the main point under discussion. At first it was expected that Charles should announce it before war was declared on Holland. But Minette felt in the end that war should be declared first. Charles, who obviously knew the great trouble it might cause, was very pleased to comply with this. From the diplomatic point of view, the longer he put off the declaration the better it would be, as long as he got the promised money from France. In fact he put it off until his deathbed. As he so amusingly put it, he had no desire to set off on his travels again.

The chief articles of the Secret Treaty were clearly stated by Mignet.

> The King of England will make a public profession of the Catholic Faith, and will receive the sum of two million crowns to aid him in the project, from the Most Christian King, to help him in the project, in the course of the next six months. The date of the declaration is left absolutely to his own pleasure. The King of France will faithfully observe the Treaty of Aix-la-Chapelle, as regards Spain, and the King of England will maintain the Triple Alliance in a similar manner. If her rights [i.e. Maria Teresa's] to the Spanish Monarch revert to the King of France, the King of England will aid him in maintaining these rights. The two Kings will declare war on the United Provinces. The King of France will attack them by land, and will receive the help of 6000 men from England. The King of England will send 50 men of war to sea and the King of France 30. The combined fleets will be under the Duke of York's command. His Britannic Majesty will be content to receive Walcheren, the mouth of the Scheldt and the Isle of Cadzland as his share of the conquered province. Separate articles will provide for the Prince of Orange. The treaty of Commerce which had already begun shall be concluded as promptly as possible.[18]

On 22 May the Secret Treaty was signed by Arlington, Clifford, Lord Arundel and Sir Richard Bellings for England, and Colbert de Croissy for France. Colbert de Croissy then took it across to Bologne to be ratified by Louis XIV, who was anxiously awaiting him. The ratifications were signed on 4 June.

To Charles and Minette's delight, Louis gave permission for her to extend her visit by ten or twelve days. Once the serious business of the treaty was completed, in spite of still being in mourning for the Queen Mother, the royal party set out to enjoy themselves. Although London was forbidden by Monsieur, they made a day trip to Canterbury to see a ballet put on by a company of the Duke of York, followed by a magnificent banquet in St Augustine's Abbey hall. The Queen arrived on 29 May, Charles's fortieth birthday, and as it was also ten years since the Restoration, the feastings and dancings were continuous. They all took to sea in yachts, accompanied by three men-of-war, which delighted Minette. Everyone remarked on how well she looked, and she seemed to have completely recovered from the terrible fatigue and stomach illness that had beset her on her journey to Dunkirk. It must have been wonderful for her to have the chance to pour out to Charles the troubles of her life with her husband, and it is possible that Charles suggested to her during this visit that if life became intolerable she should contemplate a separation from Monsieur, in spite of the new treaty with France.

Minette enjoyed meeting her sister-in-law, the Queen, and was delighted to see the Duchess of York again, and to have a chance to discuss the health of her little daughter Anne, who was still staying with her in France.

The English Court were enchanted with her, and were almost as sad as her brother to see her go. On 3 June she set sail again for France. The King and the Duke of York accompanied her some of the way. Charles was devastated at having to part with her, and came back for a last embrace three times. Colbert de Croissy remarked in a despatch to Louis XIV what a great love this brother and sister had for each other. He wrote that he 'had never seen so sorrowful a leavetaking, or known before how much royal personages could love one another. It had appeared during her stay at Dover that she had much more power over the King her brother than any other person in the world, not only by the eagerness the other ministers have shown to implore her favour and support with the King and by the favours that he has accorded simply at her request . . . but also by the King's own confession and the tears he shed on bidding her farewell.'

Fully aware as Charles must have been of the situation she was returning to, his grief in parting must have been aggravated by fears of what might happen to her when at the mercy of Monsieur and his minions.

Charles gave her 6000 pistoles towards her expenses, and 2000 crowns to build a chapel at Chaillot in memory of their mother. She stayed one night at Minimes before going on to Boulogne. The Duc d'Elboef entertained her magnificently at Montreuil. At Abbeville an escort of the King's Guards met her and escorted her to Beauvais, where Ralph Montagu was waiting to take her to St Germain. Louis would have liked to meet her, and protocol expected him to do so, but as Monsieur refused to accompany him he remained in Paris, rather than cause any more trouble between them. On 18 June Monsieur came a few miles from St Germain to meet her. Although she felt so well when she left England, the journey, which had taken over two weeks, left her very exhausted. Louis was enchanted with her, delighted with the success of her mission, and not only produced more presents for her, including a further 6000 pistoles, but also told her to keep Charles's present for herself. Monsieur was as unpleasant to her as before; when Louis and the Court moved to Versailles he begged Monsieur and Minette to come with him, but Monsieur flatly refused to go, to spite his wife. On 21 June they went to Paris for a few days and from there Minette wrote to Sir Thomas Clifford. It is the only letter in English that we have from her. She had asked Charles to give him a peerage, and Arlington an earldom for their work over the treaty. It is not surprising that Charles was anxious that she should not forget her native language. The spelling and grammar are certainly a little shaky.

¶ *Minette to Sir Thomas Clifford*

Paris, 21 June[19]

When i have write to the King from Calais i praid him to tel milord Arlingtonan you what he had promised mi for bothe. his ansers was that hi gave me againe his word, that hee would performe the thing, but that hi did not thing it fit to exequte it now.

I tel you this sooner than to Milord Arlingtonbecase i know you ar not so hard to satisfie as hee. I should be so my self, if I was not surethatvthe Kingwould not promismee a thing to faille in the performance of it.

This is the ferste letter I have ever write in inglis. you will eselay see it bi the stile and tograf. prai see in the same timethat i expose mi self to be thought a foulle in looking to make you know how much I am your frind.

for Sr Thomas Clifort

The weather was wonderful and she was delighted to leave the heat of Paris on 24 June for St Cloud. Although she was still very exhausted after the excitement of her travels, she was able to stroll in the beautiful gardens, sit and chat with her friends by her favourite fountain, and against her doctor's orders, bathe in the Seine. Turenne, La Rochefoucauld, Ralph Montagu, Madame de Lafayette, and two Englishmen, Sir Thomas Armstrong and Lord Paulett, were among her companions. On 26 June Louis summoned them to Versailles for the day, and much against Monsieur's wishes, they went. Before they left she had time to write what proved to be her last letter to Madame de Saint-Chaumont. After telling her of the joy she had in her visit, she soon reverts to the never-ending problem of her husband's behaviour. She also mentions her feelings for her eldest daughter. She had always been a very wayward little girl, her bad manners encouraged by her father. Louis was one of the few people who could control her, and he adored her. She had spent a lot of time with her paternal grandmother, Queen Anne of Austria, until Anne's death. Obviously her old governess was fond of her.

¶ *Minette to Madame de Saint-Chaumont*

St Cloud, 26 June 1670[20]

I knew you would understand the joy which my visit to England gave me. It was indeed most delightful, and, long as I have known the affection of my brother, the King, it proved still greater than I expected. He showed me the greatest possible kindness, and was ready to help me in all that he could do. Since my return, the King here has been very good to me, but as for Monsieur, nothing can equal his bitterness and anxiety to find fault. He does me the honour to say that I am all-powerful, and can do everything that I like, and so, if I do not bring back the Chevalier, it is because I do not wish to please him. At the same time he joins threats for the future with this kind of talk. I have once more told him how little his favourite's return depends upon me, and how little I get my own way, or you would not be where you now are. Instead of seeing the truth of this, and becoming softened, he took occasion of my remark to go and complain of you to the King, and tried, at the same time, to do me other ill offices. This has had a very bad effect, together with the letter which you wrote to my child, and which, they pretend, was delivered to her secretly, and has,

> I fear, increased the King's unfavourable opinion of you. I have not yet had time to defend you, but you may trust me to do the best I can for you, and to prove that I am not unworthy of the friendship which you have so often shown me. If I cannot do away with these unfortunate impressions, I will at least try to remove the false reports by which they have been occasioned. I have often blamed you for the tender love you feel for my child. In God's name, put that love away. The poor child cannot return your affection, and will alas! be brought up to hate me. You had better keep your love for persons who are as grateful as I am, and who feel, as keenly as I do, the pain of being unable to help you in your present need. I hope that you will do me the justice to believe this, and will remain, once for all, assured that I shall never lose a chance of helping you, and of showing you my tenderness. Since my return from England, the King has gone to Versailles, where Monsieur would not follow him, lest I should have the pleasure of being with him.

On 28 June Ralph Montagu visited Minette at St Cloud, and, regarding him as a friend and confidant, she discussed with him, probably indiscreetly, her success over the Treaty of Dover, and the alliance against Holland, as well as her sadness that her relationship with her husband was still as bad as ever.

On the morning of 29 June, she sat down to write a long letter to the widow of her cousin, Charles Lewis, Prince Palatine (he was the uncle of Charlotte Elizabeth, the woman who was to become Monsieur's second wife). The Princess had been trying to act as mediator between Minette and her husband. The letter is so remarkable in its clarity and detail that for many years it was considered to be a fake. A copy of it was first discovered in the collection of M. Monmerque. Miss Julia Cartwright also discovered a letter from Ralph Montagu to Arlington which evidently had enclosed the original letter for him to give to Charles. As it was written a few hours before she was struck down by her mortal illness, he felt that the King should see it, not only for its quality, and to show that she was then well enough to write such a letter, but also because it told him again that the relationship between her husband and herself was as distressing as ever. The Princess Palatine had been instrumental in helping to arrange the marriage between them, therefore she had a particular interest in trying to salvage it.

As well as Montagu's letter to Arlington, copies of the letter in French and English, the English version endorsed by Sir Thomas Clifford as Minette's letter from St Cloud, put its authenticity beyond dispute.

¶ *Minette to the Princess Palatine*

St Cloud, 29 June 1670[21]

It is only fair that I should give you an account of a journey which you tried to render acceptable in the only quarter where it could fail to meet with approval. I will confess that, on my return, I had hoped to find everyone satisfied, instead of which, things are worse than ever. You remember telling me that Monsieur insisted on three things: first, that I should place him in confidential relations with the King, my brother; secondly, that I should ask the King to give him his son's allowance; thirdly, that I should help the Chevalier de Lorraine. The King, my brother, was so kind as to promise that he would willingly trust Monsieur with his secrets if he would behave better in future than he had done with regard to my journey. He even offered to give the Chevalier de Lorraine a refuge in his kingdom till affairs should have calmed down here. He could do no more for him. As for the pension, I have great hopes of obtaining it, if only Monsieur will put an end to the comedy which he still presents to the public gaze, but you will understand that I cannot ask for this, after the way in which he behaved, unless I can satisfy the King that our domestic peace will be restored, and that he will no longer hold me responsible for everything that happens in Europe. I have said all this to him, expecting it would be well received, but since there is no prospect of the Chevalier's immediate return, Monsieur declares that all the rest is useless, and says I am never to expect to be restored to his good graces until I have given him back his favourite. I am, I must confess, very much surprised at this behaviour on his part. Monsieur wished for my brother's friendship, and, now I offer it to him, he accepts it as if he were doing the King a favour. He refuses to send the Chevalier to England, as if these things could blow over in the next quarter of an hour, and scorns the offer of the pension. If he reflects at all, it is impossible for him to go on in this manner, and I can only suppose that he is bent on quarrelling with me. The King was good enough to assure him, on his oath, that I had no part in the Chevalier's exile, and that his return did not depend upon me. Unfortunately for me, he refused to believe the King, who has never been known to utter a falsehood, and it will be still more unfortunate if I cannot help him while it is yet possible. You see now, my dear cousin, the state of my affairs. Of the three things which Monsieur desired, I can obtain two and a half, and he is angry because I cannot do more, and counts the King, my brother's, friendship and his own advantage all as nothing. As for me, I have done more than I could have hoped. But if I am unhappy enough for Monsieur to go on treating me so unkindly, I declare, my dear cousin, that I shall give it all up, and take no more trouble as to his pension or his favourite's return, or his friendship with the King, my brother. Two of the three things are hard to obtain, and others might think them of great importance, but I have only to drop the subject, and maintain the same silence as Monsieur, who refuses to speak when I desire an explanation. As for the Chevalier's return, even if my credit were as great as Monsieur believes it to be, I never will give way to blows. If Monsieur therefore refuses to accept the two things which he can have, and insists on getting the third, which must depend on the King's pleasure, I can only await the knowledge of Monsieur's will in silence. If he desires me to act I will do it joyfully, for I have no greater wish than to be on good terms with him. If not, I will keep silence and patiently bear all his unkindness, without trying to defend myself. His hatred is unreasonable, but his esteem may be earned. I may say that I have neither deserved the first, nor am I altogether unworthy of the last, and I still console myself with the hope that it may some day be obtained. You can do more than anyone else to help me, and I am so persuaded that you have my good and Monsieur's at heart, that I hope you will still endeavour to assist me. I will only remind you of one thing. If you let a good chance slip by, it does not always return again. The present moment seems to be favourable for obtaining the pension, and the future is, to say the least, doubtful. After this, I must tell you that your pension from England will be paid shortly. The King, my brother, gave me his word for it, and those persons whose business it is to see this done promised to afford the necessary facilities. If you were here we would take further steps to settle the business, for you know that I was not sufficiently acquainted with the particulars of your affairs to do more than repeat what you had told me. If I can give you any further proofs of my affection, I will do so with all the pleasure in the world.

Chapter 10

Madame se Meurt, Madame est Morte

In trying to unravel the mystery surrounding Minette's tragic death, we are lucky to have several moving accounts of her last hours on earth, one written by her friend Madame de Lafayette, one by her cousin Mademoiselle de Montpensier, and another by the English Ambassador, Ralph Montagu. All three were devoted to her. Madame de Lafayette and Ralph Montagu were with her when she died. The Jansenist monk who heard her last confession also wrote of her death. Monsieur's second wife, Charlotte Elizabeth, the Princess Palatine, recounts in great detail what she was told by Louis himself and servants who were in the household at the time. She was after all in the unfortunate position of stepping into the dead woman's shoes a year after her death, and felt that it was necessary for her own safety to get at the truth. We can, therefore, make a step-by-step journey with the unfortunate Minette through the last hours of her life.

Feeling very tired and dispirited after the great excitement of her trip to England, she had asked Madame de Lafayette to visit her at St Cloud. She arrived at ten o'clock on the Saturday night, 28 June. As it was so hot, she and Minette strolled in the beautiful gardens in the moonlight, and sat chatting by the Grand Cascade until midnight. Cheered by the presence of her great friend, she had a very good night.

The next morning she spent some time with Monsieur in his rooms, before joining Madame de Lafayette to go to Mass. Afterwards they went to the studio where her eldest daughter, the little Mademoiselle, was being painted by an English artist. At eleven o'clock they went in to dinner. Minette, who never had much appetite, seemed to enjoy her meal very much, and afterwards went back to the studio. The artist was also painting a portrait of Monsieur.

Minette settled herself comfortably on cushions at Madame de Lafayette's feet, and with her head on Lafayette's lap, went to sleep. Both Madame de Lafayette and Monsieur remarked how tired and ill she looked. When she woke up she complained of a pain in her side, which might have been indigestion after a heavy meal. She went into the drawing room to talk to Monsieur's Treasurer, Boisfranc. She asked for a cup of chicory water to be brought to her. She had, since her arrival at St Cloud, been taking some in the hot summer evenings. It was kept in a closet with a jug of fresh water to dilute it. The drink was poured out into her silver cup and given to her by Madame de Gourdon. As soon as she had drunk it she gave a cry of agony, and said that she had been poisoned. In a state of collapse, her ladies got her to her bed, where she lay writhing in agony with acute abdominal pains. Monsieur's doctor M. d'Esperit was called, who pronounced that she was having an acute attack of colic, and that there was no danger. Minette already felt that she was mortally ill and called for Monsieur, who did not seem unduly alarmed. She said to him, 'Alas Monsieur, you have long since ceased to love me, but you have been unjust to me. I never wronged you.'

Monsieur suggested that if she thought that the chicory water had been poisoned, they had better test it by giving some to the dog. Minette's maid Madame Desbordes and Madame Mecklenbourg, the irrepressible Bablon of whom Charles was so fond, gallantly offered to drink some too, and even Monsieur himself. Madame de Lafayette said they all drank out of Minette's cup. But Madame II in her account is emphatic that the cup Minette had used could not be found, and when it was finally traced it had been put into a fire to clean it.

Monsieur was by now getting seriously alarmed and rounded on M. d'Esperit for his incompetence, and taunted him that he was unable to save the life of the little Duc de Valois, and now seemed unable to help his wife. Minette was asking for a priest, and the nearest available was the Curé of St Cloud, who heard a simple confession from her. More doctors were summoned, including King Louis' physicians, M. Vallot, M. Yvelin and M. Guesclin from Paris. Every remedy they tried on her made her agony worse, one of the more excruciating symptoms being her inability to vomit properly. She was able to walk from one bed to another, but all her ladies and the doctors could see plainly that she was dying. The King and Queen arrived from Paris, with a strange lot of companions. Mademoiselle de Montpensier of course came, but Minette's old enemy, the Comtesse de Choissant, was also of the party, and the King's rival mistresses, La Vallière and Madame de Montespan, who had both been ladies-in-waiting to Minette.

Louis was deeply upset by her appalling condition; he put his arms round her to comfort her, and wept bitterly. Mademoiselle, who stood beside him, wrote that by the time they arrived Madame already had the look of a corpse. She asked for Bossuet to be sent for from Paris. Then the Jansenist priest, M. Feuillet, forestalled him. Minette, in her agony, did not deserve this type of priest to give her the last rites. Austere in the extreme, bigoted and with little or no kindly sympathy for her plight, he harangued her mercilessly on the awful state of her soul. Those who heard were shocked that he should make the dying woman feel that her entire life had been desperately wicked. It is interesting to note that Minette had three types of Catholic priest at her side when she was dying; the simple parish priest from St Cloud, the fanatical monk, and fortunately, right at the end, her kind and loving friend Bossuet.

Ralph Montagu arrived while M. Feuillet was with her, and was distraught to see the Princess, who had so delighted him in conversation the day before, so near to death. Hearing that she had said she had been poisoned, he asked her in English if this was so. Before she could reply, M. Feuillet had interrupted, warning her not to think of recriminations on her plight, but to concentrate on her soul. A maid who was standing by heard her say, very quietly, 'If this is true you must never let the King, my brother, know of it. Spare him the grief at all events and do not let him take revenge on the King here for he is at least not guilty.'

Montagu asked her where her letters from Charles were, and she told him to ask Madame Desbordes to give them to him. The poor lady was in such a state at seeing her mistress so mortally ill that she had collapsed, and by the time Montagu went to collect them after her death, Monsieur had already taken them.

Minette took a ring off her finger and asked Montagu to give it to Charles, and told him to take for himself the 6000 pistoles Charles had given her. This he refused to do, but promised to share it out among her servants.

Monsieur had at last realized that his wife was dying and appeared to be very upset. She asked to see him for the last time, and he came to her, overcome with emotion. After a time she found his lamentations too much for her so asked him to leave.

The persistent M. Feuillet was still at her side, and she asked him to give her the Viaticum. Holding the crucifix that her mother-in-law Anne of Austria had used on her deathbed, after making an act of faith, she cried out, 'My God, will not these fearful pains be over soon.' 'What, Madame, you are forgetting yourself; you have offended God twenty-six years, and your penitence has but lasted six hours; rather say with St Augustine, cut, tear, destroy, let my heart ache, let all my limbs thrill with anguish, let dung flow in the marrow of my bones, let worms revel in my breast, if only I have obtained thee, God, it is enough. . . . I hope, Madame, you will remember the prayers and protestations you have just now made to your God.' Minette's delicious sense of irony did not leave her, even in extremis, for she replied, 'Yes, sir, I hope so; in case God were to restore me to health, and I were so wretched as not to practise them, I entreat you to remind me of them. . . . At what o'clock did Jesus die, at three o'clock?' 'Do not mind that, Madame, you must endure life, and wait for death in patience.'[1]

Everyone who watched Minette's last agonies said that her courage, fortitude and spirituality were beyond praise. She was at last rewarded for her courage by the arrival of Bossuet from Paris. Her fading eyes lit up when she saw him, and she managed a smile. He was overwhelmed with grief when he saw her, and knelt down by her side, and gave her all the gentle consolation that she needed. Right at the end, she remembered to tell her maid to give him after her death the emerald ring she had had made for him. She took the crucifix in her hands again, as he gently said to her, 'Madame, you believe in God, you hope in

God, you love God?' 'With all my heart,' she replied. As Bossuet said the final prayer 'In manus tues', she died. It was three o'clock in the morning.

The whole Court was stunned by Minette's sudden, agonizing and heroic death. It was inevitable, in the light of her repeated protestations that she had been poisoned, that a firm statement on the cause of death must be made as soon as possible. It was Louis, overwhelmed at the loss of his sister-in-law and seeing the dangerous political situation that could develop if the story of poison persisted, who ordered a post-mortem. It took place late that evening, some eighteen to twenty hours after her death. The operation was performed by a junior surgeon, and Louis' two doctors, Vallot and Guesclin, and two nominated by Ralph Montagu as Ambassador, were among those present. They were Hugh Chamberlin and Alexander Boscher. Montagu was also present in a room packed with onlookers.

The certificate was signed by all the doctors present and the decision they came to was that she had died of cholera morbis. The two English doctors were far from satisfied with the result. Although they were not completely against the idea that she had died of natural causes, they stated that the junior doctor who had performed the post-mortem was extremely incompetent, and seemed to act as if he was trying to cover up the truth, rather than discover it. Boscher saw a hole in the stomach which he was not allowed to investigate, which the French doctors said was a slip of the surgeon's knife.

Although Boscher signed the certificate, he talked of his dissatisfaction with it, and wrote of the matter to Temple, the British Ambassador in Holland. In the prevailing atmosphere he dared not refuse to sign, or say all he thought.

Several medical experts have looked at the post-mortem reports for me, and they all say that the considerable lapse of time between her death and the autopsy, in the height of a very hot summer, with the lack of refrigerating facilities, would have produced severe changes in the corpse before it was opened up. The result of the post-mortem did little to quiet the rumours that had spread like wildfire throughout France and England that the Princess had been poisoned by the Chevalier Lorraine and his friends. Monsieur was not generally suspected of the crime.

According to the Chronicles of the Duc de Saint-Simon, Louis became so alarmed that the following day he called the Orléans' Maître d'Hôtel, Morel Simon, to his presence, under armed guard, and threatening him with his life if he did not tell the truth, asked if Madame had been poisoned. He answered that she had, not by Monsieur, but by the Chevalier de Lorraine who had hatched the plot from Italy, with his two friends d'Effiat and Beuvron, who were both living in Monsieur's household. He swore to Louis that Monsieur had not been in the plot, and Louis released him. If Minette had died at a less politically sensitive time, Louis might have pursued the matter further. As it was, he was determined that the poison theory should be hushed up. He even went so far as to recall the Chevalier from exile, and allow him to live in Monsieur's household again to scotch the rumours of his implication in the death. Madame de Lafayette, who was so close to Minette, followed the same line in her memoirs that Minette had died of natural causes. She had no wish to make an enemy of Louis. Ralph Montagu, on the other hand, remained convinced all his life that Minette had been poisoned.

The King, Queen and all the Court were prostrate with grief at her death. Monsieur's grief was more superficial, and he soon immersed himself in decking himself and his elder daughter and little Princess Anne in elaborate, and even preposterous mourning clothes, and in the preparations for the magnificent royal funeral that the King had ordered for his sister-in-law.

Monsieur, who understood little English, had Charles's letters to Minette translated for him by the Abbé Montagu and Madame Fiennes. Montagu was appalled at the thought of Charles's letters to his sister falling into her husband's hands, and told Louis what had happened. The King immediately demanded that Monsieur should hand them over to him. They were then returned to Charles, who presumably destroyed them. The letters that are now in the Quai d'Orsay must have been kept elsewhere, and found later.

An hour after Minette's death, Ralph Montagu wrote the following letter to Arlington, breaking the tragic news to him. It was taken post-haste by the young Sir Thomas Armstrong, who had also been in the room when Minette died. Travelling without a pause, he was the first to tell Charles of his sister's death.

¶ *Ralph Montagu to Lord Arlington*

Paris, 30 June 1670[2]

My Lord, – I am sorry to be obliged by my employment, to give you an account of the saddest story in the world, and which I have hardly the courage to write. Madame, on Sunday the 29th of this instant, being at St Clou with a great deal of company, about five o'clock in the afternoon called for a glass of chicory water that was prescribed for her to drink, she having for two or three days after bathing found herself indisposed. She had no sooner drunk this but she cryed out she was dead, and fell into Madam Mechelbourg's arms, desired to be put to bed, and have a confessor. She continued in the greatest tortures imaginable, till 3 o'clock in the morning, when she dyed; the King, the Queen, and all the Court being there, till about an hour before. God send the King, our master, patience and constancy to bear so great an affliction. Madame declared she had no reluctancy to die, but out of the grief she thought it would be to the King, her brother, and when she was in any ease for the torture she was in, which the physician called colique bileuse, she asked for me, and it was to charge me to say all the kind things from her to her brothers, the King and Duke. I did not leave her till she expired, and happened to come to Saint Clou an hour after she fell ill. Never anybody died with that piety and resolution, and kept her senses to the last. Excuse this imperfect relation, for the grief I am in. I am sure all that had the Honour to know her will have their share for so great and general a loss. I am, my Lord, Yours, etc.

An hour later his secretary added the following lines:

The bearer will tell you that Madame fell sick of a colic about 4 in the afternoon, and died, a most lamented Princess, this morning at 3. Grief will not let me add more, but refer you for further particulars to his relation, who was present at St Cloud.

Charles's grief and rage on hearing the news were overwhelming. Shouting to Sir Thomas Armstrong, 'Monsieur is a villain', he shut himself in his bedroom for five days, trying to come to terms with this terrible personal sorrow, and his deep anger at the thought that Minette had been poisoned. Always an astute political animal, in spite of his sorrow, he was well aware of the enormous political implications involved. His first reaction was to think of recalling Ralph Montagu from Paris, and for many days he refused to see the French Ambassador and the official envoy Louis had sent to England with his condolences. Lord Rochester was lord-in-waiting at the time Charles received the news, and gives a firsthand account to his wife of Charles's reaction, and the version of Minette's death which by now had reached them. Referring to this 'barbarous affair', he leaves no doubt that the court believed that the King's sister had been poisoned.

¶ *Earl of Rochester to his Wife*[3]

Pray do not take it ill that I write to you so seldom since my coming to town; my being in waiting upon the sad accident of Madame's death (for which the King endures the highest affliction Imaginable) would not allow me time or power to write letters. You have heard of the Thing, but the barbarousness of the manner you may guess at by relations.

Monsieur, since the banishment of the Chevalier de Lorraine (of which he suspected Madame to be the author) has behaved himself very ill in all things, threatening her upon all occasions that if she did not get Lorraine recalled, she might expect from him the worst that can befall her. It was not now in her power to perform what he expected, so that she returning to Paris, he accidentally carried her away to St Cloud, where having remained fifteen days in good health, she having been bathing one morning, and finding herself very dry, called for some succory-water (a cordial dewlap she usually took upon those occasions), and being then very merry discoursing with some of her ladies that were with her, she had no sooner swallowed the succory-water, but immediately falling into the arms of Madame de Chalitton, she cried she was dead, and sending for her confessor after eight hours infinite torment in her stomach and bowels, she died the most lamented (Both in France and England) since dying has been the fashion. But I will not keep you too long upon the doleful subject, it is enough to make most wives in the world very melancholy.

No one was more aware than Charles of the great importance Minette had placed on the Treaty of Dover, how hard she had worked for it, and how deeply upset she would have been if her death had caused a serious breakdown of diplomatic relations between England and France. As he gradually came to terms with his sorrow, he realized that nothing could be gained by outwardly accusing his brother-in-law and his minions of murdering his sister. His private opinions he reluctantly decided to keep to himself, and eventually received the official condolences, and even sent the Duke of Buckingham, who was almost as upset as himself, to France for her funeral. Charlotte Elizabeth, Princess Palatine, who married Monsieur a year after Minette's death, was convinced she had been poisoned, and gives a vivid account of what happened in her memoirs. Saint-Simon states in his Chronicles that Louis assured the second Madame that although her predecessor had been poisoned, it was not by her husband. She had several servants in her household who were involved in the affair, and she had the misfortune to have to put up with the Chevalier de Lorraine for thirty years, until Monsieur finally tired of him.

Madame II, like Saint-Simon, believed that Minette was poisoned through a plot between the Chevalier, who was in Italy, and Monsieur's two minions d'Effiat and the Comte de Beuvron. She was convinced that Monsieur knew nothing of the plot. Although he disliked his wife intensely, this sort of crime was not in his nature. One of the dominating feelings in his life was his great devotion to his brother, as well as a superficial affection for England and his English cousins, and he would never have risking putting himself out of the French Court for life, and in permanent disgrace with his brother.

Madame II's version of the death was that on the morning before her death, while Minette and her husband were at Mass, the footman discovered d'Effiat in the closet where Minette's carafe of chicory water was kept, with a jug of fresh water to dilute it if necessary. The footman found him wiping the goblet with a paper, and when challenged, he said that he was so thirsty he had come to get some water, and finding Madame's goblet dirty, had decided to clean it. Immediately on drinking from the goblet Minette cried that she had been poisoned, and although two ladies drank the chicory water afterwards, they did not drink from the goblet itself, as it could not be found. As Madame II describes it, when the goblet was ultimately found it had been put into a fire to be cleaned.

Louis pointed out to the second Madame that if he had believed that Minette had been poisoned by his brother, he would never have allowed him to marry again, and Louis, as a man of integrity on vital matters, should be believed.

Not only because of his deep affection for her, but to try and heal the damaging situation that had been caused by the circumstances of her death, Louis was determined to give Minette an elaborate royal funeral, even greater than the ceremonies for her mother's death. The body was embalmed and laid in state in the room where she had died, covered in black velvet, with her coat of arms emblazoned on it, under a pall of cloth of gold. Her heart was taken to the Val de Grâce and her intestines to the Church of the Celestines.

On 4 July, the long procession left St Cloud at midnight, and wound its way through the quiet streets of Paris to the Abbey of St Denis. It was headed by Mademoiselle d'Orléans, the Princess de Condé, the Duchesses of Languille, Angoulême, Aiguillon, Nemours and Mesleraye, all her household and gentlemen at arms. A family touch which would have amused Minette and Charles was an argument that broke out between little Mademoiselle d'Orléans and her cousin the Princess de Condé as to precedence, which nearly brought the whole ceremony to a halt. The coffin was placed in the Abbey on a scaffold, under a black velvet canopy, and was guarded by the monks and Monsieur's guard until the funeral on 21 August. Apparently the funeral arrangements were so complex that six weeks elapsed between her death and burial. The Abbey must have looked like a highly decorated set for one of the masques that Minette so enjoyed taking part in. The nave was draped in black velvet supported by seven-feet-high skeletons of imitation white marble. White torches made of wax, four feet high, were placed at intervals round the choir. The scaffold that held the coffin was mounted by eight steps and flanked on each corner with antique altars that held huge urns giving out clouds of perfumed smoke, probably incense. Four imitation white marble figures representing Youth, Nobility, Poetry and Music stood at the foot of the choir. Her coffin stood on an imitation black marble tomb supported by four leopards in imitation bronze, and was covered in cloth of gold edged with ermine. Her ducal mantle and coronet were placed on top.

Neither Louis nor Monsieur nor Mademoiselle d'Orléans was present at her funeral. The Queen of France, a devoted admirer, broke all precedents by going incognito, and sat in the tribune with the King of Poland, the Duke of Buckingham and the English Ambassador, Ralph Montagu. The chief mourners were the Princess de Condé, the Duchess of Longueville and the Princess Carignan. As soon as the Mass began the huge urns gave out large flames, and with the hundreds of candles and tapers, the Abbey must have been an awe-inspiring spectacle. As the vault was opened to receive her body, the members of her household broke their badges of office and flung them into the grave, with her mantle and coronet. Vernon, an English chronicler who was at the funeral, reported that 'As the coffin was put in the grave there was a general weeping, a circumstance something unusual at the great ceremonies of the internment of Princess.'[4]

Although the splendours and dazzle of the funeral are long passed, Bossuet's great oration remains. His words for her mother's death less than a year earlier were remarkable, but for the daughter his natural eloquence was inspired by genuinely deep grief at the loss of a Princess who, particularly in the last years of her life, had become an intimate friend. The outward sign of her devotion to him was there for the congregation to see: the magnificent emerald ring surrounded with diamonds flashed in the candlelit Abbey as he spoke. He wore it until his death thirty-four years later.

¶ *From Bossuet's Funeral Oration for Minette*
21 August 1670[5]

This Princess born on the throne, had head and heart above her birth. The misfortunes of her House could not crush her in her youth and already at that time we saw in her a greatness which owed nothing to fortune.... The wisest and most experienced admired the lively and piercing mind which

> encompassed without difficulty the biggest affairs, and penetrated with much ease the most secret interests. . . . Neither esteem nor all the great advantages could affect her modesty. Enlightened as she was, she never presumed on her knowledge, and was never dazzled by her brilliance . . . Madame always distanced herself from presumption and from weakness. She was equally admirable in that she knew how to find wise counsels and accept them. . . . She studied her own faults, she liked to be given sincere lessons; a sure sign of a strong spirit, not dominated by its faults and which does not fear to look at them closely, thanks to the feeling of a hidden confidence to overcome them. It was the interest of progress in the study of wisdom which held her so attached to the reading of History, which is rightly called the counsellor of Princes. . . . Under a laughing countenance, under the air of youth that seemed to promise only play she hid a sound sense and seriousness which surprised those who had dealings with her. . . . Who could think without shedding tears of the marks of esteem and tenderness which the King her brother showed to her? This great King ever more capable of being touched by merit than by blood, never failed in his admiration of Madame's excellent qualities. What was during this visit the cause of such proper admiration became for this Prince the cause of sorrow beyond bounds.

Both Minette and Charles had inherited the wit, charm and intelligence of the House of Stuart. From the earliest stormy days of the Civil War, their love and deep devotion to each other never faltered. They both loved friendship and frivolity and both had that delightful streak of irony that ran through their correspondence.

Minette had a deeply spiritual side to her nature, fortified by her education as a Catholic from her first days in France, and it was a great consolation to her at the end. Her death was more than an almost insupportable grief for Charles. It was a watershed in his life. Never again would he risk his crown for the Catholic cause, which was the in-built danger in the Treaty of Dover. The clauses dealing with Charles's outward conversion and England's return to Catholicism were quietly dropped. Only on his deathbed did Charles openly confess his Catholicism.

The sorrow at Minette's death was widely felt in her adopted country, France, and in her native country, from which she had so recently returned. The poignant, haunting lines written by Madame de Brégis, found on an engraving of her original tomb in the Abbey of St Denis, provide a fitting memorial to her.

Le Tombeau de Madame

DES pleurs, des pleurs sans fin, des plaintes éternelles,
Des soupirs, des sanglots, des cris de déséspoir!
Madame ne vit plus, et venons de voir
Le terrible succèz de ses peinnes cruelles.

Aussi cette Beauté qui fit honte aux plus belles,
Cet esprit, cet esprit admiré des maistres du scavoir,
Cette grandeur, cette grandeur suprême, et ce vaste pouvoir,
N'estoient qu'un court passage à des douleurs mortelles.

'Mais ce moment fatal de soy plein d'horreur
Devoit-il estre encor tout armé de fureur?
Falloit-il tant de maux pour perdre tant de charmes?

Ciel, qui l'avez permis, permettez ce transport,
Faites régner, faites régner vos loix,
Mais laizzez-nous larmes
Pour pleurer à jamais une si triste mort.'

Chapter Notes

Abbreviations
Cosnac: *Mémoires de Daniel de Cosnac* (1852)
CT: Codex Tenison 645, Lambeth Palace Library, London
PRO: Public Record Office, London
QO: Ministère des Affaires Étrangères, Quai d'Orsay, Paris: Mémoires et Documents Angleterre, vol. 26

Chapter 1: Une Enfant de Bénédiction
1. City Chamberlain's Accounts, Bath, no. 87
2. *King Charles' Works and Letters*
3. F. A. Knight, *Heart of the Mendips* (1971)
4. *Ellis Historical Letters*, 2nd Series, p. 316
5. Sloane MS, 1697, *Ellis Historical Letters*, 2nd Series
6. Ibid.
7. Clarendon Papers, vol. II, p. 20
8. Tanner MS no. 52, part 1, fol. 82
9. *Mercurius Civicus*, 23 April 1646
10. Tanner MS no. 59, part 1, fol. 369
11. Clarendon Papers, vol. II, p. 246
12. Browne's Dispatches, Additional MS 12185

Chapter 2: Oh Me, My Brother! Oh Me, My Mother!
1. Clarendon Papers, vol. II, p. 6
2. Clarendon MSS, vol. 49, fol. 137
3. Nicholas Papers, vol. II, pp. 90–91
4. *Memoirs of Sir John Reresby*, vol. VIII, p. 3

Chapter 3: My Dearest Minette
1. CT, no. 73
2. QO, no. 3

3. QO, no. 1
4. QO, no. 2
5. British Library, Additional MSS 18, 735, fol. 102
6. CT, no. 58
7. CT, no. 64
8. British Library, Additional MSS 18, 738, fol. 108
9. CT, no. 66
10. Julia Cartwright, *Madame*, p. 78

Chapter 4: Madame of France

1. PRO State Papers, Foreign, France: French Correspondence, 25 January 1661
2. Harleian MS 4492, fol. 27
3. Letters of Louis XIV, MS 199, fol. 17, Bibliothèque de l'Arsenal, Paris
4. *Mémoires de Madame de Motteville*, vol. V, p. 109
5. *Mémoires de Madame de Montpensier*, vol. VII, p. 11
6. Cyprien de Gamache, *The Court and Times of Charles II*, p. 424
7. *Siècle de Louis XIV*, vol. I, p. 25
8. Madame de Lafayette, *History of Henrietta of England*
9. Motteville, vol. V, p. 124
10. QO, no. 4
11. CT, no. 48
12. QO, no. 6
13. CT, no. 61
14. QO, no. 7
15. QO, no. 8
16. PRO State Papers, Foreign, France, no. 116, fol. 128
17. QO, no. 12
18. PRO State Papers, Foreign, France, no. 116, fol. 138
19. QO, no. 13
20. QO, no. 16
21. QO, no. 18
22. QO, no. 19
23. QO, no. 20
24. QO, no. 22
25. QO, no. 23

Chapter 5: A Web of Intrigue

1. QO, no. 25
2. QO, no. 26
3. QO, no. 28
4. QO, no. 62
5. QO, no. 32
6. QO, no. 33
7. *Letters of Guy Patin*, vol. III, p. 581
8. QO, no. 17
9. QO, no. 34
10. QO, no. 35

11. PRO State Papers, Foreign, France, no. 118, fol. 261
12. Calendar of State Papers, Domestic, 1663–4, p. 170
13. QO, no. 36
14. British Library, Additional MSS 18, 738, fol. 105
15. QO, no. 37
16. PRO State Papers, Foreign, France, no. 119, fols. 5–8
17. From former collection of Sir Thomas Phillips; present whereabouts unknown
18. QO, no. 38
19. QO, no. 39
20. QO, no. 40
21. British Library, Additional MSS 18, 738, fol. 114
22. QO, no. 86
23. QO, no. 40
24. CT, no. 67
25. QO, no. 42
26. PRO State Papers, Foreign, France, no. 119, fol. 218
27. CT, no. 68
28. QO, no. 43
29. PRO State Papers, Foreign, France, no. 119, fol. 162
30. CT, no. 70
31. CT, no. 71
32. CT, no. 44
33. QO, no. 44
34. QO, no. 45

Chapter 6: War

1. QO, no. 46
2. CT, no. 49
3. QO, no. 50
4. CT, no. 50
5. CT, no. 52
6. QO, no. 51
7. CT, no. 53
8. QO, no. 52
9. Coventry MS 101, fols. 24–5
10. CT, no. 54
11. CT, no. 55
12. QO, no. 54
13. CT, no. 56
14. QO, no. 55
15. QO, no. 56
16. CT, no. 57
17. QO, no. 57
18. QO, no. 59
19. Samuel Pepys, *Diary*, Braybrooke edition, vol. IV
20. British Library, Additional MSS 18, 728, fol. 110

Chapter 7: Unquiet Hours

1. PRO State Papers, Foreign, France, no. 122, fol. 9
2. QO, no. 60
3. QO, no. 63
4. Venetian State Papers, 5 October 1666
5. QO, no. 64
6. QO, no. 66
7. QO, no. 87
8. QO, no. 67
9. QO, no. 69
10. QO, no. 70
11. QO, no. 72
12. QO, no. 73
13. QO, no. 74
14. QO, no. 75
15. QO, no. 76
16. QO, no. 77
17. QO, no. 79
18. QO, no. 80
19. QO, no. 81
20. QO, no. 65
21. QO, no. 82
22. QO, no. 83

Chapter 8: Something of Majesty

1. QO, no. 85
2. Samuel Pepys, *Diary*, 25 January 1665
3. Clifford MS, British Library
4. QO, no. 88
5. QO, no. 89
6. QO, no. 90
7. QO, no. 161
8. QO, no. 92
9. QO, no. 93
10. QO, no. 94
11. QO, no. 95
12. Montagu House MSS, vol. I, no. 426
13. QO, no. 96
14. QO, no. 97
15. QO, no. 98

Chapter 9: The Treaty of Madame

1. M. Monmarque's Collection (Paris, 1819)
2. Cosnac, vol. I, p. 382
3. Ibid., p. 384
4. Clifford MS, British Library
5. Montagu House MSS, vol. I, no. 437
6. Montagu House MSS, vol. I, nos. 453–4

7. Cosnac, vol. I, p. 402
8. Ibid., p. 404
9. Julia Cartwright, *Madame*, p. 310
10. PRO State Papers, Foreign, France: Doddington, 14–24 February 1690
11. Falconbridge Despatch 25, Correspondances Angleterre, Quai d'Orsay, Paris
12. Cosnac, vol. I, p. 405
13. Ibid., p. 406
14. Ibid., p. 408
15. Ibid., p. 411
16. Ibid., p. 416
17. Négociations de Pomponne MS 601, Bibliothèque de l'Arsenal, Paris
18. Mignet, *Négociations*, vol. III, pp. 184–200
19. Clifford MS, British Library
20. Cosnac, vol. I, p. 417
21. Clifford MS, British Library

Chapter 10: Madame se Meurt, Madame est Morte

1. M. Feuillet, MS Résidu St Germain, Paquet III, No. 7
2. Historical MSS Commission, 4th Report. Bath Papers, p. 144
3. Whartonian Miscellanies, vol. II, Letter 7
4. Vernon Despatches, 23 August 1670
5. Bossuet's Funeral Oration for Henrietta, Duchesse d'Orléans, *Bossuet's Works* (1816). Translated by Patrick Reilly

Select Bibliography

Primary Sources

Letters of Henrietta, Duchesse d'Orléans to Charles II

Twenty-three in the Lambeth Palace Library, London: Codex Tenison 645; eight in the Public Record Office, London: State Papers, Foreign, France; one in the Clifford Papers, now in the British Library, London.

Letters of Charles II to Henrietta, Duchesse d'Orléans

Ninety-eight in the Ministère des Affaires Étrangères, Quai d'Orsay, Paris; five in the British Library; two (copies) in the Public Record Office, London: State Papers, Foreign, France.

Secondary Sources

Additional MSS, British Library
Bossuet's Works (1816)
Bishop Burnet, *History of Our Time* (1734)
Calendar of State Papers, Foreign and Domestic
Campden Papers
Carte Manuscripts
Clarendon State Papers
Correspondances Angleterre, Quai d'Orsay

Daniel de Cosnac, *Mémoires* (1852)
Ellis Letters
Diaries of John Evelyn (Oxford, 1955)
Lady Fanshawe's Autobiography (1830)
Cyprien de Gamache, *The Court and Times of Charles II* (1848)
Mémoires de Count Gramont, ed. Anthony Hamilton, trans. Hugh Walpole (1928)
Harleian Manuscripts
Madame de Lafayette, *History of Henriette of England* (1929)
Memoirs of Edmund Ludlow (1720)
Thomas Babington Macaulay, *History of England* (1849)
Mercurius Civicus (1646)
Memoirs of Madame de Montpensier (1848)
Memoirs of Madame de Motteville (1902)
Montagu House Manuscripts, Historical Manuscripts Commission, vol. 1 (1897)
Nicholas Papers
Charlotte Elizabeth, Duchesse d'Orléans, *Mémoires, Fragments Historique* (1832)
History of James, Duke of Ormonde (1735)
Samuel Pepys, *Diary*, ed. Lord Braybrooke (1854)
Memoirs of Sir John Reresby (1734)
Cardinal de Retz, *Mémoires* (1751)
Rushworth Historical Collection
Somers Historical Tracts, vol. IX
Tanner Manuscripts
Venetian State Papers
Vernon Despatches
Whartonian Miscellanies, vol. II (1727)

OTHER SOURCES

Maurice Ashley, *Charles II* (Weidenfeld and Nicolson, 1971)
Bryan Bevan, *Charles II's Minette* (Ascent Books, 1979)
Julia Cartwright, *Madame* (Seeley and Co., 1894)
James Stanier Clarke, *James II* (1816)
Vincent Cronin, *Louis XIV* (Collins, 1964)
Dictionary of National Biography
English Historical Review

Philippe Erlanger, *Monsieur, Frère de Louis XIV* (1953)
Mrs Everett-Greene, *Lives of the Princesses of England* (Collins, 1855)
Antonia Fraser, *Charles II* (Weidenfeld and Nicolson, 1979)
Count de Gramont at the Court of Charles II, ed. and trans. Nicholas Deakin (Barrie and Rockcliff, 1965)
Memoirs by Lady Anne Halket and Lady Anne Fanshawe, ed. John Loftis (Oxford University Press, 1979)
Elizabeth Hamilton, *Henrietta Maria* (Hamish Hamilton, 1976)
Cyril Hughes Hartmann, *Charles II and Madame* (Heinemann, 1934)
Cyril Hughes Hartmann, *The King My Brother* (Heinemann, 1954)
John Miller, *Charles II* (Weidenfeld and Nicolson, 1991)
Hesketh Pearson, *Charles II, His Life and Likeness* (Phillimore and Co., Chichester, 1960)
T. W. E. Roche, *Henrietta of Exeter* (Phillimore and Co., Chichester, 1971)
Agnes Strickland, *Lives of the Four Last Stuart Princesses* (George Bell & Co., 1872)